THE REAL A

THE REAL ASTROLOGY

John Frawley

APPRENTICE BOOKS

Published 2001 by Apprentice Books
85, Steeds Road,
London N10 1JB
England
www.apprentice.demon.co.uk

ISBN 0 9539774 0 4

Design and typesetting by John Saunders Design & Production
Printed and bound in Great Britain by
MPG Books, Bodmin, Cornwall

Contents

Introduction

Modern astrology is the pandemic of contemporary culture. Everyone in the Western world is now subjugated to a daily intake of it, and it is rapidly spreading to the rest of the globe. With its five-fold technique of sounding wondrous and exotic; never saying anything concrete; making only universally valid pronouncements; always flattering its audience, and avoiding all unpleasant or controversial subjects, it has bamboozled the modern world and insinuated itself into every medium of modern mass-communication imaginable. Thus the majority of contemporary newspapers now carry a column dispensing daily modern-astrological tips; the majority of bookshops in major Western cities now have shelves or entire sections consisting purely of modern astrology books; and innumerable and ubiquitous references are made on an hourly basis to it in countless radio and television programs, films, books, magazines, pop songs, advertisement billboards, and internet sites. Moreover, in social settings nowadays, almost every time someone's age is asked, a meaningless and tedious conversation ensues about what mutual acquaintances are what sun-sign – as if, as will later be seen, sun-sign alone meant anything intelligible, or as if more than one percent of people who indulge in these conversations had the slightest understanding of what astrology really is in the first place! Even the most pious monotheistic believers, despite the traditional strictures and bans on predictive astrology in Christianity, Islam and Judaism, will regurgitate a preformulated and well-rehearsed dose of modern astrological trivia, such that these strictures and bans themselves are perhaps no longer enough to keep people away from the subject.

Fortunately, help is at hand. In the present book the renowned and respected English astrologer John Frawley, one of the few remaining – and certainly one of the best practicing – traditional astrologers in the world, explains in rigorous detail not only what Real Astrology is but also precisely what it is not. In a logical, comprehensive but readily accessible work, John Frawley puts the weight of his experience and astrological practice behind the treasure of astrological Tradition to create not only the definitive contemporary teaching guide and introduction to the Astrological Tradition, but also the ultimate satire of modern astrology. Indeed, readers of the acclaimed magazine *The Astrologer's Apprentice* of which John was the editor will attest that there is no ink more caustic or dry than that of John's pen in dispelling astrological illusions, lies and myths, and that there is no writing funnier or more entertaining than that of John's hand when it is debunking the modern world.

This book thus presents a unique prospect amongst Twentieth Century astrological literature (and a fitting start to the Twenty-first Century astrological literature) because for the first time the layman can have access to the universal astrological tradition – universal because it is a knowledge of the stars and of the nature of time and therefore applies to all believers whatever their religious doctrines – that starts in Ancient Chaldea and Babylon, passes, essentially unchanged, through the Ancient Egyptians, the Ancient Persians, the Ancient Hindus, the Ancient Greeks, the Romans and Ptolmey, the Jewish tradition with Masha'Allah and Ibn Ezra, the Islamic tradition and Al-Biruni, the Christian tradition with Cardan, Culpepper and Lilly, and right up until the end of the Nineteenth Century, when Alan Leo and his contemporaries first began to distort it. Indeed, herein the reader can see for himself, in a way no book written in the Twentieth Century evinces, not only the distilled essence of what the astrological sages of the world for the last three thousand years have been saying and practicing – and what the ersatz horde of modern psycho-babblers and ego-massaging imposters have been saying for the last hundred years, and how and why it is wrong – but also the experience and personal tips of a practicing master of applied astrology, all in an 'easy-to-digest' and 'ready-to-teach' format. We would say that this book is the best book on astrology written in the Twentieth Century – and the only one to right its wrongs – but oddly enough this is a redundant point, because aside from the seminal work of John's former teacher, Olivia Barclay, (*Horary Astrology Rediscovered* – which as the title suggests concerns only one branch of traditional astrology, *horary*) this is the only one (at least to be published) which introduces the astrological tradition integrally and is completely faithful to the Tradition of Real Astrology.

A word of warning: as alluded to above, the intention behind writing this book was to show the falsity of modern astrology and thereby spare people its ills, dangers and lies. For this it was necessary to explain in detail what Real Astrology is. This, however, itself involves a certain danger. For although the ultimate purpose of all the traditional sciences, including astrology, was to teach the knowledge of God through showing the perfection of His handiwork, and although there are certain branches of astrology which are clearly beneficial to man in body and soul (such as, for example, Astrological Medicine), there are also, even in Real Astrology, certain branches which are strictly forbidden by the three monotheistic religions (Judaism, Christianity and Islam): namely 'astrological magic' (or at least, as will be seen, those forms of it that harm or have selfish ends) and predictive astrology (or at least, as will be seen, those forms of it that do not take into consideration ultimate Divine causality, and Divine Freedom to change the forms of even 'predestined events'). Therefore if the reader uses the knowledge gleaned from this book in the wrong way, and tries to practice these forms of astrology, he or she should know that they do so at their own peril! Indeed, in the Holy Qur'an we see that even when astrology (at least in its current form) was first transmitted to man, in Ancient Iraq (*The Holy Qur'an* 2:102) it was accompanied with a similar warning:

> *Solomon disbelieved not; but the devils disbelieved, teaching mankind magic and that which was revealed to the two angels in Babel, Harut and Marut. Nor did they (the two angels) teach it to anyone till they had said: "We are only a temptation, therefore disbelieve not (in the guidance of God)".*

Hence Real Astrology must be respected, and as with all forms of real knowledge – or indeed as with anything that is precious – it brings with it the responsibility and moral imperative that it be used correctly, for the benefit of others or *ad majorem Dei Gloria*. So *caveat emptor!*

Victor Laude

Acknowledgements

I must first thank Victor Laude for his generosity with his time, knowledge and wisdom. My thanks also to Slobodan Paich, who first showed me that there are more things in heaven and earth, and to those from whom I have learned astrology, particularly Olivia Barclay.

Suzanne Knight has enthusiastically deployed her secretarial skills at the shortest of notice, while the staff of East Finchley Library have hunted down recondite texts with remorseless efficiency and good humour. Lesley Hughes and Dawn Spence have been of invaluable assistance at the production stage. Throughout this work, the blessings of a wife and family supportive and forbearing far beyond the call of duty have become ever more apparent; my gratitude must always fall short of their deserts.

Solomon disbelieved not; but the devils disbelieved, teaching mankind magic and that which was revealed to the two angels in Babel, Harut and Marut. Nor did they (the two angels) teach it to anyone till they had said: 'We are only a temptation, therefore disbelieve not (in the guidance of Allah).'

The Holy Qur'an, 2:102

We shall show them Our portents upon the horizons and within themselves until it will be manifest unto them that it is the Truth.

The Holy Qur'an, 41:53

What would a science, a philosophy, a technology be like, which, while not abandoning the outward operations of observation, experiment and analysis, nevertheless remained firmly grounded upon awareness of the Word within, the source and meaning of all?

Cyprian Smith

Key

♈	Aries	ruled by Mars
♉	Taurus	ruled by Venus
♊	Gemini	ruled by Mercury
♋	Cancer	ruled by the Moon
♌	Leo	ruled by the Sun
♍	Virgo	ruled by Mercury
♎	Libra	ruled by Venus
♏	Scorpio	ruled by Mars
♐	Sagittarius	ruled by Jupiter
♑	Capricorn	ruled by Saturn
♒	Aquarius	ruled by Saturn
♓	Pisces	ruled by Jupiter

♄	Saturn
♃	Jupiter
♂	Mars
☉	Sun
♀	Venus
☿	Mercury
☽	Moon

☊	North Node of the Moon
☋	South Node of the Moon
⊗	Part of Fortune/Fortuna

♂	Conjunction	same degree, same sign
♂	Opposition	same degree, opposite sign
△	Trine - 120 degrees	same degree, 4th sign round
□	Square - 90 degrees	same degree, 3rd sign round
✶	Sextile - 60 degrees	same degree, 2nd sign round
℞	Retrograde	appears to be going backwards

1

Introduction to Traditional Astrology

Six hundred years ago, the king summoned the royal astrologer into his august presence. A messenger ran from the throne-room, down the winding corridors and up the spiral stairs, brushing aside cobwebs and the odd slumbering bat, into the dusty chamber at the top of the Black Tower where the astrologer had his den. "Come with me," he said, "The King wishes to consult you." The astrologer picked up his astrolabe and a couple of attendant spirits and, limping valiantly as fast as his aged frame could carry him, hobbled after the messenger.

Reaching the King's throne-room he wiped his trembling hands on his long, snow-white beard and bowed low. "We are thinking of marrying the princess of Ruritania," the king boomed, "Is this is good idea?"

"Well, your majesty," the astrologer replied, "You're a Leo and always like to be the centre of attention and she's a Pisces so she's dreamy and other-worldly. There's not much hope for you. Your lucky number today is 6."

"Thank you," said the king. "You have set my mind at ease. Take this golden ducat for your pains, and tell your bat he is now Duke of Estragon."

This did not happen.

Six hundred years ago, the king summoned the royal astrologer into his presence. A messenger ran from the throne room, down the winding corridors and up the spiral stairs, clambering over candle-making kits and macrame plant holders, into the loft-space at the top of the Black Tower where the astrologer was enjoying a rebirthing session. "Come with me," he said, "The King wishes to consult you." The astrologer picked up his astrolabe and a selection of flower remedies and, limping valiantly as fast as his fragile archetype would permit, hobbled after the messenger.

Reaching the King's throne-room the wiped his trembling hands on his aura and bowed low. "We are thinking of marrying the princess of Ruritania," the king boomed, "Is this a good idea?"

"Well, your majesty," the astrologer replied, settling himself comfortably onto the Complete Works of Jung, "I see from your chart that you had a difficult childhood and are far more sensitive than other people realise. You have a vocation as a healer and unfulfilled creative potentials."

"Thank you," said the king. "I understand the whole situation much better now. Take this golden platitude and add it to your collection."

This did not happen.

Six hundred years ago, the king summoned the royal astrologer. 'I'm thinking of marrying the princess of Ruritania," he asked him. "Is this a good idea?"

"Well, your majesty," the astrologer replied, "I see from the chart that the princess will attract poets, thinkers and artists from across the continent and make your court a renowned centre of learning. The marriage will create a lasting bond between the two kingdoms and her father will be a valuable ally in the forthcoming war against the barbarians. But all of your children will predecease you, so after your death the throne will pass to your wicked brother, who will oppress the people."

"Thank you," said the king. "That gives me something to think about and some concrete information on which to base my decision. Now get back to your studies."

This did not happen either; but it is a much closer picture of what astrology has been through most of its history.

Modern astrology is rubbish. As a practising, professional astrologer I find it necessary to make this clear from the start. What passes for astrology today is nothing but a travesty of the science as once practised.

Our first familiarity with the subject comes almost invariably through the Sun-sign columns of the newspapers, usually when we are hoping for some favourable omen that this is the day when Mr or Ms Perfect is finally going to notice us. Here we find invaluable advice such as 'avoid accidents' and 'be careful with sharp objects'; precise predictions such as 'public events may start late' and 'small items may be lost' (note the word 'may'); or penetrating character analysis such as 'your relationship needs are rather complicated and not easily satisfied'.[1]

The scientific critics have trouble grasping the possibility that there is, even today, rather more to astrology than is given in these columns. Most people, however, have a more or less vague awareness that there is 'something else', that it is possible to have one's own birth-chart cast, which offers the promise of greater insight into one's nature than the simple knowledge that one is a Leo or a Taurus. Indeed there is 'something else'; but unfortunately this something is of little more value than the newspaper columns, typically consisting of a mish-mash of half-understood psychoanalytical jargon, vague enough so that whoever hears it can find it applies to themselves. "You're deeply sensitive," "You had a difficult childhood," "You find even close relationships somehow unfulfilling," Yes, we think, that's me to a 'T'.

Modern astrology thrives on the natural human propensity to relate anything

---

[1] All quoted from a random sampling of the genre.

that is heard to oneself; as we are all made of the same materials in different proportion, all the vague psychological generalities are inside us somewhere. "You're deeply sensitive," and even the most hardened thug thinks of the time he stroked a puppy. This is a basic trance-induction technique – say anything and the listener will immediately be reminded of an occasion when it happened to them: "You're thinking about the countryside." You certainly are now. This is the cosy base on which modern astrology is built, as the client is taken on a drowsy tour of the more acceptable parts of their own psyche to reassure themselves that they are really more wonderful than those horrid people outside will ever appreciate. The guiding rule of all modern astrology is that the astrologer must never, ever say anything that might possibly discomfit the client. Having the undivided and uncritical attention of another person for an hour is no doubt pleasant enough; but if that is really all that astrology can offer, it is hard to understand why it has for so long occupied so prominent a place in the intellectual life of cultures across the globe, accepted and practised by minds of uncommon power and subtlety.

As with the king in our story, anyone consulting an astrologer in the past wanted some specific, verifiable information. Will my wife stay faithful and can I get my hands on her money? Where is my stray cow? When is a good moment to attack this castle? Will the harvest be good this year? Unlike his modern counter-part, the astrologer in days past was making clear, verifiable statements. If he told the client he would find his cow in the pound in the next village, the client would go to the next village and look. For the astrologer to retain any credibility, either a reasonable proportion of his statements must have been correct, or his clients must have been remarkably foolish. If, as the sceptics would have us believe, our ancestors regularly came back from the pound having found no cow, yet still believed in the wisdom of the astrologer, we might reasonably expect that the human race would have died out from sheer stupidity. It did not.

So let us consider (and 'consider' means 'to study the stars') an example of the traditional astrological methods with which our forebears would have been familiar, seeing how traditional astrology actually worked, so we may judge its value for ourselves. Fear not – no technical knowledge is needed to follow the process.

A lawyer had mislaid some share certificates belonging to a client: they had been in her office, where they belonged, and then it was noticed that they were no longer there. At the very least, this could have been extremely embarrassing; it had potential to cause serious financial implications for her company, so she asked an astrologer a question, "Where are the share certificates?" Using the technique of *horary* astrology, probably the most common branch of the art in centuries past, the astrologer set a chart of the stars as they stood at the moment the question was asked.[2] This horary chart provides a picture of the situation

---

[2] November 27th 1995, 5.51 pm GMT, London.

Chart 1: Where are the Share Certificates?

which, by following set rules or pathways to judgement – no subjective intuition or psychic powers are involved – the astrologer reads to provide an answer to the question.

If we consider the question as a drama, each of the planets in it represents one of the characters in that drama. Our first task is to identify which planet is playing the part of the chief character in this particular play: the share certificates. The chart, as you can see, is divided into twelve sections, called *houses.* Everything in the universe, no matter how big or how small, past, present or future, animate or inanimate, real or imaginary, is regarded as falling within the scope of one or other of these houses. The horizontal line across the chart represents the horizon; the houses are numbered from one to twelve in anti-clockwise order from the eastern (left-hand) horizon. In this instance, the share certificates are regarded as falling into the fourth house; being at the bottom of the chart, this house is concerned, among other things, with buried treasure and hence mislaid objects: the share certificates are our lawyer's 'buried treasure'.

The planet playing the part of the certificates will be the one that rules the zodiac sign on the leading edge, or *cusp,* of that house. In this chart, Virgo (♍) falls on that cusp. Virgo is ruled by Mercury (☿), so Mercury represents the certificates. All we need do now is locate Mercury in the chart. This will give us the whereabouts of the certificates.

Houses 1, 4, 7 and 10 are known as *angular* houses; had we found Mercury in one of these it would have indicated that the certificates were close at hand, or near where they ought to be. Houses 2, 5, 8 and 11 – the middle houses in each quadrant – are *succedent;* had Mercury been in one of these, we should have judged that they were a little distance away. In this context, perhaps they would have been in the next room rather than the one where they should have been. The remaining houses, 3, 6, 9 and 12 are *cadent;* finding our significator in one of these suggests that the certificates are a long way off. This is puzzling. Why are the documents a long way away?

The chart explains how this has come about. Mercury, at 7 degrees of Sagittarius (♐) is very close to the Sun (☉), at 5 degrees of Sagittarius. Mercury moves faster than the Sun, so we can see that they must recently have been together and Mercury is now separating from this contact. A contact – known as an *aspect* – that is about to happen when the chart is cast refers to something that is about to happen in the world; similarly, a contact that has already happened when the chart is cast refers to something that has already happened in the world. This, incidentally, is a distinction that has been largely forgotten by modern astrology; we must assume that the modern astrologer has never waited for a bus: if he had, he would be aware of the significant difference between things that are applying and things that are moving away. As with buses, so with aspects. This contact with the Sun is the only thing of note that has recently happened to Mercury; perhaps it is the clue that we need.

To find out what the Sun represents in the chart – which role it is playing in our drama – we look first to the house that it rules. In this case, this is the third house, as Leo (♌), the sign ruled by the Sun, is the sign on the cusp of that house; so the Sun could well represent something connected with the third house. Among the many concerns of the third house are all forms of communication, including the post. If the documents (Mercury) have been in recent contact with the post (Sun), this might explain why they are now a long way off (cadent house). This is a plausible story; we can run with this until we find it either provides us with the solution that we require, or leads us into a blind alley, from which we must backtrack and take another path.

So the documents seem to have been bundled up with some other papers and put into the post by mistake. They are now a long way off. This is interesting, but neither use nor consolation. We need to find out what will happen to them. Moving away from the Sun, Mercury is approaching Jupiter (♃). As Mercury moves much faster than Jupiter, it will soon catch it. Jupiter rules Pisces (♓), the sign on the cusp of the tenth house. The tenth is the house of work, career, the office. This is promising: the documents are coming to the office.

But, woe and alas! Mercury is at 7 degrees of Sagittarius, Jupiter is at 21 degrees of that sign. For Mercury to catch Jupiter it has to pass through 18 Sagittarius, where there is an aspect with Saturn (♄), sitting at the top of the chart at 18 degrees of Pisces. This is not good. Saturn is a thoroughly nasty piece of work and best avoided. In traditional astrology we deal with *benefic* planets, Jupiter and Venus, and *malefic* planets, Mars and Saturn. Benefics are helpful; malefics are not. Modern astrologers have no truck with this. The idea of malefic planets was fine for the simple folk in days of yore, but the moderns claim (apparently in all seriousness) that we are far too sophisticated for such things now. We inhabit a Jungian universe, where we make psychological gold out of any base matter that crosses our path; but is this really true? Given the envelope with the cheque and the envelope with the bill, do we not prefer the envelope with the cheque? Our day-to-day world is constructed on these black and white lines of good and bad: maybe the bill will be of long-term benefit to me by teaching me financial discipline, but I'd still rather have the cheque. This does not imply that we live totally on some childish level of pleasure versus pain, demanding metaphorical ice-cream on all occasions; it merely recognises that there are things which are fortunate and things which are not. If every cloud has a silver lining, we do not necessarily find it. This is all the more relevant in horary astrology, where the fact that someone has bothered to pose a question almost invariably implies that there is a desired outcome: a benefic is what facilitates that outcome, a malefic is what hinders it. Here, our querent seeks the return of her documents; by obstructing this outcome, Saturn is most definitely malefic.

In horary, we are concerned almost always with the next aspect only. If that does not produce an outcome, game over. Realistically, we must acknowledge that the chance of the documents, arriving for no reason in some strange office, being posted back is not high: we know with just what frequency businesses return our phone-calls; how much the less chance then of someone taking the trouble to return the documents. Saturn is the planet associated with inertia and obstruction, which suggests that natural reluctance to make an effort will prevent the return of the certificates to the office.

But help is at hand. The Moon (☽) is at 15 degrees of Aquarius (♒). It moves very much faster than any other planet, even Mercury, so we see it separating from the aspect with Mercury that it made at 7 degrees of Aquarius and applying to an aspect with Jupiter, which it will reach at 21 degrees of Aquarius. Planets in adjacent signs do not make aspects with each other, so as Aquarius is the next sign to Pisces, the Moon escapes the interference from Saturn and carries the documents back to the office. This is known technically as *translation of light:* the Moon picks up the light of Mercury and carries it to Jupiter, joining the two planets together. The involvement of the Moon, carrying the documents home, makes sense: the documents are not going to post themselves back to the office; we need the involvement of a third party.

The Moon's movement allows us to gauge the timing. The question was asked on a Monday evening; the documents had last been seen the previous Wednesday. The Moon's position at 15 degrees of Aquarius represents the "Now" of the question – Monday – so the aspect with Mercury (the documents) which the Moon made at 7 degrees of Aquarius can be taken as the time of their last sighting on the previous Wednesday. So the Moon's motion from 7 to 15 degrees shows the time from Wednesday to Monday. By proportion, then, the distance from the Moon's current position, 15 degrees, to its position when it makes the aspect with Jupiter, 21 degrees, will show the time that must elapse before the documents return. The astrologer's judgement was that they would arrive back in the office on the Friday, and so they did.

This is exactly the kind of clear, straightforward judgement that would have been sought throughout most of astrology's long history, and that is still obtainable today, provided only that the methods of the true astrological tradition are used rather than their distorted modern counterparts. Modern astrology is incapable of providing such a judgement. There are two reasons for this. One is a matter of preconception: it no longer aims to do so nor does it believe it possible; the other is a question of tools, as, for reasons which we shall explore later, in its passage into the modern world astrology has been completely and unrecognisably transformed and most of the tools with which it once worked thrown overboard.

Modern astrology demonstrates an absolute obsession with the inside of one's head. The traditional astrologer began with the assumption that his client was reasonably well appraised of what was happening between his ears; what he did not know, and therefore wanted information about, was what was happening in the world outside.

So psychologically oriented are we now that the world outside has but small importance, being seen only as provider of grist to our mental mill: what is of paramount significance is whatever mood the individual might be indulging at that moment. When necessary, traditional methods of astrology can provide psychological analysis of great subtlety, the more so for being cast in concrete terms rather than psychoanalytic jargon; one of its great strengths in practical use is the determining of what might be happening in other people's psychology – whether, for example, one's opponent in a court case is determined to battle it out or if he will settle at the first sign of conflict. But most of its aim, although by no means its highest goal, is to give an indication of what might happen in the world.

Suppose I am to drive from London to Glasgow and wish to know when I will arrive. I look at the map to see how far it is. I check the TV travel information to see if the road is being dug up. I look at the weather forecast to see if rain will slow my journey. There are still imponderables. A modern astrologer might tell me that my desire to drive to Glasgow has something to do with my *puer aeternus;* an astrologer working with traditional methods will tell me rather more usefully that there will be a pile-up on the direct route, so if I take that road I will be stuck for several hours in a tail-back. The function of astrology is to give a clear, dispassionate overview of the situation in question, whether that situation be the whereabouts of the documents or my travel plans, the fate of nations or a man's life and his spiritual strengths and weaknesses. The greatest caution must be exercised when peering into the future, for all things are subject to the Will of God and the workings of His Will are not always scrutable by man; nor is it desirable that we should behave as if they were. But the clear analysis of a situation, beyond the fog of our wishes, fears and ignorance, has, for some thousands of years since the Revelation of the science to man in Babylon, been highly prized.

The edited highlights of the following chart point the difference between the traditional and modern approaches. The chart is borrowed from a lecture by a respected teacher of modern methods. He explained that one of his students had had her handbag snatched three times in a matter of days. She had not lost anything of great value, nor had she been hurt, but she had, obviously enough, found this an unsettling experience. She asked the teacher to look at her birth-chart to see what was happening to her. The diagram shows only the relevant planets.

The key, as correctly identified by our lecturer, is the aspect between Saturn (♄) and the Moon (☽). At the time when these events took place, Saturn in the sky was returning to the same position it had held at the moment of the student's birth. This is known as a *Saturn return* and occurs to everyone at around 29 years of age, marking one of the major turning-points in the life. The planet returning to its original position activates, as it were, the potential stored at that point. The aspect between Saturn and the Moon connects this return with the student's emotions. Our teacher's considered opinion was that she could expect to experience something unpleasant, but that there was no way of knowing whether this would be an external event or an internal feeling of unhappiness. This was, indeed, the whole argument of his lecture, that it is impossible to tell whether things shown by the chart will happen in the outside world or as states of mind. We might think that it would be useful to know which, but this desire indicates only what undeveloped folk we are.

With the poor tools of modern astrology, and its even poorer aims, this argument is correct. Let us look at the same small section of a chart from a traditional perspective. Saturn is the Great Malefic, the Big Bad Wolf in the chart; we do not like it. When it is well-placed, in a sign where it is strong – such as Capricorn or Aquarius – it can behave itself and confer unexciting but valuable benefits such as discipline, gravity and endurance; in Pisces, where it is here, it is weak, so it is going to bring misfortune. It aspects the Moon, which is on the cusp of the second house, which is the house of possessions. Saturn is the planet of boundaries; here, it is weak and associated with possessions; we might suspect an inherent difficulty on questions of what is mine and what is thine surfacing throughout the life. The twelfth house, where Saturn is placed, is the house of secret enemies; so, more specifically, we have a proclivity towards malicious secret enemies afflicting her possessions.

Pisces, the sign in which Saturn falls, is one of four signs called 'double-

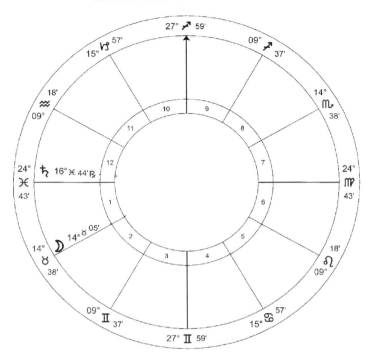

Chart 2: The Snatched Handbags.

bodied' and thence indicative of duality; so there is more than one secret enemy afflicting her possessions, or more than one occasion when this will happen. The Moon is in Taurus, where it is strong, much stronger than Saturn; the possessions, as it were, are stronger than the secret enemies, so her assailants are not about to drive up in a truck and empty her house. The loss will be only small. Taurus is a feminine sign, ruled by Venus, so we are considering some specifically feminine small possessions. Being by nature fixed and earthy, Taurus is associated with holding; a small feminine possession that holds things is known as a handbag. The angle of the aspect from Saturn to Taurus is 60 degrees (that is, they are two signs apart = one sixth of the zodiac; one sixth of 360 degrees is 60). This is called a *sextile*, and whatever a sextile indicates will happen easily: the thefts happened easily. Had it been a 90 degree aspect, indicating that they happened with difficulty, we would have expected her to be hurt. So we have the repeated theft of a handbag by persons unknown occurring without hurt. We can then take the characteristics of Saturn combined with the characteristics of Pisces to give a close physical description of the first of the thieves. Yes, we have the benefit of hindsight – but so did the modern astrologer who was unable even to decide even whether this unknown unpleasantness would be an event or a state of mind.

The great attraction with things psychological, of course, is that they are totally unverifiable. The astrologer can say what he likes about them and nobody can prove him wrong. The car-mechanic, who either fixes the car or fails to fix the car, might envy this ability to turn everything into a subjective question of mood. On the odd occasion when the astrologer says something with sufficient clarity to render it capable of contradiction, the client might object: "But I don't feel like that at all"; but the client is under a misapprehension, not realising the true nature of their own feelings. I recently judged the birth-chart of a client who had previously had the same task performed by a leading practitioner of the modern astrology. "She kept talking about my childhood," he complained, "Even though I told her I wanted to understand the present trends in my life. She kept talking about my problems with my mother. I told her I had always got along well with my mother; but she just said I was refusing the face the issue." "I've fixed your car," says the mechanic, "It's just sulking. Here's my bill."

Out in the real world, we have documented accounts of the accuracy that astrology could provide. The astrologer Guido Bonatti was consigned by Dante to the fourth bolgia of the Inferno; the Earl of Mount-Serrant had a rather higher opinion of his abilities. When the Earl was besieged, Bonatti advised him that if he were to sally out and attack his enemies at a certain time he should defeat them, forcing them to raise the siege. He, however, would receive a dangerous, but not mortal, wound in the thigh. The Earl attacked as advised. Despite being outnumbered, victory was his; following his fleeing opponents, he was wounded in the thigh, but the advice had enabled him to make the necessary provision for treatment, so he survived.[3]

Luca Gaurico – not only a renowned astrologer but also Bishop of Dijon – judged from Henri II's birth-chart that the king should be killed in his forty-first year by being struck in the eye with a lance whilst jousting.[4] The sceptic might claim that the prediction works on the subject's psychology, which suggestion renders the event likely to happen; if we consider the contortions that Henri's psychology would have had to manifest in his body in order to present his eye to the moving lance-point, it is simpler to accept that the astrologer just got it right.

The number of astrologers who published predictions of the outbreak of plague in London in 1665 and the Great Fire a year later, or who, like Ebenezer Sibley, foretold that in 1789 "some very important event will happen in the politics of France, such as may dethrone, or very nearly touch the life of, the king, and make victims of many great and illustrious men in church and state, preparatory to a revolution or change in the affairs of that empire, which will at once astonish and surprise the surrounding nations,"[5] contrasts strongly with

[3] Henry Coley, *Address to the Reader,* in William Lilly's edition of Bonatus' *Anima Astrologiae,* London 1676; reprinted Regulus, London, 1986. Coley cites Fulgusos, L.8, c.11.

[4] John Gadbury, *Collection of Nativities,* p. 23; London, 1662; reprinted Ascella, Nottingham, n.d.

[5] In his *A New and Complete Illustration of the Celestial Science of Astrology,* London, 1784-8, III, 1050-1; quoted in Patrick Curry, *Prophecy and Power,* p. 135, Polity, London, 1989.

the general failure of modern astrologers to predict such notable events as the outbreak of the Second World War.

Traditional and Modern Compared: Adolf Hitler

If this astrology was so successful, we might reasonably wonder what happened to it. Why was it replaced by the tepid banalities with which we are familiar today? Before exploring why and how this happened, let us conduct a test of at least as much scientific validity as any of the tests by which the scientific sceptics claim to have tested astrology. We shall take the birth-chart of a well-known person and subject it to cold readings by an astrologer from the past and one from the present. Unfortunately, all the ancient astrologers whom we invited to take part in this experiment were otherwise engaged, being fully occupied turning in their graves at the state of modern astrology; so we shall have to use their writings. In the interest of scrupulous scientific fairness, we shall do the same with our representative modern.

We shall take as our subject a life whose proclivities are well documented: that of Adolf Hitler.[6] Hitler was a man of some note, so it is not surprising that

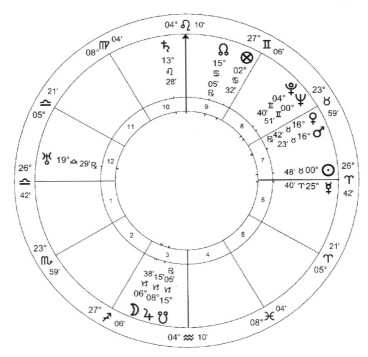

Chart 3: Adolf Hitler.

[6] April 20th 1889, 6.30 pm LMT, 48N12 13E02.

he is mentioned in almost all introductions to astrology written since the war. What is surprising is that in the great majority of these books he is cited as an example of an Aries, that is, as someone who was born while the Sun was in the astrological sign of Aries. His character is taken to exemplify the typical Aries traits – self-importance, impetuosity, ardour and the like. That the Sun was not actually in the sign of Aries when he was born – as is readily verifiable – shows both the amount of effort expended on most modern astrological writing and the amount of credence which can be given to its conclusions. Hitler was born at 6.30 local time on April 20th 1889. The Sun had left Aries and entered Taurus the previous day, almost 24 hours before his birth. Few writers have bothered to check this, looking merely at that invaluable reference source, the Sun-sign column of their daily newspaper, which tells them that Aries finishes on April 21st. But the time at which the Sun moves from sign to sign varies by up to around a day from year to year. Rather than exemplifying the characteristics of an Aries, Hitler does in fact exemplify the characteristics of a Taurus, such as stubbornness and resilience. That we could also pass him off as a Gemini (orator), Cancer (overwhelming), Leo (dictatorial), Virgo (stomach pains) or any other of the signs demonstrates exactly how much truth there is in these sun-sign platitudes.

Even those modern astrologers who have taken sufficient trouble to look at Hitler's birth-chart rather than just copying from whatever worthless book falls into their hands frequently confess a certain bafflement. While it is apparent that this is not someone whom we would necessarily wish to invite to tea, the depths of his nastiness elude astrological modern techniques. From the traditional perspective, however, these depths are quite clear.

The traditional method of judging a natal chart begins with assessing the temperament. This is, as it were, the cloth from which the person is cut. All the detail which we later see must be judged against this background, as if the details were embroidery on a garment. No matter what is embroidered, the fundamental question when determining for what purpose the garment is fit is whether the material is a delicate silk or a tough denim. So in the person. Is he predominantly choleric, phlegmatic, sanguine or melancholic – or a mixture of two of these?

This balance is calculated according to the respective measure of hot, cold, moist and dry qualities, manifesting in their four possible combinations as earth, air, fire and water (that is, cold and dry, hot and moist, hot and dry, and cold and moist respectively). The ideal would be a perfect balance between them all. Man – and more specifically, the male human – is the best balanced of all God's creatures (woman being colder and more moist than man), although there are, of course, extreme variations within that. The tradition holds that the best balanced of all men was the Prophet.[7] What we must determine is the exact nature of the mixture of hot, cold, moist and dry in the particular person whom

---

[7] See Jalalu'd-Din Abd'ur-Rahman As-Suyuti, *Medicine of the Prophet*, p. 3, Ta-Ha, London 1994

we are considering, mixture being the literal meaning of *temperament*, and also of *complexion,* which was originally a synonym for temperament, but is now applied only to the outward appearance rather than to the whole of the being.

In most people there are one or two of these qualities which are notably strong, and one or two that are similarly weak. This balance shows which of the temperaments the person has: choleric, which is, in modern parlance, fiery; phlegmatic (watery); sanguine (airy) or melancholic (earthy). Far from just describing a set of mental habits, this balance tells us also about the person's appearance, the illnesses from which they are likely to suffer, and much, much more. Geoffrey Chaucer, for example, who was a skilled astrologer as well as a poet, could describe a character by his temperament – 'cholerick', perhaps – knowing that just that one word would give his readers a good idea of not only this character's general mode of behaviour, but also his appearance. Having this basic understanding of temperament is vital if we are to put the details which we find later in any meaningful context. It is all very well knowing that the native will murder his granny; but does he beat her to death in a fit of choleric fury, or does he slowly poison her from sanguine curiosity? Only a knowledge of the temperament will tell.

To see just how significant temperament is, and how fixed we are in whatever temperament is our own, we might consider actors. Even they, who are skilled at adopting different personae, will not act outside their own basic temperament. To do so would appear ridiculous, for unconsciously we all understand that temperament and body type are indissolubly mixed. Indeed, one of the easiest and most reliable forms of comedy is to cast someone against their natural temperament. Whether it is Jim Carrey trying to be John Wayne or John Wayne trying to be Jim Carrey, the product is guaranteed to be hilarious. Our temperament never leaves us. Even when we lose our temper-ament, we act according to type: the fiery, choleric person will hit someone; the airy, sanguine type will unleash his stinging tongue; the watery, phlegmatic person will burst into tears. So we begin to see how important it is to grasp this if we are to understand the person as a whole.

The modern, if attempting to look at Hitler on anything approaching this level, would note the number of planets in earth signs (Sun, Mars and Venus in Taurus; Moon and Jupiter in Capricorn) and decide that he must be earthy by nature. Far from it: in traditional terms, the temperament is strongly choleric, or fiery. The choleric is today the least fashionable of the temperaments, the ideal of the warrior, which the natural mode of expression for choler, being now acceptable only in distorted or trivialised forms. In itself, however, the choleric is no worse than any of the other temperaments. Sanguine always gets a good write-up in the text-books; but we must remember that the people who write these books are necessarily more likely to be of airy, sanguine nature: any imbalance is a falling short of perfection.

So Hitler is choleric; the problems start when we consider how this choleric fire is going to find outlet. By its own hot, dry nature, Mars is the planet with natural affinity to the choleric temperament. Finding a strong, well-placed Mars in the chart would suggest that the native can successfully integrate his nature into society as a warrior – in modern terms this often manifests as the professional athlete. Hitler's Mars, however, is in a dreadful state, as we shall see shortly. The Sun, which is also hot and dry and so might also allow positive expression of this choler, is also very weak. This choleric temperament, we begin to see, is going to manifest itself in the most appalling ways.

At this stage in judgement, our attention is struck by the placement of some of the *fixed stars* – that is, what we normally refer to as 'stars' as opposed to the 'wandering stars' or planets. Most fixed stars, most of the time, are mute notes in a birth-chart; the ones that matter are those on angles, particularly the Ascendant or Midheaven, and those within about a degree of the planets, especially the Sun or the Moon. They are almost entirely ignored by modern astrology: as the following shows, this is something of an omission. On the Midheaven is Praesepe, known to the Chinese as 'Exhalation of Piled-up Corpses'. The Midheaven is the place in the chart particularly associated with career, or public image. We need hardly say more – but, of course, we shall: it brings 'disease, disgrace, adventure, insolence, wantonness, brutality'.[8] The Sun is on a thoroughly unpleasant star, Sharatan, which 'causes bodily injuries, unscrupulous defeat, destruction by fire, war or earthquake', while the Moon is on Facies, giving a violent death. Like Praesepe, Facies afflicts the eyesight, much the more so if in conjunction with one of the luminaries (the sources of light); this works on a metaphorical as well as literal level – although Hitler's physical eyesight was weak but not unusually so, his inability to see in metaphorical terms was remarkable. Finally, in itself of much less significance but important by virtue of its angularity, is Mercury, falling on Vertex, the Andromeda nebula, which repeats the testimony of afflicted sight and violent death.

Having laid the foundation to the traditional judgement, let us subject this chart to our blind reading by two astrologers, one ancient, one modern. Our modern writer, plucked at random from the shelf, but by no means among the most down-market of the genre,[9] outlines her method of judging a natal chart. We start by assessing the sign on the Ascendant (note that in this reading we as yet know nothing of what we have just just described above: this is where we begin). With Libra on the Ascendant, our native is "an easy-going, charming and kind personality who is diplomatic, co-operative and will do anything for peace and harmony. (He) is intellectually intelligent but inclined to indecision and easily influenced by others. (His) faults are indecision, being frivolous, too easy-going, untidy and an inclination to sit on the fence."

We must then look to the Ascendant ruler, Venus. Falling in Taurus and the seventh house, our native is "pleasant, kind, faithful, appreciates good manners;

---

[8] Quotations on fixed stars from the standard reference: Vivian Robson, *The Fixed Stars and Constellations in Astrology*, London, 1923; reprinted, Ascella, Nottingham, n.d. Robson's work is a compendium of traditional views.

[9] P. Tillot, in *Tybol Astrological Almanac for 1999*, pp. 15-30, Tybol, Preston

has a love of luxury, especially the home; good voice; good taste; interested in gardening; can be very possessive" and is concerned about, but has problems with, close relationships. The Sun in Taurus adds a stoical nature and further concern with relationships. The Moon in Capricorn gives a "reserved and cautious nature; ... ambitious and hard worker... has a drive for success," while in the third house it shows "thinking strongly governed by emotions; prone to day-dreaming; soon tire of monotonous routine."

We can then continue through various other points too tedious to list. In fairness, we must point out that the Venus in Taurus will be moderated by its conjunction with Mars. That is, the "pleasant, kind, faithful, etc" will be conditioned by "very practical; has great determination; usually very peaceful." The square aspect from Saturn would also limit the Venus qualities owing to a need of "a great deal of respect/attentions from others; has responsibilities whether wanted or not; develops a strong sense of values to do with leisure/pleasure/authority/power."

Once this list of points has been noted, the astrologer reaches the next stage, called 'synthesis'. This is when all the various points have to be joined together to make a coherent picture. If we imagine a recipe which reads "Carefully weigh out all your ingredients, then toss them into a bowl in whatever order takes your fancy," we have an idea of the art of synthesis. We have weighed out the ingredients according to this typical modern method; we shall leave our reader to blend them together to give an accurate picture of Adolf Hitler.

For our blind reading from the past, we shall turn to Claudius Ptolemy.[10] Remembering that our assessment of the temperament has already provided us with all the information above, we can concentrate our attention on just one point: the salient Venus/Mars conjunction. This is squared by Saturn, but more importantly, by the traditional technique of *antiscion,* Saturn falls exactly on this conjunction, bringing all three of these planets into immediate contact. Antiscion is a technique almost entirely forgotten today, without which an accurate judgment of a chart is impossible; it gives what is literally the shadow of each planet (this must not be understood in the Jungian sense), or what in practical terms amounts to an alternative placement of each planet. This is not the place to enter into into the technical details, but trust me, dear reader, it works, and in this instance brings Saturn exactly onto Mars and Venus.

The relative strengths of the planets is something else that is largely ignored by the moderns. In Hitler's chart, there is no strong planet. To use the technical labels, Jupiter is in its *fall;* the Moon and Mars are in their *detriment;* Mercury and the Sun are *peregrine.* This is a strong indication of the degeneracy of the nature. Even Venus, which has strength by virtue of falling in its own sign, Taurus, is grievously handicapped by being retrograde and by its immediate contact with the two malefics, Mars and Saturn. This contact is all the more serious because both the malefics are weak, and the weaker the malefics are, the

10   *Tetrabiblos,* trans. F. E. Robbins, p. 343, Heinemann, London, 1940

worse their effects. Occurring in fixed signs, this gives an unshakeable malaise. With most of the planets above the horizon (the horizontal axis of the chart) and in angular houses, this will find its outlet in the world: were the planets hidden below the horizon, Hitler would have spent his life thinking dreadful thoughts, rather than acting them out.

According to Ptolemy, this planetary combination "in honourable positions makes his subjects neither good nor bad, industrious, outspoken, nuisances, cowardly braggarts, harsh in conduct, without pity, contemptuous, rough, contentious, rash, disorderly, deceitful, layers of ambushes, tenacious of anger, unmoved by pleading, courting the mob, tyrannical, grasping, haters of the citizenry, fond of strife, malignant, evil through and through, active, impatient, blustering, vulgar, boastful, injurious, unjust, not to be despised, haters of all mankind, inflexible, unchangeable, busy-bodies, but at the same time adroit and practical, not to be overborne by rivals, and in general successful in achieving their ends." This is if the combination is "in honourable positions", so this is the good side. In Hitler's chart, it is most definitely not in an honourable position, with all these planets severely afflicted, so its outcome is not so favourable. Ptolemy suggests that in these cases, it "makes his subjects robbers, pirates, adulterators, submissive to disgraceful treatment (we might recall Hitler's sexual predilections), takers of base profits, godless, without affection, insulting, crafty, thieves, perjurers, murderers, poisoners, impious, robbers of temples and of tombs, and utterly depraved." All these points would manifest through the choleric, but degenerately choleric, temperament.

We might feel that Ptolemy has given us a picture somewhat closer to the mark than the peace-loving gardener that our modern blind reading has produced – not bad for someone writing almost 2000 years before the birth and without the opportunity to revise his opinion of that "easy-going, charming and kind" Libran Ascendant in the light of the considerable attention that Hitler's horoscope has attracted since his rise to fame. It is no doubt true that we could find a modern astrologer who, if presented with the details of the time and place of Hitler's birth, could give a more accurate analysis of his character from a blind reading; but our example modern is representative, and it should be noted that the general tone of astrological writing in even the late Nineteen Thirties was that the world could look forward to an era of peace and plenty courtesy of that nice Mr Hitler. We must also note that while our modern does at least claim to be an astrologer, there is no evidence to suggest that Ptolemy ever cast a horoscope in his life. He was merely an encyclopaedist recording current practice. That an astrological layman could give so accurate a picture is entirely through the validity of the traditional method. We must also point out that were Mr Hitler to wander into a contemporary astrologer's den, he would no doubt hear what a difficult childhood he had, how his creative drives are frustrated and how he feels that even those closest to him fail to understand him completely, probably finishing by being told that he has a vocation as a healer.

2

The Rise of Modern Astrology

In 1895 Alan Leo took it upon himself 'to modernise the ancient system of Astrology'.[1] His work is the cornerstone around which the ramshackle edifice of modern astrology has been constructed. Had astrology been in healthy condition, however, the work of one man, no matter how determined he might have been to reform, deform or undermine her, would have been absorbed into her swelling tide; as it was, the poor trickle that was all that survived of this once mighty river proved easy to divert.

It pleases the more misty-eyed of the astrologically inclined to gaze back fondly upon some distant era when Astrologosaurus Rex ruled the earth, making accurate predictions at which all around fell down in wonder. This golden era seems never to have happened. For as far back as we can trace astrological writing, we find contemporary attacks from sceptics – notably because no astrologer has ever managed to get everything right all the time: then as now, one man sees only the failures while another sees only the successes. It is always possible to disparage a mountain for the fissures in its sides, or to praise a grain of sand for its solidity. Traditionally, however, even the most vehement attacks on astrology were not so much over its validity *per se,* but over the extent to which it could be said to be valid. Even the most adamant of sceptics usually accepted astrological influence on the weather and the rise and fall of kingdoms. It is only over the last four hundred years that there has arisen a widespread literature denouncing astrology's slightest claim to credibility.

The myth of the glorious past is not a modern invention. In the 17th century, we find astrologers such as John Partridge hankering after this golden age, claiming that modern astrology is so corrupt that we must go back to the ancients to find it in pure form. His work *Opus Reformatum* is an attempt at 'Reviving the True and Ancient Method laid down by the Great Ptolemy',[2] although its resemblance to Ptolemy is no closer than that of the Pre-Raphaelites to any of the pre-Raphaelites. As with Rossetti in the world of art,

---

[1] *Modern Astrology,* first issue, 1895; quoted in Patrick Curry, *A Confusion of Prophets,* p. 123; Collins & Brown, London, 1992

[2] London, 1693, title page. Reprinted Ascella, Nottingham, n.d.

Partridge's desire to return to his roots is the result less of a sound under-standing of what those roots actually were than of an acute awareness of a malaise in the world within which he worked.

As was the custom in his day, Partridge published an annual almanac. This was much the equivalent of an astrologer writing a newspaper sun-sign column today: it was a guaranteed money-spinner and placed one's name firmly in the public eye. There were many of these almanacs on the market, so the appear-ance of yet one more for the year 1708, published under the previously unknown name of Isaac Bickerstaff, would have occasioned little interest, had it not been that first in the list of prophecies of notable deaths that every almanac was expected to carry was not 'a notable duke' or 'a prince of foreign climes' or some such, but Partridge himself, who was to die "upon the 29th of March next, about eleven at night, of a raging Feaver".[3]

Bickerstaff's work attracted great attention, even being translated into several languages. On March 30th, an elegy on Partridge's death was published, soon followed by an anonymous letter, describing in exact detail, complete with a death-bed confession of his astrological sins, the unfortunate astrologer's last hours. "I am a Poor, Ignorant Fellow, Bred to a Mean Trade," he is said to have gasped, "Yet I have sense enough to know that all pretences of foretelling by Astrology are Deceits."[4] Partridge's own almanac appeared as usual later in the year, including his protestations that he was still alive and well. Bickerstaff rushed into print again, defending his prediction. Amongst other evidence, he pointed out that it was well known that many almanacs continued to appear long after the death of their putative author. Partridge's attempts to prove himself alive were hindered by a falling out with the Company of Stationers, which refused him a licence to publish for the next three years. In intellectual circles, if not on the street, he rapidly became a laughing-stock.

This incident is symptomatic of the change in the spirit of the age, percep-tion of which had prompted Partridge to publish his *Opus Reformatum* nine years earlier. Isaac Bickerstaff was a *nom de guerre* of Jonathan Swift, self-appointed champion of the new Enlightenment, in whose brave new world astrology had no place. As always, the critics display the greatest disinclination to the framing of a cogent argument: Swift's main complaint against Partridge was that he had once worked as a cobbler. This apparently proves that astrology is nonsense. Swift's attack was emblematic of a sea-change in the affairs of man. Astrology was becoming incomprehensible to the new intellectual order, or, to be more precise, the new intellectual order was framing its vision of reality in such a way that astrology no longer made sense. We must also note that whereas the plentiful criticism of astrology in the past had come almost entirely from those with a knowledge of the subject, Swift was among the first in the glorious line that would regard ignorance as sufficient qualification for judgement.

---

[3] *Esquire Bickerstaff's Most Strange and Wonderful Predictions,* London, 1708
[4] *The Accomplishment of the First of Mr. Bickerstaff's Predictions,* London, 1708

The new world-view exemplified by Bacon, Descartes and Newton cut the ground from beneath astrology's feet, leaving it suspended without visible means of intellectual support. Without a plausible rationale, even when it worked it seemed like sleight of hand, whereas before, in the world-view that had held until the Renaissance, its workings had seemed perfectly natural. Although the new developments, like Baconian science, can be seen as an articulation of a changing zeitgeist, as long as this articulation was current only in the small world of the intelligentsia it mattered little. As it filtered down to transform the perception of common-sense held by the man on the Clapham omnibus, astrology's understanding public disappeared. Astrology no longer made sense not only to the intelligentsia, but also to the man in the street. We see this incomprehension today in the scientific attacks on astrology: these never raise valid issues, but concentrate on points such as the way in which planets cast their influence or whether or not a planet is ever literally 'in' a sign – and whether these signs even exist. To an astrologer these arguments sound like wilful ignorance, but they are not: the incomprehension is inevitable as the scientist's world-view is now so totally alien from that in which astrology is a coherent part. Astrology's fall from grace was caused by the movement of society away from the traditional principles that had guided it. Astrology's basic ideas no longer made sense within the *Weltanschauung.*

The idea of the absolute pre-eminence of the Divine, the Truth that was once central to all man's conceptions, however far he may have strayed from the precepts which that Divinity laid down for his behaviour, has been forgotten in our headlong rush towards the technological paradise. This Truth, in its manifestations through the revealed faiths, was once a kind of lingua franca and now is no longer widely spoken. So astrology, which as one of the lesser manifestations of this spiritual tradition is built within the walls of its concepts, no longer has a common language with modern man. Those who are content with the modern, secular, materialist world regard this lack of a common tongue as a sign of their progress; those who think otherwise regard it as a tragedy. As science took step after step down the pathway opened at the Renaissance, with common-sense tagging along a few steps behind it, it moved ever further from astrology. The so-called 'new' physics is sometimes said to be a rediscovery of ancient truths in modern terms, but this is far from true: a clear understanding of these ancient truths reveals that the new physics is even further from them than the old. If we trust that the path beaten by the scientists is a valid one, this gap would cast serious doubt on the verity of the ancient sciences. As we look around us, however, much as we may admire the technological rabbits which the scientists are so adept at pulling from every conceivable hat, the intellectual, moral and spiritual bankruptcy of the world created by modern science so impress themselves upon us that this view cannot be seriously entertained.

The world in which Alan Leo found himself had Darwinism rapidly making itself at home in the house built by Newton and Descartes. In this world of secular mechanical materialism, astrology had lost its audience; it was no longer understood. It was not unreasonable, then, that Leo should have decided that something should be done to rebuild the bridge of understanding between astrology and the public. The means by which he sought to achieve this, apart from being almost totally ineffective – as we may witness through the frivolous view of astrology common today – were utterly pernicious, destroying the sacred science even as he sought to revive it.

There is one way and one way only to render astrology intelligible to the modern mentality. This way is to change modern thinking until it accepts the principles on which astrology is founded. Let us suppose that astrology is a plate of broccoli. We know that our child would benefit from eating this nutritious vegetable, but he has no wish to do so as he fails to understand its benefits. So we take the broccoli away, replace it with a bowl of ice-cream, and when the child empties the bowl we congratulate ourselves on our success at making him eat the broccoli. We could hardly reach such a conclusion without being aware of our self-delusion. Yet this is exactly what Leo (and his many followers) have done with astrology. In order to make it intelligible they have transformed it until it bears but the scantiest resemblance to what it really is – just as ice-cream and broccoli bear some slight resemblance in that they are both edible, but otherwise have little in common.

Leo remade astrology in the terms of Theosophy, which was itself a rendering of Victorian scientific materialism into something which to those of little discrimination could pass for spirituality. The garbled mish-mash of spiritual jargon from which Theosophy was constructed was sufficiently vague and sufficiently broad to accommodate any visitor who had the decency to suspend critical judgement before entering its portals; most importantly, so thin was the pseudo-spiritual veil which it threw over the common-sense world-view of the time, that it was readily comprehensible. Its influence extended far beyond those who became card-carrying members of its societies; today, its odour pervades the whole world of 'Alternative Religion' and 'New Age Spirituality'. For three-quarters of a century the writings of the overtly Theosophical dominated the astrological literature in the English language; that which was not written by them could not help but be coloured by their influence. Every one of the major astrological organisations in Great Britain at the end of the Twentieth Century is directly descended from the Astrological Lodge of the Theosophical Society, founded by Leo in 1914. Grown men who are usually capable of composing their features into a mask of sanity are reduced to the most acrimonious squabbles over the rightful possession of Leo's pen, which to them has powers somewhat similar to the Holy Grail.

Why anyone seeking knowledge of astrology should wish to possess the Infallible Pen is unclear, as its original owner's connection with astrology is not dissimilar to Robert Oppenheimer's connection with Hiroshima. The world of Theosophy is quite alien from the metaphysics of astrology. Humanity, the theosophist astrologers would have it, is divided into those of 'evolved' or 'unevolved' souls, the former being distinguished by their conformity to the norms of late-Victorian middle-class behaviour. Any configuration in the chart will be judged according to the stage of evolution of the chart's owner – one man's mystical experience being another man's drunken binge. It is not possible to ascertain the state of the soul from the chart itself, so the astrologer must rely on his own judgement of the client: possession of the correct school tie or knowledge of the appropriate strange hand-shake is a reliable indicator of evolution. The astrologer himself, it almost goes without saying, is a highly evolved soul, and well-equipped to determine the state of evolution of his fellow man.

Leo's inclination was to the use of astrology as character analysis rather than as predictive tool; one of his favoured slogans was 'Character is Destiny'. This propensity was furthered by his trial and conviction on a charge of "pretending and professing to tell fortunes". Leo's claim that he had pointed only 'tendencies' to certain happenings, rather than clear and definite forecasts, proved no defence, so he fled still further from the concrete into the delineation of character. While it might at first seem that the absence of any clear information in the astrologer's judgement would be a liability, quite the opposite proved to be the case. By concentrating on holding a rose-tinted mirror before the client's face and avoiding saying anything that could be contradicted by fact, Leo achieved the great break-through which he had sought.

Convinced that concrete statement was undesirable, Leo set about neutering astrology to make it impossible. Techniques were arbitrarily mangled, interchanged or excluded: as there was no longer an aim of stating anything verifiable, this could be done at whim without fear that the new methods might be exposed as invalid. Indeed, the more it was done the further the dire spectre of plain accurate judgement was banished into the fog.

Times continued to change, so to keep astrology abreast of the intellectual vernacular, further changes had to be made. The Darwinist impulse behind Theosophy was succeeded in the popular imagination by the investigation of the unconscious by the psychoanalysts. Jung's active interest in astrology proved an open door. First through it was the American Dane Rudhyar, who combined Theosophy and Jung to produce an even more appealing flavour of intellectual blancmange. The amount of Jungian verbiage in this mix was gradually increased, notably through the work of the current Queen of the Bookshelves, Liz Greene. Although the work of Greene and her associates falls neatly between two stools, being scorned by both psychologists and those with a working knowledge of sound astrology, its ability to reflect exactly the picture of himself that the reader or client wishes to see has made it immensely popular, less as a form of astrology than as part of the literature and practice of 'self-help'.

In the past, the astrological consultation was a simple request for information; it would become a medical matter only if the client were actually ill and astrology were being used as a tool in the diagnosis and treatment of his illness. Mimicking the psychoanalysts, the psychological astrologers have made a medical model of consultation the norm in all circumstances. The implicit assumption is that the client is in a mess (and if you're not in a mess, it is only because you don't understand your situation clearly enough) and the astrologer, being a Person of Knowledge and Wisdom, has sufficient mental clarity to be able to sort him out. It is indeed a requirement in the leading school in the field, Greene's *Centre for Psychological Astrology*, that the student undergoes extensive therapy. We might note that it is not a common requirement in schools of surgery that the student go under the knife in order to become a better surgeon.

This medical model extends beyond the consultation to the astrologer's view of himself, for in the debate about professional validation that continues among astrologers it is taken for granted that such validation should be styled in the medical fashion and achieved by the affiliation of astrological organisations with medical or quasi-medical bodies. A great many astrologers regard themselves as working within or complementary to the health services; yet only in the very rarest instances do these astrologers deal with patients having a definable ailment that they might be expected to succeed or fail in curing. Safer far to offer 'counselling', with no definable result and often no definable aim, other than the transfer of a cheque from client to astrologer.

We might compare the traditional and modern models of astrology by seeing the client as a man standing on the kerb of a busy road. The traditional astrologer looks up and down the road and tells the client if there is any traffic coming; his modern incarnation tells the client what dark childhood trauma is responsible for him wanting to cross the road in the first place, and then walks off and leaves him where he is. If we regard the former as rather the more useful of the two, no doubt our own childhood traumas are clouding our judgement.

The psychological has now ousted the Theosophical as the dominant – indeed, almost the only – trend in astrology. Within its orb, sharing its fixation with the world between the ears and its uninterest in whatever happens outside it, we find the manifold varieties of New Age astrology. Five minutes inside a bookshop turns anyone into a guru; knowing the names of the planets entitles him to cast his wisdom in astrological terms. There is also a growing trend to the intuitive. Many are they who will proudly proclaim that never have they stooped so low as to study astrology with anyone, but have developed an intuitive understanding of the subject. Those who use their services no doubt also patronise dentists with an intuitive knowledge of dentistry and electricians with an intuitive knowledge of wiring. Even among those who have studied the subject, there is a general horror at the idea of following rules of practice when judging a chart: the done thing is to pick at it until one gains an 'intuitive' understanding. This is apparently not the same as judging it solely in the light of one's own preconceptions. The leitmotiv of any astrologer's judgement is the words "for me...": "For me this Saturn means..." "For me this aspect means..." This does not mean that the astrologer has no idea what the significance of that Saturn or that aspect actually might be; it means that this significance has been vouchsafed to him alone, by virtue of his highly developed psychic powers.

Those whose psychic powers are most strongly developed abandon astrological convention altogether and enter the realms of 'esoteric astrology'. There are many books with just such a title – somewhat strange, we might think, as the esoteric by its very nature is loathe to proclaim itself in the market-place: we might as well find a sign saying "This way to the Secret Headquarters." To be an esoteric astrologer, one leaves to lesser mortals all the usual ascriptions of planets and signs – ideas such as Venus ruling Taurus, for instance – and reshuffles the pack, dealing the cards in an order that the uninitiated might take for random, but which is revealed to the writer by personal contact from some angel or other – usually one whose knowledge of astrology and things of the spirit is somewhat shaky. This personal revelation is a fine thing, as it avoids the necessity of learning anything and removes one from all criticism. The most sensitive will introduce a few new planets which are of too subtle a vibration to have been detected by the rest of humanity. Viewing the chart from this perspective, the esoteric astrologer can then discourse learnedly on the state of his client's soul, a disquisition even less capable of contradiction than the nebulous descriptions of the client's psyche beloved by the exoteric practitioner. Alan Leo's own exercise in this area, the original *Esoteric Astrology,* was judged even by Charles Carter, a fellow Theosophical astrologer, as "a big volume containing virtually nothing worth reading"[5] – the first of a noble tradition. It is notable that the the esoteric 'teachings' in which these works are framed are never those of the revealed faiths, the spiritual doctrines too having been personally dictated by one or more of the aforementioned channels.

For reasons which are not visible to the unaided eye, all with which we have so far dealt is, incredibly, known as 'serious' astrology. Its practitioners go to the greatest pains to distance themselves from 'popular' astrologers, awarding themselves any number of mickey mouse qualifications entitling them to put whole scrabble sets of random letters after their names in order to convince gullible punters that they are in possession of high knowledge (we should note that the great astrologers of the past seem not to have felt the need to boast their learning: the ability to perform was what mattered. Even at the height of his fame, the great William Lilly styled himself only a 'student' of astrology). Popular astrologers, we are told, plying their trade in newspapers and magazines, deal only in vague platitudes and saccharine generalities designed to make their public feel better: as different from serious astrologers as chalk from chalk.

The day when the newspaper sun-sign column was written by the office junior has largely passed: the greater number of these columns are now the work of 'serious' modern astrologers feeling the need to turn a penny. In 'serious' circles this is widely looked upon with disapproval, as if these renegades were letting the side down, like some officer of empire allowing the natives to see

[5] Quoted in Curry, op. cit., p. 145

him without full uniform. Although it is difficult to see that the average newspaper column contains (could possibly contain) a greater number of banalities than the average psychological astro-analysis, it must be admitted that the existence of this form of journalism – for, as an internationally syndicated exponent explains, the sun-sign column is a branch of journalism, not a branch of astrology[6] – does provide the great majority of people with their guiding impression of astrology. There is a certain number who have some awareness that there exists something else, maybe connected with birth-charts, but most are sure that a knowledge of one's sun-sign and its supposed characteristics is all of which astrology consists. On revealing that one is an astrologer, the second question – after "What are this week's lottery numbers?" – is invariably "I'm a Scorpio and my boy-friend's a Pisces: will we get along?"

There is a measure of truth in the division of mankind into twelve groups according to the section of the zodiac occupied by the Sun at birth. There is a measure of truth in the division of mankind into groups according to the country of nationality; but as the number of countries compared with the number of sun-signs indicates, this division is far more subtle than that based on zodiacal signs. Yet no one thinks to ask "I am an American and my boy-friend is Australian, will we get along?" There is a profound meaning in the sun-signs: these are the twelve gates by which we may enter Heaven; but in the day-to-day world of our secular lives, the analysis of character by sign is no more accurate than the analysis of character by nationality. If we were to distil essence of Australian it might perhaps be more rumbustuous, more interested in sport and with a greater affection for beer than essence of Moroccan; but to judge any individual Australian or Moroccan by these characteristics would be foolish. We could indeed, if possessed of certain facts, make predictions by nationality. If we know that the Australian cricket team is losing heavily, the weather across that continent will be dreadful and the price of lager is about to rise, we might predict that "Australians will be gloomy today". There will, however, be a large number of Australians, even beer-drinking, sun-worshipping sports fanatics, who will be perfectly cheerful. If we consider a prediction such as "Australians will receive a major career boost today," and bear in mind that the number of Australians in the world is markedly smaller than the number of Leos, Aquarians or any other sun-sign, we see the fatuity of the average sun-sign column. We shall not consider the below-average sun-sign column, carrying helpful tips for the day such as 'avoid accidents', nor shall we puzzle our heads wondering why an Aries might win the lottery with one lucky number while a Taurus should win it with another.

It is sometimes claimed that the proliferation of these columns demonstrates the healthy condition of contemporary astrology; in which case an abundance of stinging nettles shows the beauty of a rose garden. Or that, although worthless in themselves, they play a useful role by creating an environment in which

[6] Personal conversation.

astrology is accepted and thence encouraging those with a serious interest to pursue it further. It is rather true to say that they play a destructive role, accustoming the public to fantastic predictions which cannot possibly come true and deluding them that this is all that astrology has to offer. The general belief that this is all there is to astrology is repeatedly demonstrated by the scientists, who gleefully cast aside any semblance of scientific method, look at a few sun-sign predictions and conclude that astrology is therefore rubbish. We cite the representative instance of Paul Couderc, astronomer at the Paris Observatory, who glanced at the birth-dates of 2,817 musicians and concluded that no one sun-sign was more likely than any other to produce a musician. As scarcely even the most superficial of modern astrologers, let alone any astrologer with a mastery of the craft, would claim that it does, it is hard to see that this shows anything except that M. Couderc has far too much time on his hands.[7]

Sun-sign columns are hugely popular. Even the less disreputable newspapers, who some ten or twenty years ago would have been horrified at the suggestion that they might publish such things, now proudly proclaim the prowess of their own house astrologer as a powerful weapon in the battle for readers. What, we may then wonder, is the attraction? A favourable horoscope in one's morning paper gives a little fillip, a shot of emotional caffeine, to perk us up as we start the day. We may know that it is nonsense and not consciously expect it to be fulfilled, but the statement that today is a good day for love engages our hopes with the promise that life need not always be like this, just as we may know that our chances of winning the lottery are negligible, but in buying the ticket we purchase the fleeting dream of change. Even if the horoscope advises caution, we are left with the feeling that all will not be lost; our doughty Aries, Taurus, Gemini, Cancer... virtues will enable us to battle through. It is as if we were soldiers at the front, crouched in a fox-hole. The general passes briefly by, giving us a smile and a cigarette. He leaves, and we are still in the foxhole; but our morale is that much better for his visit.

For most people, most of the time, the little shot of confidence that the sun-sign column brings is sufficient. But there are hardened cases, who have become inured to the effects of the newspaper column. They have switched papers to find a better astrologer; they have bought magazines with detailed monthly forecasts; but they have tried this kick so often that it no longer works: they must go in search of stronger stuff. So they send away for a computer-generated reading of their birth-chart; or in the most desperate cases they slink into the astrologer's lair in person, cross her palm with silver and sit open-mouthed as she reads them like a book. But still, they invariably find, it does nothing beyond giving a fleeting feeling that life is not as hopeless as it seemed.

With the concentration of modern astrology on 'character delineation' and its abandoning of the tools necessary if it is to say anything at all specific, astrologers can offer nothing other than the holding of a flattering mirror before

---

[7] P. Couderc, *L'Astrologie, Que Sais-je?* pp. 86-89, Presses Universitaires de France, Paris, 1961.

the client's face. Whatever it is that is given by this willingness to focus exclusively on the client for an hour, saying nothing disturbing, it has less to do with astrology than with validating the client's poor stressed ego with sugared words. What is said may contain little in the way of truth, but long practice has enabled it to hit just that satisfying mark.

Proudly the modern astrologer proclaims, "I do not predict; I do not advise." But what then, other than massaging egos, does he do? "I consider the underlying planetary patterns in the chart." If we were to turn on the TV and hear the weather-forecaster saying "I'm not going to attempt to tell you what the weather will be like tomorrow; nor will I advise you on whether you need to carry an umbrella – but I can tell you that summers in this country are usually hot and dry," we might justly wonder why we bothered turning the dial. If we were to wonder what effect the movements of planets in the sky now over sensitive points in our birth-charts might have, the comment of a leading astrologer, "Who are we to know how they are going to manifest?"[8] might strike us as a dereliction of duty (imagine our weather-forecaster asking, "Who am I to know how this cumulonimbus will manifest?"). But we would be missing the point. Modern astrology's job is not – under any circumstances – to say anything that might conceivably be taken down and used in evidence; its sole purpose is to pander to the ego. People nowadays do not consult astrologers when they are feeling on top of the world; they seek their services when they are confused and uncertain; what they seek is assurance, and this is exactly what the modern astrologer provides. We hear from time to time of purveyors of computer-generated chart readings who do not bother to change the details of birth-date and time from client to client, but send each client exactly the same reading. Most of those who receive these universal readings accept them as their own, and not without reason, for they contain the three magic phrases:

> You are important
> People do not fully understand you
> Your vices are quite endearing, really.

Into three lines we have the distilled the modern astrological reading, guaranteed to satisfy every client. We cannot reasonably imagine that such fluff would have enticed a long series of great minds to devote their utmost efforts to the study of the science that produced it.

In sum: the efforts of various well-meaning but gravely misguided individuals have remade astrology in a form that attempts to make sense to the modern mind; but they have failed miserably because, bereft of the philosophical base from which they have torn it, astrology can make sense to no one. Astrology is no longer intelligible, not because it has been disproved in any final sense, but because the philosophical ground has shifted. Modern society no longer under-

---

[8] Quotations in this paragraph are verbal comments at meetings of the Association of Professional Astrologers, London, 1999.

stands the cosmos in a way within which astrology makes sense. By the criteria of the modern world – and, it must be stressed, by these criteria alone – astrology is indeed nonsensical.

That astrology and the modern world-view are incompatible is commonly taken as disproof of astrology; yet it can equally well, and rather more plausibly, be seen as disproof of the modern world-view. They cannot both be correct; one or other is wrong. We see the arguments only from within the camp of the modern world, through the tinted glass that the modern world provides; yet the victors write not only the history, but also the philosophy. Only if we accept that our contemporary society is superior to all the normal societies that have gone before, societies centred on the simple truth of revealed faith, can we accept that this society's view is correct and that the philosophy behind astrology is therefore wrong. The tangible evidence for this claim is not persuasive.

To understand the traditional astrology it is necessary to realise that it is not – as is usually presented today – a retrospective branch of astrology, which implies that there is a valid relationship between it and modern astrology. Traditional astrology is not a branch of astrology which happens to rely on ancient authorities: it is the tradition of astrology itself. As a traditional science, that is, a science in the true sense of the word as opposed to the sciences of today which are what could with exact accuracy be described as 'pseudo-sciences', the object of astrology is the greater understanding of the Divine, of the Creation and of Man's place therein. The words of al-Ghazali on anatomy are just as true of the celestial science: "The science of the structure of the body is called anatomy: it is a great science, but most men are heedless of it. If any study it, it is only for the purpose of acquiring skill in medicine, and not for the sake of becoming acquainted with the perfection of the power of God."[9]

There are valid and invalid objections to astrology. A large section of the critical literature – mainly past rather than present – does not deny its workings, but points the pitfalls of man's involvement with it. Some of this criticism argues that it is impious for man to pry into the workings of the cosmos, peering into forbidden realms of knowledge. Other works make plain the foolishness of worshipping or attributing independent powers to the individual stars, a confusion that is one manifestation of man's unfortunate habit of mistaking agent for cause: we see the messenger arrive with a letter and praise the messenger if it bears good news. Neither of these arguments reflect on astrology itself, only on man's attitude towards it. Any form of knowledge is a test: how is it to be treated? The Qur'an speaks of the challenge of knowledge: '*We are only a temptation, therefore disbelieve not (in the guidance of Allah).*'[10] Astrology, no less than knowledge of nuclear fission, can be misused. If it

---

[9] Al-Ghazali, *Alchemy of Happiness,* p. 38. Albany, N.Y, 1873. Quoted in Seyyed Hossein Nasr, *An Introduction to Islamic Cosmological Doctrines,* pp. 97-98, rev. ed., Thames & Hudson, London, 1978
[10] 2:102. Pickthall translation.

perverts man's faith, or causes him to set that faith aside, it is pernicious; if it leads him to walk on the straight path, it is a blessing. If either astrology itself or any of its elements come between man and God, it is being misused, for implicit in its teachings is the truth that all power is with God, and all things are subject to His will. It is here that we see most clearly exposed the crux of the problem: why astrology is not accepted in the modern world, and why the form in which it survives in that world is but a mockery of its true form. In a determinedly secular world, there is no room for a true scheme of knowledge, for the existence of such a scheme exposes ruthlessly the paucity of the premises on which this secular knowledge is founded.

The efforts to remake astrology in the terms of Twentieth-Century western culture have inevitably distorted it out of all recognition. First it was remade in the form of Theosophy, then in that of Jungian psychoanalysis, then in that of West Coast New Ageism. Each of these new languages gained it an audience; but although the audience could understand the concepts in which astrology was now framed, what they were hearing bore little resemblance to its true nature. It is the hubris of modern man that "if I don't understand it, it will have to change." The stars have been around for a lot longer than we have: if we wish to understand them, it is we who must change; we cannot change them to fit our preconceived illusions of how things should be.

Nor can we subject astrology to any meaningful test by the criteria of modern science. These criteria are essentially technological: the endless quest for the better mousetrap, as man seeks to dominate the universe. The criteria of astrology are sapiential. We can no more judge the one by the other than we can judge the ability of a basketball player by the number of home runs he has scored. Lamentably, astrologers too have been sucked into the devouring mist that promises validation of astrology by scientific means. Their first action is invariably to abandon all knowledge of astrology. It is not only the scientists who conduct 'experiments' based around the existence or otherwise of a correlation between sun-sign and profession, an existence which no astrologer competent in the techniques of the tradition would expect to find. Astrology concerns itself with qualities, not quantities; its results are not measurable by strictly quantitative methods such as statistical analysis. "How much do you love me?" "Forty-two centimetres." The answer clearly has nothing to do with the question – yet this is exactly the answer which those modern astrologers who claim to prove anything by statistics are providing.

Thus the essence of the problem – the cause of the famished condition in which true astrology lingers into the modern world – is that there can be no such thing as humanistic astrology. Astrology is a sacred science – take away the sacred and we have nothing. Many of the modern schools proudly proclaim themselves as purveyors of 'humanistic astrology'; the others have their humanism dressed up in a mockery of faith, but are nonetheless founded in ideas that are fundamentally anti-spiritual. The consequences of this cannot be other than what we have: narcissism through stellar oracle. Modern astrology, in whatever form it masquerades, even the so-called 'esoteric' astrology, is a poor creature bereft of all inner meaning. Its primary use is to provide validation for the bewildered of the world, stroking fragile egos to convince them all is well. The scorn it attracts from the sceptics is fully deserved, albeit given for the wrong reasons. If traditional astrology is a cathedral, where man comes closer to his Maker, its modern offshoot is nothing but a bordello, promising everyone the particular comfort they feel they require, yet giving not one of them what he really needs. The following chapters introduce the possibilities offered by the real astrology that flourished so long and so richly before the advent of what is known as the Enlightenment.

3

Horary Astrology

Not only in the structures by which it seeks to comprehend the universe, but also in the structures of the science itself, astrology is remorselessly hierarchical. That well-known tenet of Hermetic doctrine, so carelessly bandied by so many who flee screaming from the very thought of cosmic hierarchies, 'As above, so below,' implies quite clearly that there is an above and there is a below. This understanding runs throughout astrology; there is no astrology without it: no matter how attached we may be to our egalitarian social beliefs, they will not work when applied to the cosmos.

The traditional authorities laid down a strict hierarchy of 'subjects fit to be judged', matters into which astrologers might usefully pry. The subjects are as follows:

1: States and great nations
2: Dynasties and families
3: Kings and potentates
4: Individual nativities
5: Elections
6: Horary questions

In the hierarchy of importance, the traditional texts always start from the top and work downwards; this can be seen in any description of the planets, which will always start with Saturn and work in through the celestial spheres to finish with the Moon. We might contrast modern texts, which typically start with the Sun and then work in exactly reverse order from the Moon outwards, noting that this order conforms neither to astrological theory nor to the modern model of the structure of the solar system and is thus totally arbitrary. The beauty of astrology is that it gives a completely coherent intellectual model; the modern mockery of astrology is nothing but a random pastiche.

As might be expected, traditional didactic texts start the student from the bottom and lead him gradually upward. So the first subject to be covered is the lowest on the list: horary astrology, which is the art of answering specific questions by judging an astrological chart for the moment at which the question is asked. The traditional teacher has a careful belief that it is better to start with what is easier and work towards what is more difficult. The study of modern astrology invariably begins with birth-charts, which is akin to confronting children in the first year of elementary school with the differential calculus. A few of those who master natal astrology will find their way to a study of horary, as if that small proportion who study maths at university were finally to be introduced to the multiplication tables. This might not be unconnected with the lack of mastery prevalent today.

From horary, we come to electional astrology. This can be seen as horary back-to-front: while horary takes the moment and judges the likely consequence, in electional astrology we take the desired consequence and look for the moment most likely to produce that result. Only then do we come to the thorough study of natal astrology; for only through having attained mastery of horary and elections will the student have acquired sufficient knowledge to be able to soundly judge the infinitely more complex matter of a human life.

But even natal astrology, the be-all and end-all of the craft today, is but a stepping stone on the path to the three highest sections in our list of subjects, which together comprise 'mundane' astrology: the astrology of the world, traditionally considered the flower and the crown of astrological learning. The lowest branch of mundane, kings and potentates, is but a short step from natal astrology. Here, we judge the life and reign of individual monarchs. With dynasties and families we take a longer view, watching the rise and fall of royal families; from there we pass to judgement of the fall and swell of history as empire follows empire and dominance passes from nation to nation. As we might expect, we see here not just a hierarchy of meaning, but also a hierarchy of technique: in horary, we are much concerned with the movements of the Moon, the lightest of the planets; in mundane, we deal primarily with the 'great chronocrators', the time-keepers of the cosmos, the outermost planets, Jupiter and Saturn. Following the traditional pathway, we shall start our ascent with a consideration of horary.

Of all the forms of traditional astrology, it is horary that falls most strangely on the modern ear. The idea that a question can be asked, a chart of the stars drawn for that moment and the answer to that question deduced from what it shows sounds bizarre. It stretches the theories of planetary causation that are foisted onto astrology somewhat beyond their reasonable limits, implying as it does that, for instance, Saturn should suddenly find itself responsible for someone's lost ear-ring and have to dash around the cosmos deciding what shall happen to it. To the modern mind, horary makes no sense at all, even less so than tarot or I-Ching, where the questioner does at least have contact with the cards or the coins: the stars are immutable and are not to be shuffled to match the state of the querent's unconscious. Yet work it does, and with great accuracy, providing verifiable, concrete answers to the questions asked, whether these questions be on public issues, the major business of a person's life, or even day-to-day trivia such as "Where is my watch?" or "Have I got time to have a bath before the repair-man arrives?"

Horary was the staple of most astrologers' business in the past, for a variety of reasons, only one of which is the material fact that few people knew their date and time of birth with any accuracy (even today, the accuracy of most given birth-times is doubtful: almost everyone lacking the dubious privilege of being born into a family of astrologers seems to be born on the hour or on the half-hour). When the king summoned the court astrologer to find out if he should marry the princess or invade the next kingdom, horary is what the astrologer would almost invariably have used. Quick, precise and efficient, it provides more bang for the astrological buck than any other form of the craft, and hence, as it allows for quick turnover and impressive results, found favour with skilled professionals. One sets the chart and finds the answer 'instantly', according to William Lilly, one of the masters of the craft. Instantly is perhaps an exaggeration, but in his day (the Seventeenth Century) the norm was for an astrological consultation lasting some fifteen or twenty minutes. This brief time would include social niceties and payment, the asking of the question and explanation of the situation, the astrologer adjusting his daily chart for the exact moment at which the question was asked, his telling the client – if a 'convincer' were necessary – where on their body they had warts, moles or scars (all deduced from the chart), and finally judging the chart and giving the answer. Quick, precise and efficient.

If we liken the conventional idea of the birth-chart reading to general medical practice, horary is like surgery: it cuts straight to the point. By concentrating on one issue alone, it gives a close and detailed focus on that issue, in a way that is not possible from a birth-chart, without – if at all – the exercise of greater amount of subtlety than most astrologers possess and a greater amount of work than most clients can afford. A birth-chart reading, for instance, may suggest that the native is likely to marry this year; it will not, however, say whether Bill or Tom is the man in question, or that it is unwise to plan the reception outdoors because it is going to rain on that day. Similarly – and this is perhaps the most immediately impressive use of astrology – it will not reveal the whereabouts of your lost cat/ring/handbag/whatever. From the practitioner's point of view, the client, even if asking for a birth-chart reading, will usually have some specific issue on their mind; it is far simpler to deal with that issue than to attempt to unravel a whole life-time of specific issues – most of which do not concern the client at that moment.

The assumption behind horary is that the question is an existent thing in its own right. It is conceived when it enters the mind, and born when it is understood by the person who is in a position to answer it: in this case, the astrologer. So the astrological chart cast for the moment at which the astrologer understands the question is, as it were, the question's birth-chart. This holds true even if the question is understood at what is, apparently, a completely random moment, such as the moment at which the astrologer picks the letter containing the question from his door-mat, or when he returns a message left on an answerphone: logically, a request for information is born only when it reaches the ear of the person who can provide that information. The relevance of even these supposedly chance moments to the issue at hand can be seen from the frequency with which the charts cast for them show verifiable events in the past which are datable from the chart. In fact, even though it is not done consciously, the querent exercises precise control over the moment of the question. Often, if the question is being asked by phone, the querent will hesitate, make small talk, change his mind, change it back again, ask the question, decide not to ask it, change its form – and then finally decide "OK, this is it: here is the question." This can invariably be shown as a quite unconscious process of fine-tuning, often waiting for the moment when the Ascendant of the chart (which always represents the querent) moves from one sign to another. In the traditional cosmos, there is nothing random; there is no pure chance. Everything is connected and everything has meaning.

That the querent chooses this particular moment to ask this particular question is a consequence of absolutely everything that has happened in his life up to that point. There is a reason why this querent phones the astrologer while working, while that one waits until her lunch-break; why this one boldly picks up the phone and dials, while that one hesitates and puts it off. The differences – far more plentiful and mostly far more subtle than these examples – that these sundry actions reveal in the querents are directly pertinent to the question asked; thus also the differences in the astrological chart consequent upon these pertain to the judgement of that question.

The great majority of horary work is predictive, for which it has incurred the wrath of both the churches and modern science to a greater extent than any other form of astrology; many astrologers, indeed, both past and present have condemned horary for just this reason – and not only the ones who lack the knowledge to make it work. Alan Leo denounced it as 'THE CURSE OF THE SCIENCE AND THE RUIN OF THE ASTROLOGER',[1] although it had been the making of many abler than he. The desire for prediction does usually betray a lack of trust in God, and as such is not to be encouraged; we are reminded again of the warning given with what was revealed to the angels Harut and Marut in Babylon: *We are only a temptation, therefore disbelieve not (in the guidance of Allah)'.*[2] Yet the very possibility of being able to predict from the stars, and the intricacy of the structure of the universe, can also be a light on the path to God. For this, however, both artist and querent must always be aware that all is subject to the Will of God. This statement, so stressed by the traditional authorities, seems to the sceptical modern as a 'get-out clause'; but it is an intrinsic part of the whole attitude, without which judgement is impossible. In our astrological hierarchy, the lesser is ever contained within the greater; the fate of a man is contained within the fate of his country, and since there is no greater than God, the spheres of the universe are enclosed by His will. Judgement is also evidently always subject to the

---

[1] Alan Leo, *Modern Astrology,* II/VII:10 (1896), pp. 434-7; quoted in Patrick Curry, *A Confusion of Prophets,* p. 165 Collins & Brown, London, 1992. Leo's capitals.

[2] The Holy Qur'an, 2:102.

fallibility of the astrologer, though even the traditional authorities emphasise this rather less.

Finally, in this section, it must be said that since the republication of William Lilly's classic text-book, *Christian Astrology*, in 1985, horary, understood or misunderstood to varying degrees, has begun to establish a beachhead for itself in the modern world. Within modern astrological circles, indeed, the words 'horary' and 'traditional' are more or less synonymous, however much this misrepresents the vast depth of traditional astrology. By seeing the tradition as offering only horary, which the moderns lack the techniques to perform, they can avoid having their own strange ideas of natal astrology challenged by other ideas that actually work. Horary cannot be done at all with modern method – as those text-books which attempt to demonstrate such a method make perfectly clear.

"When Will the Repairman Arrive?"

Let us consider an example to show how simple horary can be. I had been told that the electricity repair-man would arrive at some time that morning. I wanted to have a bath, so, knowing that nothing is more certain to make the

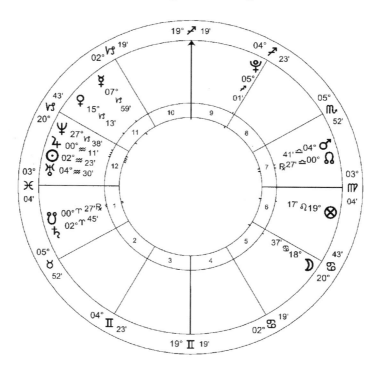

Chart 4: When will the Repairman Arrive?

door-bell ring than settling into the tub, I cast a horary to find out exactly when he would arrive.[3]

The querent is always shown by the planet ruling the Ascendant, in this case Jupiter(♃). At 0 degrees of Aquarius, Jupiter has no strength; being so close to the Sun (☉), the most destructive position a planet can hold, confirms my total lack of power in this situation. Trapped in the twelfth house, the section of the chart concerned with imprisonment, there is nothing I can do other than wait. The repairman's position is quite different. He is shown by the Moon (☽), ruler of the sixth house, as repairmen are rumoured to be our servants. In its own sign, Cancer, it is very strong: he is in control of the situation.

I had expected to see his planet applying to aspect – probably by conjunction – either the Ascendant or my significator. The distance his planet would have to travel in order to complete the aspect would then show the time that must elapse before his arrival. I was horrified to see his significator, which is moving round the chart in an anti-clockwise direction, just entering the sixth house, the house of servants. This can be read quite literally: the repairman is going into his own house. The Moon makes no major aspects to any of the traditional planets before leaving its sign: this is further confirmation that he is going nowhere except home. And so it proved.

Horary judgements are only rarely as straightforward as this, largely because horary questions are only rarely this simple: profound as may be my desire for my bath, "When will the repairman arrive?" has none of the emotional complexity of the tangled situations from within which querents usually pose their questions. The principles, however, remain the same. Muddy situations inspire muddy charts, but the same few simple rules applied patiently and with care will unravel the most knotted bundle of conflicting passions.

Horary can deal with a variety of differing types of question. Questions of state seek an understanding of how things actually are at that moment, looking for information that is veiled from the querent, such as "Where are my keys?" or "Am I pregnant?" We can peer back into the past, with queries such as "Did the cleaner steal my ring, or did I just lose it?" Most often, however, questions are directed into the future, asking if, how or when a certain event will take place.

The technical principles for judging charts set for such questions as these are in essence simplicity itself. Most significantly, for all that they must be applied with subtlety of understanding, these techniques are fixed. There is not the slightest question of intuition, except in the sense of Polyani's formulation of intuition as 'tacit knowledge' – that is, the way that a mechanic knows what is causing that squeak without necessarily being able to articulate the reasons why, large experience having made certain stages in the reasoning process redundant. Any competent astrologer looking at the same chart should, allowing for human fallibility, reach the same conclusions. Intuition in the common under-

[3] January 22nd 1997, 9.07 am GMT, London.

standing of the word – or even in its higher and original meaning of intellection as regards a particular fact or allotment of knowledge – has nothing to do with it: the client can get 'intuitions' from his next-door neighbour; from an astrologer he requires the truth.

These techniques involve first locating the planet that signifies the querent; then the one that signifies the thing they are asking about. If these planets meet by aspect, we have the possibility that the thing will happen; if they do not, it won't. Once we have found that an aspect is there, bringing the two planets together, we must assess the strength of the planets, in order to determine whether they are strong enough to make the event happen; then we evaluate the nature of their connection with each other to find out if they both want the event to happen. If the planets are adequately strong, if they share an interest in making the event happen and if they meet by aspect, we may judge – within as always the possible limits of prediction, as all is ever subject to the will of God – that the event will come to pass.

So if the question were "Will Susie go out with me?" and the chart showed my planet and her planet coming to immediate aspect, this would be an encouraging start to judgement. The aspect provides, as it were, the occasion, without which nothing happens. If both our planets were strong, the chart would look rosier still, as we both have the ability to act. Suppose her planet were weak: no matter how desperate she was to go out with me, any obstacle would prove too much for her to surmount. The chart would show the nature of the obstacle: perhaps she is afflicted by the planet that would represent her father, so we could judge that he will not let her see me. Finally, we examine the way in which the two planets regard each other. In this situation, the ideal would be for my planet to be in a sign ruled by her planet, while hers falls in a sign ruled by mine: this would show intense mutual feelings. If her planet were not in any part of the zodiac ruled by mine, we would judge that she is not interested in me. As the asking of the question implies a certain level of interest, we might expect my planet to be in some part of the zodiac ruled by hers; if, however, it were in one of my own signs it would show clearly that I have no real interest in her, but just want the kudos of being seen with Susie, the prettiest girl in the school. We might make do with planets that do not indicate any interest in each other, but do show a shared interest in something else, as evinced by their both being in parts of the zodiac ruled by a third planet: we don't think much of each other, but we do both want to go to the dance.

As with the lovely Susie, so with any other issue. In the example about the repairman, his planet is very strong, while mine is weak: he can choose what happens, while I cannot. His planet is in a sign ruled by itself: his main priority is his own business. His planet is in Cancer, a sign where my planet, Jupiter, is said to be exalted; this is an important dignity, so I am clearly of some significance to him; unfortunately of not nearly as much significance as he is to himself. In sum, he has the power, while I don't; he is more interested in himself than in me; there is no aspect to bring us together. In this instance, I would happily have settled for an aspect without any indications of his interest in me: I should have been happy if he had turned up; I would not have minded if were thinking of something else while he was working. If the context were different and I were asking about Susie, the amount of interest she had in me would be of the utmost significance.

Suppose I ask "Will I get this job?" My planet strong in the chart would indicate that I have the ability and qualifications to merit it. My planet could be weak in either of two ways: if it is in a part of the zodiac where it has no power, it would suggest that I am weak of myself – in this context, I lack whatever is necessary to get the job. It might, however, be in a congenial part of the zodiac but be afflicted by another planet or by being in an unfortunate part of the sky relative to the horizon: I have the necessary skills, but something gets in the way – maybe I arrive at the interview drunk (my planet weak by being in the house of self-undoing), or perhaps my undoubted abilities are overshadowed by the urgent need to find a post for the chairman's new son-in-law (my planet afflicted by another). Even if my study of the chart revealed that I lack the strength to deserve this job, all might not be lost. Perhaps the planet representing the job has something in common with my own, so I dig out my old school tie or rehearse the secret handshake knowing that this will outweigh my inadequacies. But for all this, if the two planets representing me and the job fail to meet each other in aspect, nothing will happen. No matter how promising the situation, I will not get the job: perhaps the company decides not to hire new staff after all; perhaps great-uncle Silas dies, relieving me with his riches of all need to work: the chart will indicate which.

Where is my fish?

Before turning to a consideration of the basic tools with which astrology works, by which we assess the relative strengths, interests and possible actions of the actors in whatever drama we are watching, whether it be the non-arrival of the electricity man or the demise of a great empire, let us examine a last example of horary, which makes clear some of the apparently problematical issues surrounding this branch of astrology more even than any other. This chart was judged by one of the greatest masters of the craft, William Lilly.

Lilly practised during the Seventeenth Century, acquiring a reputation for accurate, specific astrology stretching far beyond the shores of his native England, a fact that presents us again with the two options: either our ancestors were singularly stupid, or he had to at least some measure the abilities which he claimed. The bulk of his practice was in horary; his surviving notebooks show him dealing with some 2000 clients a year, a depth of practical experience which combined with a huge breadth of study to enable him to write *Christian Astrology*, a text-book of horary and natal astrology that was, suffering varying degrees of distortion, to be the standard work on the subject until Alan Leo put the dying corpse of astrology out of its misery two and a half centuries later.

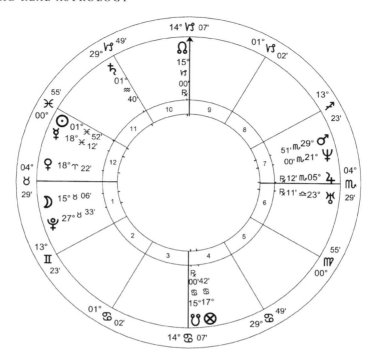

Chart 5: Where is my Fish?

Lilly had ordered some fish and a bag of Portuguese onions to be sent from London to his home, just up-river in Hersham. But when the warehouseman arrived at Lilly's house, instead of delivering the goods he told the astrologer that the warehouse had been broken into and the fish stolen. Lilly set a horary chart to find the thief.[4]

In a question of theft, a planet without strength placed in an angular house often shows the thief, while the Sun or Moon in the Ascendant in one of its own dignities shows that the thief will be discovered. Here, Jupiter (♃) is without strength and angular, while the Moon (☽), in its dignity, is in the Ascendant. Jupiter is the natural ruler of the rich and noble, but Lilly decided that a gentleman was unlikely to burgle warehouses to steal fish. He did, however, take note of the sign that Jupiter is in: Scorpio, a water sign. The Part of Fortune, which falls at 17 degrees of Cancer, represents the querent's 'treasure' in the chart; Lilly's treasure here is his missing fish, so its being in Cancer, another water sign, is of significance. Mercury (☿), ruler of the second house in the chart, and as such significator of Lilly's property – his fish – is in the third water sign, Pisces. Considering this evidence and the circumstances of the theft, Lilly decided that the thief must be connected with the water, probably by

4 February 20 1638 n/s, 9.00 am LMT, Hersham

working on the river (Jupiter in water sign) and the fish must be in some moist place (Part of Fortune and Mercury in water signs).

The Moon usually works as secondary significator of the querent, so its immediate formation of an aspect with Mercury (the property) shows that the querent will recover it. Unfortunately, Mercury is very weak in Pisces: the aspect shows that the fish will be recovered, but this weakness shows that it will be found in less than pristine condition. Lilly judged that he wouldn't recover the fish intact, but that he would get some of it back. The chart has told him that he will discover the thief and recover some of the goods. This judgement has been made by the application of fixed rules: Lilly is not employing his intuition.

Apart from a weak planet in an angular house, the thief can also be shown by the ruler of the seventh house. Here, this is Mars (σ). Mars is on the point of leaving Scorpio ($\mathfrak{M}$), which is its own sign. This suggested that the thief had recently moved house, or was just about to do so (the technical term *house* was commonly applied both to sections of the chart and to the signs of the zodiac). Combining the indications of the two possible significators of the thief, Jupiter and Mars, Lilly was able to work out a physical description of the man. After making enquiries, he heard of a fisherman with a reputation for thieving who had just moved to a house by the river, as was shown by the chart's emphasis on water signs. Tall and well-built with fair complexion and reddish-yellow hair, his appearance was typical of Mars combined with Jupiter. Lilly had his suspect.

Armed with this combination of astrology and detective-work, he approached the local magistrate, who readily granted a warrant to search the man's house and provided him with a bailiff to enforce it. They found part of the fish, at which the thief confessed all, explaining that the rest had already been eaten. Lilly grumbled at the man's wife about the fate of his Portuguese onions – not knowing what they were, she had made soup out of them – but then relented and let them keep the remains of their loot.

As we have seen, the discovery of the thief and the retrieval of the fish are shown, clearly and according to set rules, in the chart; but these predictions depended on certain actions to make them happen, actions which need not, apparently, have been taken. The chart guided Lilly to the thief. Having found the thief, many people would not have confronted him. This was a small community: Lilly might have been frightened of the consequences of his accusation, or uncertain of his judgement and scared of embarrassment if he had got it wrong. He wasn't. This was the same Lilly who, shortly after arriving in London as a young man, had performed a mastectomy on his master's wife, and who was later to risk execution with his vehement astrological propagandising on behalf of Parliament during the Civil War: he wasn't one to back down from a challenge. Then, to allow the prediction to come true, Lilly had to be in a position to obtain a warrant to search the thief's house. Few modern astrologers would find much sympathy arriving at their local police station waving a chart and claiming to know who had stolen their belongings. Lilly had a strong reputation as a worthy citizen and an accurate astrologer. The wealth he had gained through his astrological practice had made him the magistrate's social equal, so he would have found no problem in obtaining the warrant.

Lilly's character and circumstances were necessary factors in the accuracy of the prediction. But it it is reasonable to think that had the circumstances, including Lilly's character, been different, he would not have asked this particular question at this particular time. If, for example, he were timid, he might well have spent another hour worrying about the situation before asking the question, resulting in a different astrological chart; if his reputation as an astrologer had not made him the social equal of the magistrate, he could probably not have afforded to order the fish in the first place. The chart itself is a product of the man and the situation just as much as whatever takes place in the life; unless we are to make the rather bizarre, but currently fashionable, assumption that life is a succession of random events, the two must be meaningfully connected. There is only one possible set of circumstances that could have led to that exact prediction being made at that exact moment. That set of circumstances is the one, and the only one, that had actually arisen. Anything else exists only in the world of hypothesis, as the product of man's tireless fancy.

It is easy to see now why most modern astrologers, from choice or ignorance, have no truck with horary, and why many of them become surprisingly excitable when the subject is raised: the prospect of there being a verifiable, accurate astrology based on sound principles inevitably touches a sore spot.

Some moderns have managed to deal with the threatening intrusion of reality into their nebulous dream-world by breeding an unearthly creature called 'psychological horary'. This strange product of genetic engineering knows nothing so vulgar as providing a simple answer to a simple question, but must delve into the psychological motives for that question having been asked. Had William Lilly been foolish enough to have demanded of one of these astrologers "Where is my fish?" he would have received the response "What does your fish mean to you?" What strange psychological quirk makes you want to know what has happened to the fish that someone has stolen from you? In this way, reality is reduced to its customary place as an adjunct to the client's psyche, and what happens in the life is of no importance other than as a means of casting light on our own kaleidoscope of whirling mental fixations. We might note in passing that such attitudes absolve us from the necessity of any engagement in the world, for whatever we may perceive as wrong-doing is merely our psychological projection, and so we may justifiably admire ourselves in our mirror while the world burns around us.

We might suspect that William Lilly would have given the enquiry "What does the fish mean to you?" a short and dusty answer; we might certainly suspect that using the chart only to analyse this question would not have put the fish on his dinner-table – but to think such thoughts reveals our lack of sophistication: "What does your dinner mean to you?" Any question is construed as an invitation to the contemporary astrologer to trample through the querent's psyche. Whilst some may find this titillating we cannot but regard it with abhorrence. Indeed, René Guénon has pointed out that what the mind keeps unconscious it keeps unconscious for good reason; it does not do to go poking around in it.[5] The amount of psychic detritus we see all around us is not unconnected with the Twentieth-Century fashion for doing just that. All manner of unsavoury genies have been released from bottles in which they slumbered quite safely; they are not easily returned.

While we are most certainly wrong to reduce the great benefit of horary astrology to a means of psychological analysis, we are wrong also to think that the importance of horary is in the immediate results that it offers. Whether we can find the lost ring or determine whether the repair-man will arrive on time is not, in the great scheme of things, a matter of any significance. As horary is the doorway to astrology, the celestial science, we are given a few sweets to tempt us inside. We are provided with some immediate verification of the truth behind the science; yet it does not do to place too great an importance on these proofs. The point, as always in astrology, is to look beyond towards the Divine. *"We shall show them Our portents on the horizons and within themselves until it will be manifest unto them that it is the Truth,"*[6] but we must not become attached to the portents: the signpost is not the destination.

[5] *The Reign of Quantity,* p. 279. 3rd edn. Sophia Perennis, Ghent, USA, 1995
[6] The Holy Qur'an, 41:53

4

The Nature of Time

Before venturing further up the hierarchy of astrological knowledge, we must devote some attention to the principles through which astrological judgement is drawn. The first conception which we must address is the nature of time itself, for it is time that is astrology's basic concern, the material with which it works.

To the scientist, ten past three is just like any other time. Certain things may well happen then – the kettle may boil, the train may arrive, he might think of his mother – but there is no reason why these things could not just as well have happened at nine minutes past three, or twenty to four, or any other time. If we compare time to a landscape, the scientist looks out over a vast featureless vista. There are no mountains, lakes or swamps; there are no areas of barren land, no patches of fertile soil. Time is homogeneous; no one moment has any qualities different from any other.

The astrologer sees time quite differently. To him each moment is different from its fellows, just as you and I are different from ours. The landscape of time that the astrologer sees from the window of his tower is just as varied as any physical landscape: it has its mountains and plains, its dry deserts and lush pastures. To him, whatever happens at ten to three is a part of the particular quality of ten to three; if an apparently similar event happened at twenty to four – the kettle boiling, for instance – it would be subtly different.

The classic scientific experiment treats time as a stable constant. The experiment is something that, all other things being equal, can be repeated at any time without change in its result. This, the scientist would hold, shows that time is indeed a constant and the basic supposition of astrology is false. Leaving aside the fact – which the scientific literature itself confesses – that this claim is actually untrue, we can see that the scientific experiment, which is deliberately constructed 'outside life' as it were, is of so simple and so gross a nature that it will *almost* invariably bludgeon its way to the same conclusion. Dealing with life as it proceeds in all its subtlety and complexity, what may or may not be the result of an artificial experiment is irrelevant. It is notable that when science turns its attention to more subtle realms, such as particle physics, experiments become rather less well-behaved.

To the scientist, the words 'ten past three' tell all there is to be known about that particular moment; to the astrologer, the words 'ten past three' are nothing but a convenient label to assist identification, and no more describe the nature of that moment than the number on my door describes the nature of my house. What astrology does – that of which the whole craft of astrology consists – is to describe that actual individual nature of moments of time as they exist in particular places. The means by which astrology achieves this description is by reference to the relative positions of the planets. This is what astrology is, and this is all that astrology is: *a means of describing the individual nature of moments of time.*

The moments which we choose to describe are those of significance in whichever context we are working. They might be the moment of a birth, of a marriage, of the foundation of a empire, or of the asking of a question. Knowing the context and understanding the nature of the moment, the astrologer may, within strictly circumscribed limits, make an informed judgement as to what is likely to follow. There is nothing magical in this: once we accept that time varies in the same way as place, the possibility of prediction inevitably follows. If I understand the nature of a piece of ground and I know what seed a farmer is about to sow in it, I can make an informed prediction of what will grow there and how it will flourish; if I understand the nature of a piece of time and know the act that someone intends making at that moment, I can make an informed prediction of what will follow and how successful that act is likely to be. Bearing in mind always that all things at all times are subject to the will of God, so no matter how inevitable my prediction might seem, whether based on astrology or horticulture, it can always fail.

This variable quality of time is part of our common-sense experience. I know that I can meet my friend today and we will spend an enjoyable hour, with neither of us wanting to part; I can meet the same friend in the same place and do the same things on another day, and we will both be watching the clock wondering if we can politely leave yet. The scientist would point to physical variables: I am wearing a different shirt, my friend has toothache and a tax demand; the astrologer would claim that above and beyond these things the nature of our meetings is determined by the differing quality of the time at which they take place. Or in the field of sport: Superstars United may have spent millions of pounds assembling a team of all the talents; they may be vastly superior in all areas to No-hopers Town; but sport would lose all its interest if we did not know that on the odd occasion, for no apparent reason, No-hopers Town will bring their glorious opponents firmly down to earth. The astrologer would suggest that this is indicated by the nature of the moment at which the event happens.

The words of Ecclesiastes are familiar: "*To every thing there is a season and a time to every purpose under the heaven.*"[1] Today, in a world which ignores the variable nature of time, this is taken to mean "everything has to be done at some time or another." But it means exactly what it says: there is a specific time to every purpose. "*A time to be born, and a time to die; a time to plant, and a time to*

---

[1] Ecclesiastes. 3.1

pluck up that which is planted; a time to kill, and a time to heal; a time to break down, and a time to build up; a time to weep, and a time to laugh; a time to mourn, and a time to dance; a time to cast away stones, and a time to gather stones together; a time to embrace, and a time to refrain from embracing; a time to get, and a time to lose; a time to keep, and a time to cast away; a time to rend, and a time to sew; a time to keep silence, and a time to speak; a time to love, and a time to hate; a time of war, and a time of peace." [2] We find elucidated in these verses the one essential principle of astrology: time differs in its nature. Understanding the nature of a moment gives us insight into that which happens in that moment, or the consequences of what has happened or of what will happen in that moment. That which is done in its time will prosper, that which is not will not, as surely as seed that is sown in fertile ground will grow and that which is sown in barren will fail. And acts that are not the work of man will happen when they will, just as "*in the place where the tree falleth, there it shall be.*" [3] Many are the modern sciences that devote close study to the variations in the nature of place; astrology is the traditional science that devotes close study to the variations in the nature of time.

These variations in the quality of time are difficult for us to appreciate, because we cannot see time: we see only its effects. We can easily see the nature of place, and so act appropriately: we do not sow our seed on a concrete waste. The only way by which we may see time is by observing things that change regularly with time, such as the position of the hands of a clock – or the places of the planets. The study of astrology is what enables us to understand these changes in time, and to shape our actions accordingly.

Clock Time and Real Time

Acting according to the nature of time becomes ever harder, as our culture distances itself from any awareness of the real phenomenon of time. Time is something to be conquered. Just as most of the space on Earth has been beaten into shape, so we seek to do the same with time. 24-hour shopping; the desire to appear forever young; ubiquitous electric lighting; strawberries available all year round: no matter how convenient some of these developments may be, they all distance us from our awareness of the true nature of time. It is not insignificant that the glare of the electricity in our streets makes it ever harder to see the stars, the markers of true time.

Astrological time – or, to be more correct, the astrological definition of true time – is rather different from the time in daily use. To be sure, astrologers make full use of the common conventions: we set a chart by the clock and only the most perverse would arrange a meeting 'at the start of the next Mercury hour'. Clock time is a useful thing; the astrologer does not suggest that it is in any way wrong, no more than he suggests that astronomy is wrong: the

---

[2] ibid. 3. 2-8   [3] ibid. 11.3

astrologer suggests only that clock time, like astronomy, is a thing devoid of meaning, and true time is the meaning that it lacks, just as astrology is the meaning without which astronomy, no matter how fascinating, is useless.

We see here the theme that runs as a thread throughout this book: one level of truth does not deny the veracity of another level of truth. The relationship of astrological to clock time is much the same as the relationship of esoteric to exoteric truth. Both levels are true; that one is true does not deny the other; but take away the esoteric and the exoteric remains but a husk. Clock time is a useful thing, but since the level of meaning given by astrological time has become virtually forgotten, what was adopted as a convention for man's convenience has become a snare from which he is unable to escape.

Astrological time is shown by a series of interlocking cycles. We are familiar with some of these: the daily cycle of Sun around the Earth; the monthly cycle of Moon around the Earth; the annual cycle of Sun against the stars. Conventional approximations to the term of these three cycles give us our day, month and year. There are longer cycles, some stretching into many thousands of years, marked by the movements of the outer planets. There are minor cycles, down to the smallest units of time. The long cycles delineate the long patterns of time: the rise and fall of faiths or empires. Of more immediate day to day significance is the interplay of the short cycles of hour and day.

Astrological hours differ from clock hours in that they are not uniform. Each clock hour is the same length as every other; the astrological hour, however, is one twelfth of the time between sunrise and sunset (or between sunset and sunrise if it is a night hour). As the length of time between sunrise and sunset varies not only from day to day but also from place to place, the length of the hour varies not only with the time of year but also with geographical location. In temperate latitudes, natural hours vary in length from around 40 clock minutes in winter to around 80 clock minutes in summer. As the start and finish of each hour is determined by the exact moment of sunrise, this will vary from place to place: it is quite possible that on one side of town it is the third hour of the day, while on the other it is still the second.

This sensitivity to both place and season is of great significance. Each hour is said to be ruled by one or other of the seven planets known in the classical world. The qualities of that planet will be most apparent during an hour that it rules. Each day is also ruled by one or other of the planets: Sun-day, Moon-day, Mars-day, Mercury-day, Jupiter-day, Venus-day and Saturn-day, in the order of the week (the astrological rulerships are clearer in French: Mardi, Mercredi, Jeudi, Vendredi). The astrologer would suggest that if I wish to propose to Ermintrude, I would be better advised to wait for a Venus hour on a Friday (Venus-day) than to risk being sent away with a flea in my ear by doing so on a Mars hour on a Saturn-day. Similarly, if I am in a different town to my true love, the advent of a Venus hour might fill my heart with fond thoughts of her; I may rush to the phone to whisper sweet nothings, only to find that it is a Saturn hour where she is, so my charms are not well received.

The strength and exact nature of the ruling planets' influence on their subject hours will vary first according to the day – a Venus hour on a Venus day being rather different to a Venus hour on a Saturn day – and then according to that planet's placement in the sky, relative to the zodiacal signs and the other planets. If Venus during that hour is in Taurus, where it is strong, and helpfully aspected by benevolent Jupiter, she can work at her best. If she is in Aries, where she is weak, and aspected by restrictive Saturn, her influence will be hindered. In both cases, it will be coloured by the nature of the planet aspecting her.

The hours proceed in an endless cycle in the traditional order of the planets: Saturn, Jupiter, Mars, Sun, Venus, Mercury, Moon, Saturn, Jupiter, etc. The day starts at sunrise (not midnight). Each day takes its planetary ruler from the hour that starts at sunrise on that day: this explains the apparently random order of the days, which we might at first glance have expected to follow the order of the planets, running Saturn-day, Jupiter-day, Mars-day and so on. So the first hour of Monday is ruled by the Moon; the second by Saturn, the third by Jupiter. Following the order through the twenty-four hours of the day, we find that the first hour after sunrise on Tuesday (Mars-day) is Mars, the first on Wednesday is Mercury. It is notable that if the urge towards decimalisation – a trend that abandons measure on the human scale in favour of the purely rational – is ever applied to time, dividing the day into two periods of ten hours each, renaming the days of the week after their starting hour would re-order them into a reversal of their traditional order (Moon-day would be followed by Mercury, Venus, Sun, Mars, Jupiter and Saturn-days). It is unlikely that the consequences of this rigid reversal of nature would be fortunate.

Finding the ruler of any particular hour is a simple enough operation. From the times of sun-rise and sun-set which are available in most diaries and annual ephemerides, work out the length of the day and the night on the date in question. Divide both of these times by twelve to find the length of each day hour and night hour on that date. Then, taking sun-rise as your starting point, work out how many hours have so far elapsed and thence which hour you are in at that time (eg the tenth, or the fourteenth). The first hour of each day, and consequently also the eighth, fifteenth and twenty-second, is ruled by the planet that rules the day (Moon for Monday, Mars for Tuesday and so forth). The intervening hours follow the order of the planets as above. For example, Wednesdays are ruled by Mercury, so the first, fifteenth and twenty-second hours of any Wednesday are ruled by Mercury. The second, sixteenth and twenty-third are ruled by the Moon; the next by Saturn; then Jupiter; then Mars, the Sun, Venus and back to Mercury.

Even though the dominance of the artificial conception of clock time has severely restricted our openness to the changing nature of true time as it flows past, a glance at the start of the week shows that traces still survive. The first hour of the week, as dawn breaks on Monday, is a Moon hour on a Moon day. We might expect the pervasive influence of such an hour would be to bring out the baby (Moon) in us: weak, undisciplined, wanting only to snuggle up and sleep. But the next hour is ruled by Saturn, planet of discipline, duty, and, indeed, of time itself: a most unwelcome visitor to our snug, babyish, Moon-day world. We must assume that those who feel themselves free of all astrological influence have never hurled an alarm-clock across the room first thing on Monday morning.

The use of the unequal, astrological hours and the equal, mechanical hours existed side by side from the earliest times: a water-clock measures time in just as even and mechanical a fashion as a clockwork clock (although it can be and sometimes was modified to tell unequal hours). These types of hours each had their different uses, the equal hours being most useful for commercial purposes. In those days commercial considerations were not the measure of the whole of life. By the late Middle Ages, the growing emphasis on equal, mechanical hours becomes apparent. The thirteenth-century Italian astrologer, Guido Bonatti, claims, after describing the principles of planetary rulership of the unequal hours, that the principle can be just as well applied to equal hours, though he says this without much conviction.[4] He is nodding in the direction of growing current practice as the importance of commercial life grew and began to shoulder aside the idea that time has its own, varying nature.

The most obvious variation in the nature of time is that at certain hours it gets dark. The human being has a natural tendency to stop work when this happens. The codes of the medieval guilds typically prohibited their members from working after dark: that this prohibition needed to be made suggests that even then the desire to turn a penny was undermining the natural relationship with time. As mechanical clocks became more common, this natural relationship became ever more tenuous.

It is perfectly possible to build a mechanical clock that will tell the unequal, natural hours: complicated, yes, but when we consider the intricacy of many medieval clocks, with their record of celestial motions and complex striking mechanisms, it would be unwise to deem it beyond the wit of the age to have developed such if such had been wanted. Some were built when clockwork was introduced into Japan, but there is no record of there being any attempt to build one in Europe, the cause for which lies with those who were paying for the clocks to be built – primarily the merchant classes. Their requirements were for merchant-friendly clocks telling equal hours "so they could grind a full hour's worth of labor out of workers in the gloomiest and briefest days of winter."[5]

This points the basic conflict between the two systems of time – if conflict there must be: the one has financial rewards; the other pays its wage in the coin of human well-being. The one demands that man conquer time, forcing it into an arbitrary plan to suit his short-term convenience; the other suggests that man is well served by accommodating himself and his desires to the nature of

---

[4] *Liber Astronomiae, Part III*, p. 50; trans. Robert Hand; Golden Hind Press, Berkeley Springs.
[5] Alfred W. Crosby, *The Measure of Reality – Quantification and Western Society, 1250-1600*, p.82, Cambridge University Press, 1997

time as it flows by. That man may impose his own artificial pattern upon the surface of time does not, of course, mean that the nature of time itself alters one jot: Monday morning remains Monday morning; the being responds to darkness whether that darkness falls at 4pm or 10pm.

As commercialism planted its satanic mills across the land, Tom Wedgwood, son of the more famous Josiah, came up with his hare-brained scheme for Etruria, which took to an extreme the wish to destroy the natural connection with time. In this model village, every moment would be strictly regulated, most importantly in the lives of the children. There would be no time wasted on play or fallow idleness. The natural world was far too confusing, so 'the child must never go out of doors or leave his own apartment', which would itself be a completely controlled environment: 'plain grey walls with one or two vivid objects for sight & touch'.[6] Every moment would be spent on a taut time-table of work and moral improvement. The ideal man, he decided, to run this loony utopia was William Wordsworth; but his plans came to grief when he realised his chosen dictator thought his time excellently spent gazing at a fallen tree. Wordsworth was horrified at the idea, his revulsion contributing much to the genesis of *The Prelude,* in which he details the vital importance of apparently random stimulus to the growing mind. It is not coincidental that the most famous scion of the Wedgwood family is he who has made the mechanical model of man the cornerstone of modern thought: Charles Darwin.

We may have avoided these disciplined utopias, but the imposition of artificial time and the expunging of our connection with time as an organic, living force has been none the less total for the more insidious means by which it has arrived. In our electric cities, we scarcely notice nightfall as the light is turned on. In winter, the person who does not behave exactly as in the height of summer, but feels instead a natural desire to enter a state of semi-hibernation has something wrong with him: he 'suffers' from seasonal affective disorder. Each winter in Britain there is debate on whether the time natural to that place, as approximated by Greenwich Mean Time, should be abandoned in favour of Central European Time – that is, time as it is in Prague, a thousand miles to the east. The clock time of the hours of darkness under GMT is not convenient. Exactly why the British should live their lives according to the time in the Czech Republic is unclear – except that it favours commercial policy. The common-sense answer to the problem, which is that everyone should simply stay in bed longer on dark mornings, adapting themselves to the nature of time in that place, is never seriously raised.

As we can see, the determining factor of an astrological hour is the position of the Sun. The hour is calculated as a fraction of the Sun's journey from one horizon to the other (rather than as a product of atomic decay, which is our current definition) and which particular hour it is – whether it is a Venus hour or a Mars hour, for example – is shown by the Sun's position relative to the

---

[6] Quoted in Stephen Gill, *William Wordsworth, A Life,* pp. 130-1, Oxford University Press, 1990

Earth. The Sun is the manifest symbol of the Divine in our cosmos; the hour-ruler, the planet that has rulership over that particular section of the Sun's journey, is the filter through which the Sun's light is directed, the particular fragment of many-coloured glass staining the white radiance of eternity at that particular moment. The stained glass of the great cathedrals of Europe embodies this notion.

This idea has another manifestation, which makes the nature of the hour-rulers much clearer – and also shows more clearly how we have lost touch with the true nature of time. An angel is, literally, a messenger: endless numbers of them speed and post o'er land and ocean on errands from God. They are, as we are, differentiated in their essence, and will be called into service accordingly. For an errand of mercy, Gabriel might be sent; on an errand of justice, Michael, and so on, the angel being the visible channel of the Will of God in the same way as the hour is the visible colouring of the white radiance of the Sun. It is, for example, a particularly sad hour that Shelley summons from all years to mourn Adonais. We find another expression of the same phenomenon in the Greek literature, where, for instance, Pallas Athena will appear to our hero and tell him a crafty ruse. Muslims, Christians and Jews might describe this as a visit from an angel on orders from God; translated into astrology, this becomes a Mercury contact. All carry the same message from the same Source.

Angels, like hour-rulers, were once rather more familiar to man than they are today. There exists a vast literature of angelic appearances, which we now choose to regard only as fairy-story or, at best, symbolism. But we have no reason for disregarding it other than its not fitting our current preconceptions. When William Blake tells us he bumped into an angel on Peckham Rye, we are able to write this off as the testimony of an obvious loony because the scientists assure us that such things cannot possibly happen. These are the same scientists who tell us that cows eat sheep; but it is Blake who is the loony. Evidence for appearance of angels declined hand in hand with use of the natural astrological hours. Like the astrological hours, the angels are still there, but man has become more and more reluctant to notice them. In the seventeenth century, the astrologer William Lilly lamented that even then it was no longer easy to communicate with angels, as they speak 'like the Irish, much in the throat'.[7] We might suspect that the problem is less with the angelic powers of enunciation than with the growing hardness of our hearing.

Clock-time, which was once a convenience, became a commercial necessity with the age of the factory. The natural rhythms of time, to which the human organism responds by its very nature, are not suited to the inexorable rhythms of the machine. The owners of the factories found it expedient to override these natural rhythms by imposing regular clock time on their employees. The imposition of clock over natural time was done quite deliberately and, as historians have

[7] *William Lilly's History of his Life and Times from the year 1602 to 1681, written by Himself*, p. 199; London 1715, reprinted Ascella, Nottingham, n.d.

documented,[8] often, with a surprising degree of perceptiveness, quite consciously as a means of breaking the will of the work-force. We still see today the bizarre ritual of giving a clock to someone who retires – at the very moment when he no longer needs it. It is as if a freed slave were to be given his shackles as a souvenir.

The astrological view of the world does not admit the possibility of random coincidence. It is, therefore, no coincidence that clock-time rose to dominance with the Reformation, or that clock-making was 'a typically Protestant industry'.[9] The one thing as the other were direct consequences of the loss of understanding of the concept of essence, that existence of the divine spark within creation which lies at the heart of the traditional view of the cosmos. Being born from this incomprehension, the clock spread its germs in its wake, like a traveller bearing a plague wherever he set foot. Where once we had our family angels, we now have a clock, and would find it a hard job indeed to convince a visiting alien that we do not worship it. The ubiquitous clock has enforced the tacit acceptance of an essence-free reality; yet this view is a lie, and true, traditional astrology is one of the few voices in the western world still able to speak the truth.

Considering astrology as the study of the varying nature of time, we can better understand the absolute bafflement with which modern scientists regard it. By their lights, astrologers are studying something that simply does not exist, which is not the sanest of pursuits to which to devote one's energy. An understanding of astrology, however, makes it plain that the preservation of what few vestiges of contact with true time we still have is a matter of the utmost urgency. We are like an endangered species of animals, becoming ever fewer in number as its environment is destroyed. As human beings – as distinct from mechanical creatures in human form – time is our environment. Allowing the building of a world of endless twenty-four hour shopping-malls imperils our very existence.

---

[8] See for example E.P. Thompson, *The Making of the English Working Class*, passim; Gollancz, London, 1963; or his *Customs in Common*, chap. 6, Merlin, London, 1991

[9] Christopher Hill, *Intellectual Origins of the English Revolution Revisited*, p. 170, Oxford University Press, 1997

5

The Order of the Cosmos

Astrologers work from a geocentric model of the universe; that is, one where the Sun still goes round the Earth. This is conventionally known as the Ptolemaic model of the universe, which in the realms of science has been superseded by what is conventionally known as the Copernican model, where (in broad terms) the Earth goes round the Sun. There are a handful of eccentrics who have followed the scientists and practice a heliocentric astrology, but their influence is as trivial as their thinking. This persistence in the use of the geocentric model, it might be supposed – and often is so supposed by vociferous scientists who really ought to know better – proves that astrology is hopelessly outdated and nothing but empty superstition. Far from it.

When I am explaining the structure of the geocentric, Ptolemaic universe to classes of beginning students, there is always someone who raises the issue, "Yes, this is all very well – but it's not real, is it?" on the assumption that the Copernican model which we have all learned in school is real. This is a question which cuts to the very heart of astrology and exposes exactly what it is that astrologers are actually doing.

We all know what is real. The desk at which I am writing this is real; the room in which I sit; the keyboard on which I type; the fingers which are doing the typing: these are all real. Yet we live in perhaps the only culture in the history of the world that has ever had this particular idea of reality. Come back in a hundred years time: the desk, the keyboard, the fingers, most probably the room itself – none of these will exist. For most cultures through most of history the idea that these things might be real would be utterly absurd: nothing that is so ephemeral could possibly be real; for something to be real it must be lasting for at least something longer than the flicker of an eyelid which it takes for all I see around me to pass away. So the idea of what is and is not real is not quite as clear cut as it might seem.

The geocentric universe pictures what is real; that is, what is true in the eternal world of the spirit. Yes, the Earth goes round the Sun in the purely material conception of reality, but this is neither here nor there. On a physical level, the popular substitution of the Copernican for the Ptolemaic universe replaced one more-or-less accurate model of what happens with another more-or-less accurate model of what happens; in purely practical terms this has made not the slightest difference to anybody, except by allowing infinitesimally more accurate predictions of the positions of the planets, an improvement of no interest to anyone without an extreme Virgo nature and far too much time on their hands. On the deeper and more relevant levels of spiritual truth, the substitution of the one for the other was the replacement of a model demonstrative of profound truths with a model demonstrative of trivia, a substitution which has had cataclysmic consequences for mankind.

The ancient world was well aware of the heliocentric model; it existed side by side with the geocentric. As the focus of interest was not on this superficial material reality, little attention was paid to it. The geocentric model exactly pictured the spiritual truth of the structure of the universe and provided a perfectly adequate means of tracking its material phenomena, as exemplified by plotting the positions of the planets. The typical school history lesson tells us that the Ptolemaic model was hopelessly inadequate, so when Galileo publicised the heliocentric model its accuracy was greeted with gasps of admiration from across the civilized world. This is quite untrue. It was, in fact, some two hundred years before the Copernican system could plot planetary movement with the same degree of accuracy achieved by the Ptolemaic. Its adoption had little to do with scientific accuracy; a lot to do with the period of the Reformation and the changes it brought in political and religious belief.[1] This mirrored a huge and determined shift of interest from the spiritual to the material or, in philosophic terms, from the essential to the accidental. We might note in passing that the persistent use of a geocentric cosmos that proves the stubborn foolishness of astrologers is perfectly acceptable in other fields. As Kuhn explains: "Most handbooks of navigation or surveying open with some sentence like this: 'For present purposes we shall assume that the earth is a small stationary sphere whose center coincides with that of a much larger rotating stellar sphere.'"[2] The asylum in which astrologers are to be confined has some highly respectable inmates.

The Geocentric Cosmos

The exact mechanics by which the traditional model of the cosmos works has never been a matter of undisputed agreement. Within the basic framework, accounts of how the design can present the visible phenomena have varied; but this is a matter of technology and of trivial significance. All the apparatus of epicycles and deferents which adorned the most familiar example of the geocentric model were needed to save the phenomenon, to describe what could be seen, but were never of more than minor importance in astrology. They were, as it were, technical decorations to please minds attracted by that sort of thing. The important part was the basic structure. Or, to put it another way, the basic geocentric structure was the spiritual truth and in fact is as true today as it has

---

[1] See Thomas S. Kuhn, *The Copernican Revolution,* Harvard University Press, 1957, for a detailed account of both the material structure of the Ptolemaic model and the history of the introduction of the Copernican system.

[2] ibid. p. 38

always been; the technical explanations of how this structure produced the visible phenomena were in the realm of the material, and have been superseded by the heliocentric model of the cosmos in common use today.

Traditional descriptions of the cosmos always start at the outside and work inwards, as if peeling away layers from an onion, because the creation consists of a series of concentric spheres created by God. The outermost of those with which we need concern ourselves here is *the sphere of the zodiac*. This sphere is utterly invisible, and carries no stars on it. What it does carry are the signs of the zodiac, which have no connection with the constellations that bear the same names. The scientists would have us believe that far back in the distant past, a particularly imaginative cave-man, falling back exhausted after dragging his wife around by the hair, looked up at the sky. "My goodness," he exclaimed. "That group of stars up there looks just like a man pouring water from a jug which he is carrying on his shoulder." "I say!" cried all about him, "So it does. Let those stars be known as the water-bearer for ever after." And so taken were our ancestors with this picture of a man pouring water from a jug held on his shoulder that they spread the news of this discovery far and wide, and anyone who dared to suggest that those same stars looked like a bunch of carrots or a man riding a sabre-toothed tiger was ostracised until he realised the error of his ways. When reading scientific claims like this, it can be difficult to remember that it is astrologers who are very silly people.

The truth, of course, was nothing of the sort. The signs of the zodiac are a division of the zodiac into twelve equal sections. They are differentiated one from another by the process of creation. The primal matter of the created cosmos is not itself manifest. It comes into manifestation as (what appear to us as) hot, cold, moist and dry. Onto these four possibilities fall the three modes of creation: the out-going, which carries the initial impulse from the source into the creation; the expansive, which maintains and explores within the creation; and the returning, which turns the impulse back towards its source. These three principles falling on the four qualities of hot, cold, moist and dry give (3 3 4) twelve combinations. Each of these combinations has its own distinctive nature: for each an image was revealed which describes – one picture being better than a thousand words – that nature. These are the signs of the zodiac.

Once the image mirroring the nature of each sign was known, a likely-looking bunch of stars that were in roughly the right place was joined together to give a picture of that image. Because, by the mercy and wisdom of God, the creation is congruent all the way down, there existed a likely-looking bunch of stars close enough to each of the required points of the zodiac, the apparently random arrangement of which stars fitted the image which it was to portray. Close enough, but not exactly at, for no material form can ever perfectly reflect the essence, and zodiac sign to constellation is as essence to material form. You will read again and again in books of both astrology and astronomy that there was once a time at which the signs of the zodiac and the constellations which share their names coincided. This is not true.

The zodiac, insofar as – being nominally a circle – it starts anywhere, starts at the Spring Equinox, the image of the initial creative impulse from the Divine. This is called 0 degrees of Aries. Everything in the zodiac is measured from here, just as all longitude on Earth is measured from Greenwich. When the Sun reaches this point each year, day and night are of equal length with the days increasing and thus the year starts. Once, some 2000 years ago, the Sun appeared to enter the astronomical constellation of Aries on this same day. But this does not mean that the constellations and the zodiac signs were all neatly aligned: they were not. The signs of the zodiac are, by definition, equal segments of 30 degrees each; the constellations, being merely the material form of these signs, fail to live up to the masterplan. They are a mess, though they do lie across the Sun's path through the sky: the line of the ecliptic. Some of these constellations, like Leo, are huge, stretching far across the sky. Some, like Aries itself, are small and quite insignificant, having no really bright stars. They are not separated by strict boundaries, but overlap: most of Aquarius, for instance, lies above rather than behind Capricorn. Bits of other constellations, like the notorious 'thirteenth sign' of Ophiuchus, intrude into the procession. So, although the point of the Sun's entry into the constellation of Aries once happened at astrological 0 degrees of Aries, nowhere else did the Divine Plan imaged in the zodiac match its material form. The constellations are the first mirror of ourselves, forever falling short of their inherent possibilities, but still linked to those possibilities as shown by their sharing the same name.

The idea of name is an important one to understand: our modern conception, which is quite wrong, is that name is an optional label which can be stuck onto something as we will. The tradition tells us, however, that it is far more important than that: name is mysteriously one with the named, at least in sacred languages. It is not an arbitrary compound of sounds applied by coincidence. Hence the importance given to the Name of God in the scriptures. Our given name often mysteriously captures our essence or potential; our surname describes our material form or social function (Long, Whitehead, Butcher, Baker). By taking a saint's name at, for instance, confirmation we share in the essence of that saint. So the fact that the name of the constellation (Aries, Taurus, Gemini) – which names were inspired, as were their symbols – is that of the zodiac sign is of great significance.

The constellations of Aries, Taurus and the rest, together with all the other stars in the sky, are carried on the next sphere within the sphere of the zodiac – the next layer of the onion. This sphere, *the sphere of the fixed stars,* moves, albeit slowly, relative to the sphere of the zodiac, producing the phenomenon of the precession of the equinoxes. That is, the Spring Equinox no longer takes place when the Sun enters the visible constellation of Aries, but moves backwards and is presently near the beginning of Pisces, almost a whole sign away. Again, the modern text-books get it completely wrong, saying that the equinox moves through the constellations. It doesn't: the constellations move relative to the equinox. This is an important distinction, even though the material result is the same whichever way the movement is expressed. It is matter which falls short of essence, not the other way round.

The movements which astrology measures and by which it works began, the tradition tells us, only with the Fall. Before that, there existed a perpetual Spring, but a Spring in which all trees and plants brought forth both fruit and flowers, for the seasons (and with them the inevitability of death) did not yet exist. Milton, working from a sound knowledge of both astrology and theological tradition, describes the process in *Paradise Lost*. As soon as Adam and Eve taste the apple, God orders his angels to rearrange the cosmos, first pushing the Sun into its elliptical motion, so Earth feels for the first time 'cold and heat scarce tolerable' as it travels

> from the north to call
> Decrepit winter, from the south to bring
> Solstitial summer's heat,

then setting the planets in motion:

> to the blank moon
> Her office they prescribed, to th'other five
> Their planetary motions and aspects
> In sextile, square, and trine, and opposite
> Of noxious efficacy,

and teaching the fixed stars 'their influence malignant when to shower.'[3]

These changes in the heavens produced – as man did not fall alone, but took the whole cosmos with him – all the unpleasantness that had been absent from Eden: contention, beast ravening on beast, tumult, illness, fear and pain. The essential nature of the cosmos is as a series of spheres; the material form has the Sun moving in an ellipse. It is this difference – the movement away from the perfectly spherical – that gives us the precession of the equinoxes. The difference between essence and form is shown clearly in the story: from being happily at one with God, as soon as they are fallen, Adam and Eve realise their material nature and are suitably horrified and ashamed at its shortcomings. We see here the difference between the zodiacal signs and the constellations that share their names.

The sphere of the fixed stars is the limit of visibility in the cosmos. The sphere of the zodiac and those spheres beyond that, which are of metaphysical importance but of no immediate, practical relevance to our astrology, have no material form in any sense tangible to us. So the fixed stars are the closest things that we can actually see to the Divine. As we might then expect, they are of particular astrological significance at the major turning points of life, especially the entering and leaving of it.

The zodiac, then, reflects the three modes of creation – the 'out-going', the 'expansive' and the 'returning' – working through the four fundamental

[3] Book X, ll. 650-60

distinctions in which the prime matter manifests: hot, cold, moist and dry. We are still speaking here at a level far beyond anything tangible to humankind. This combination of the 3x4 is, as it were, the blueprint for Creation. It is more manifest than the initial creative impulse within the Divine, but its relationship with our daily perception of reality is not dissimilar to that between architect's plan and house: the plan most definitely exists, but you cannot live in it.

Hot, cold, moist and dry are principles that are not in themselves capable of entering manifestation. To do this, they combine into the four elements of traditional science: fire (hot and dry), air (hot and moist), earth (cold and dry) and water (cold and moist). These are still far different from those substances of the same names with which we are familiar, or even from the physical states of solid, liquid, gas and energy to which earth, water, air and fire loosely correspond; but we are beginning to approach the tangible. The element fire is, as it were, 'essence of fire'; water, 'essence of water'; earth, 'essence of earth'; and air, 'essence of air'. These material forms, however, point us in the direction of understanding the elements. The blueprint is drawn in the fieriness of fire, the wateriness of water, the earthiness of earth and the airiness of air.

The modes of creation work through these elements as cardinal (out-going), fixed (expansive) and mutable (returning). This gives us our twelve signs, one cardinal, one fixed and one mutable in each of the four elements: Aries being cardinal fire, Taurus fixed earth, and so on. This is our blueprint, our potential for creation. But to continue with our building metaphor, the blueprint exists all at once: it cannot be manifested all at once. If we wish to build a house from plans, we must take one step at a time: we cannot build the roof at the same time as we are digging the foundations. So to enter into manifestation, the same principles of 3 and 4 must exist in extension (3+4) as well as at once (the 'blueprint' form of 33 4). The 3+4 gives us the seven planets of the traditional cosmos, realising the possibilities of Creation in extension. This can take place only through the medium of time, which fact brings us back to what we are studying: the gradual realisation of the possibilities of the Creation through the medium of time, as shown by the changing positions of the planets relative both to each other and to the original blueprint as indicated by the signs of the zodiac.

The *outermost of the planetary spheres* lies immediately within that of the fixed stars. This is *the sphere of Saturn,* and it carries something of the same meaning as the sphere of the stars, as the gateway to and from the Divine. But whereas the fixed stars are activated only every now and again in each of our horoscopes, Saturn is operative all the time. It is the planet of justice (hence its exaltation in the sign of the balance, Libra), and as such it is not popular. For our modern, sentimental idea of divine justice – a belief that everything will sort itself out in the end, no matter how we live – is not at all the justice on which the cosmos is built: the inexorable truth that if we identify ourselves with essence we will live with essence, while if we identify ourselves with the material we will die with the material. Saturn is the gateway to the divine, but it is a strait gate and narrow is the way that leads through it.

Modern culture is strongly anti-saturnian. As such, the manifestations of Saturn are white-washed out of existence. Saturn rules death: death happens only in hidden, secret places. It rules age: our dreadful ideal is to live in a perpetual adolescence. It rules values: but there are no values in today's world. It rules sacrifice: but even the path to God is now one of indulgence – Heaven forbid that we might actually have to alter our behaviour in some way to reach Him. Saturn rules agriculture: where we reap exactly what we sow. It is time, by which our tangible experience is bounded, but which is also our gateway to God. It is wisdom; but wisdom, people now like to believe, is packaged and sold sugar-coated in the bookshops.

Saturn is known as the Great Malefic, a term with which modern astrologers find fault. Contemporary man is so much more sophisticated than his forbears that these terms of malefic and benefic no longer apply to us, they say. It is flattering to be told that I am more sophisticated than Shakespeare, but I am not quite vain enough to believe it. The tradition in astrology deals in malefics and benefics. The greater and lesser malefics, Saturn and Mars, are not nice. Their actions in our lives are often things we would much rather not encounter. The greater and lesser benefics, Jupiter and Venus respectively, are far more 'user-friendly', promising an existence of sugar and spice and all things nice. Given the choice, we opt naturally for them.

Another aspect of our modern sophistication, the contemporary astrologers tell us, is that we now have such rich inner lives that it is impossible to judge from an astrological chart whether any event will happen in the world or just inside our heads. Pre-Twentieth Century man reflected on nothing but his plough and the back of the horse that was pulling it. Poor fellow. We might rather suspect that the necessity of inventing a box to live our inner lives for us shows a vast internal void in modern man that his ancestors never experienced.

Jupiter, the great benefic, is a much more popular fellow than his dour compeer Saturn. Jupiter's is the next concentric sphere on our journey inwards. The jolliness of his nature is too much stressed today, for he is more than just the planet of parties and ice-cream. The word 'jovial', derived from the Latin name of the planet, has become progressively trivialised in our language until it describes just someone who has been at the sherry. True, a common manifestation of Jupiter's expansive nature involves unbuckling one's belt, but his real nature is as a spiritual guide, and in this he does not work alone, but hand in hand with Saturn. They are the carrot and the stick, 'Thy rod and Thy staff' which comfort me though I walk through the valley of the shadow of death. Saturn is the rod, that beats me onto the straight path; Jupiter the staff that pulls me out of the thorns. They are expansion and contraction, mercy and justice. We like mercy – or at least, we think we do: we like it until it is shown to the man who has wronged us.

A second related pair of planets holds the spheres on either side of that of the Sun. These are *Mars,* embodiment of force, and *Venus,* embodiment of conciliation. If all were functioning as it should, Mars would be the ardour that takes us to God, Venus the desire for reconciliation that fuels that ardour; as such, they are two different sides of the same principle. But all is not functioning as it should. Mars is the faculty of volition in its dynamic mode; but unless this will is rightly guided, Mars becomes a nuisance, especially if it is other people's manifestations of it with which we come into contact. Venus, too, although usually rather more pleasurable and hence a popular little planet, is no less disruptive if it is not rightly directed.

The power of Venus is today greatly under-rated. She is, after the Sun and Moon, by far the brightest object in the sky, the only object other than the luminaries capable of casting a shadow. If we reflect for a moment on the influence of the advertising industry, we begin to see something of her power, for not only the pretty face that is used to sell us something, but almost every motive that is played upon is Venusian. In practical terms, she is just as much a malefic as Mars, leading us far from our true path. Our present age is totally under her sway; even in things of the spirit, we spurn the Saturnian sense of sacrifice or even the martial ardour that will transform itself to win its goal (just as an amorous teenager will change all his interests at his sweetheart's behest), waging Holy War within itself, and expect instead a religion to accommodate our peccadilloes, promising us Heaven without leaving our armchair. The common antidote to too much Venus in society is a burst of fundamentalism, with ill-guided Mars trampling all its path. Without the right guidance that is pictured by the sphere of the Sun lying between them, each of these twin planets can be as dangerous as the other, our common problem being a reluctance to apply them within ourselves, to fight the internal *jihad* and seek conciliation with what is good within ourselves, it being the easier course to turn them outwards, fighting and lusting after others.

Within the sphere of Venus lies that of *Mercury*, planet of reason. During the French Revolution, high-point of the so-called Enlightenment under which we now live, the goddess Reason was ceremonially enthroned as the supreme deity. It was not, of course, the goddess herself, but an actress; so the reason which claims to rule our lives is itself but a mockery of what reason truly is. At no point in recorded history has the quality of reasoned thought been lower, despite the morass of words all around us, a fact which has more than a little to do with the widespread incomprehension of astrology. In our coincidence-free astrological cosmos, we must note that the mercurial breakthrough of the printing-press occurred together with the Reformation, on whose effects we have already remarked. All the planets are dependent upon right guidance; which is why we find the Sun holding the central sphere.

The innermost sphere is that of the *Moon*. Everything above this level is held to be unchanging; below this is the sublunar world, 'the world of generation and corruption' where things come into being and pass away, the world where we live. The histories tell that a major impetus to the abandonment of this spiritual model of the cosmos was the sighting of a nova, known as 'Tycho's star' after the astronomer Tycho Brahe who was one of the first to comment on it, which shattered man's illusions about the unchangeability of the supralunar worlds. It was evident that this nova was happening far beyond the sphere of the Moon, so things at that level must be changeable after all. If even the spheres can change, the gradual logic ran, nothing is certain in our universe. This resulted in a general lessening of faith; but its cause was not as the histories tell us. The problem was not that the nova indicated change in the spheres, but that this was regarded as significant. Tycho's star was not the first nova that had ever been seen, and previous ones had not somehow managed to keep their supralunar nature hidden from prying eyes. In the past, it was accepted that what was important was the essential model, the idea of the thing; if the material form had its quirks that failed to agree with it, this was just a reflection of the fallen nature of the cosmos, of the inevitable differences between material and essential. By 1572, when the nova became visible, man had so greatly identified himself with the material that he judged the material to be of greater significance: if the essence failed to fit with the material form, the essence was wrong. It is as if the priest were to sneeze during the ritual, and the human frailty of the sneeze were to be accorded more importance than the spiritual reality of the ritual. This gave a major impetus to the abandonment of the spiritually correct model in favour of its material brother. Man was remaking the cosmos in his own fallen image: where Copernicus trod, Ronald MacDonald was not far behind.

In this account, we have skipped lightly past *the sphere of the Sun,* to which we shall now return. It can seem odd that what is proclaimed as the spiritual model of the cosmos is in fact centred on the Earth – or, more precisely, on mankind. Surely our current, heliocentric model, centred on the Sun, the image of the Godhead, must be the spiritually correct one? From our rather partial modern point of view, perhaps; but this is not to be relied upon. The position of the Sun in the geocentric model clarifies this confusion.

The Sun is the image not of God, but of the manifestation of God in the universe. In the manifested spheres of the cosmos, that of the Sun holds central place. It is also true to say that the Earth is central, but in a different (more material) manner of speaking. The Sun is, we might say, the essence of this model; it is its central heart. If we consider the manifest spheres in order, with * indicating the sphere of the fixed stars and ⊕ the Earth, we find the Sun in the centre.

$$* \qquad ♄ \quad ♃ \quad ♂ \quad ☉ \quad ♀ \quad ☿ \quad ☽ \qquad ⊕$$

If we take the spheres of the planets in order on either side of the Sun, folding, as it were, the cosmos around this central point, we find the following pattern:

$$☉$$
$$♂ \qquad\qquad ♀$$
$$♃ \qquad\qquad ☿$$
$$♄ \qquad\qquad ☽$$

This is the pattern of the rulerships of the zodiacal signs: the signs ruled by Mars (Aries and Scorpio) are opposite those ruled by Venus (Libra and Taurus), as are the signs ruled by Jupiter (Sagittarius and Pisces) and Mercury (Gemini and Virgo) and Saturn (Capricorn) and the Moon (Cancer). We see here a different pairing of planets to that discussed above. Saturn as ruler of Aquarius rounds off the pattern, opposing Leo, the sign of the Sun. Aquarius is the symbol of man, the most humane of the signs, and we find here again the polarity of human and divine. Sun and Saturn are each of them the planets closest to God: Saturn as the outermost sphere is closest in an almost geographical sense, insofar as we can talk of being geographically close to God (spiritual geography being a less materially-bound science than its earthly cousin); the Sun as the essence of the system is by its nature the image of the divine manifestation.

We can also complete the pattern by adding the two outermost of the manifested spheres:

$$\odot$$

$$\begin{array}{cc} \mathord{\mars} & \mathord{\venus} \\ \mathord{\jupiter} & \mathord{\mercury} \\ \mathord{\saturn} & \mathord{\moon} \\ * & \oplus \end{array}$$

This points the balance between man and the fixed stars, the creation of both of these embodying the principles of plenitude and yet of similarity, there being, it is held, a star for each one of us. The stars are as the angels, or as the Names of God, of which there are any number. The planets, being just 'wandering stars' are of their nature, being those of their number that move, or are in action: these are the ones that 'speed and post o'er land and ocean' while the others serve by standing and waiting; the planets thus are those qualities of the Divine manifestation which are most strongly potentialised. Thus, while the Divine qualities are infinite, for the purposes of the creation there is a twelve-fold potentiality manifested from among this infinitude (as shown by the twelve zodiacal signs from among the whole number of stars) and on this twelve-fold potentiality is woven a seven-fold actuality (as shown by the seven planets) that displays the web of the creation.

This model, with its interweaving patterns of truth of which we have barely scratched the surface, was carelessly jettisoned in favour of a strictly one-dimensional model which fitted man's new obsession with the material world, showing truth solely in material terms. To be blunt, yes, the Earth goes round the Sun – but so what? It makes not a jot of difference to any one of us. As is plainly apparent if we but look outdoors, the Sun goes round the Earth, and that is what is important.

The fashion for thinking of the cosmos in only heliocentric terms had far-reaching consequences. An awareness of these consequences and of their inevitability was what prompted the Church to suggest to the propagators of this new fashion that they exercise some circumspection before opening their mouths. We have been taught that the cardinals were the Bad Guys trying to stifle the heroes of free thought; this is a somewhat partial point of view, argued by those who benefit – or think they benefit – from the decay which this free thought impelled. It is possible that a world in which our greatest concern is to make ourselves appear sexy by drinking a different brand of cola is superior to the ordered world of pre-Renaissance thought, structured to facilitate the accomplishment of man's spiritual duties, but this superiority is by no means as unquestionable as those who profit from this view would have us believe. While Galileo and his peers acted in good faith, they acted also with a total lack of foresight, displaying not only an absence of awareness but also a complete absence of concern for the consequences of their statements – in which they show a paternal resemblance to our contemporary scientists who cut and botch and clone, intoxicated by their own cleverness, with a brazen unconcern for the long-term result.

The over-riding significance of the switch from geocentric to heliocentric world-view was the change in value from spiritual to material of which, as we have seen, it was both consequence and cause. It might perhaps have been theoretically possible to retain a balance between the spiritual and material view, stating the material and utilising it for technological convenience, but this possibility existed only at a theoretical level: as Adam first proved and our newspaper and television proprietors well know, offer Man a baser choice and he will gladly take it. Weighted by greed and lust for innovation, the scale plummeted in favour of the material choice. Our scientists point to their proud technological achievements as evidence that their view is correct; but how correct their view of the cosmos might be has not the slightest relevance to the correctness or incorrectness of any other view. We might liken the cosmos to a book. We can use it as a step to increase our height, so we can achieve the technological feat of reaching that packet of biscuits on the top shelf; we can open it up to make a tunnel through which we can run our model train; yet for all these wonders, the supreme truth is found only when we read what is inside it. Science has forgotten that there are words to read within the cosmos. The heliocentric model was developed by a series of scientists who dropped their eyes from the divine to the material.

The most significant particular change with the adoption of the 'new' view of the cosmos was not the whereabouts of the Sun, but the belief in an infinite universe that follows from this model. It was forgotten that Man is a unique creation; it was immediately thought that there might be myriads of other Earths scattered through the endless depth of space. Man was evicted even from this substitute Eden into which he had wandered in exile from the first. With the possibility of infinite, equally significant, worlds, all sense of value was doomed, with the inevitable results amid which we live.

God too, from enfolding the cosmos, has been pushed out to some infinite distance, where He was soon forgotten. The Sun, symbol of His manifestation, was made central, but no longer central to the cosmos, only to one little, obscure corner of it. Although our immediate perception tells us otherwise, we are assured by the scientists that there are far bigger and brighter stars than our Sun: bigger and better gods. Even in spiritual terms we see the consequence of this: every far-off faith is more attractive than that to which we are born, as if we have the choice of being warmed by suns other than our own.

6

The Outer Planets and the Asteroids

The idea of the plurality of worlds implicit in the new, heliocentric model of the cosmos proved hopelessly confusing for man. Man was faced, however, not just with infinite numbers of suns beyond our own petty system, but extra objects within it, for among the first things Galileo saw through his telescope were the four brightest moons of Jupiter. The first of the new planets, Uranus, was discovered in 1781. Some of the more fanciful astrological writers claim that the ancient Chaldeans knew of it, as at magnitude 6 it is just on the threshold of naked-eye visibility. Believe this and you will believe absolutely anything. John Flamsteed, the Astronomer Royal who founded the Greenwich Observatory, tracked it and designated it as a star in the constellation of Taurus – *34 Tauri* – and there is no evidence that it was ever regarded otherwise. As the Chaldeans seem carelessly to have omitted to leave any record of their knowledge of Uranus, the reasons for ascribing such knowledge to them are rather harder to see than the planet itself.

Neptune was spotted in 1846, followed in 1930 by Pluto. Thousands of other bodies are now known, including asteroids by the bucket-full and strange objects like Chiron, whose astronomical designation changes with the breeze. As if this were not quite enough, modern astrologers insist on inventing more, some which are completely hypothetical, and some which they claim to have located but which cannot yet be seen, as mankind has not quite reached that stage of spiritual evolution. The ability to determine the existence and position of these not-yet-sighted planets does of course show that those who do so are in the very vanguard of mankind's spiritual advancement (never mind the question of why then they have not found something better to do). Strangely enough, the awareness of all these additional bodies has not provided the slightest increase in accuracy of astrological judgement; indeed, the more of these bodies astrologers use in their work, the further removed from any verifiable reality their work tends to be. The general principle behind these innovations seems to be: "I can't be bothered to study the traditional method sufficiently deeply to achieve any accuracy with it, so I will invent a new system of my own."

Once the astronomers discovered the new planets, forward-thinking astrologers, lacking the ability to leave well alone, felt the need to incorporate them in their work, doubtless fearing lest they be left behind by modern progress in the sciences. To do this, they faced the problem of finding a role for them. This was not easy: the system with which the tradition had worked was self-contained and exclusive; everything was in there somewhere; there were no omissions waiting for a new discovery to look after them. Most importantly, the system represents truth, the real cosmological order. But modern astrologers, who had not sufficiently studied the traditional model to be aware of its signifi- cance, took pity on these new arrivals, who had no sign to rule. Most of the traditional planets had two signs: this was most unfair, and so – democracy being the watchword of the age – our new planets had just as much right to a sign as their elders. It was then decided that Uranus should rule Aquarius, Neptune Pisces and Pluto Scorpio. As, however, Mick Jagger can own more than one house, it is hard to understand why Jupiter and Saturn, who are probably of greater significance in the cosmic order, should be barred from doing the same.

The need to incorporate these new planets into the system is itself erroneous, and betrays an ignorance of that system. The workings of the traditional system are based on light and the providential appearance of the Heavens to the naked eye: a planet with no light has no power, hence the weakness of whichever of the luminaries is darkened at an eclipse. The new planets and other miscellaneous objects have no appreciable light. They cannot be seen from Earth without artifi- cial aid. Some of them cannot be seen from Earth with artificial aid. Light is the visible manifestation of truth, the substance of creation. These objects lack it, and are irrelevant to us. Of course, they are "there"; but they are there in the same way that ultraviolet and infrared wavelengths of light are "there". These extremes of the spectrum exist and with artificial aid can be made visible to the human eye; but they are irrelevant to us. So too are Uranus, Neptune and Pluto.

These outer planets have captured the imagination of the astrological world. Astrological circles resound to the desperate striving for kudos as each astrologer trumps the next with tales of the dire placement of the outer planets in their birth-chart, or of the degree of havoc that they can expect from the forthcoming transit of whichever of them strikes him as the most dramatic. Not even an awkwardly placed Saturn carries the astrological glamour of a natal outer-planet square. It stamps its victim as a man set apart from his fellows, an ubermensch, destined to wrestle brigands on the alpine precipices of the heart. These outer planets are figures of romance. The great delight taken in contemplating their obscure movements has one simple cause: we have framed the supposed meanings of these bodies in our own image; but not just the tawdry, day-to-day image which we much prefer not to see: this is a picture of dark and seductive passion, the elemental and brooding Heathcliff nature in which, as we plod through our dreary daily round, we like to think we share. This picture is woven of several different strands.

As the traditional system, so redolent with truth, has been forgotten, the modern astrologer must make up some new kind of 'truth' to explain the significance of the outer planets. They are, we are told, the higher octaves of the seven traditional planets, and have become visible to us and relevant in our lives because of our increasing spiritual awareness. The fact that all these new planets seem to be more or less malefic is explained by the inability of stubborn mortality to cope with their higher vibrations. The arrogance of the idea that mankind is now more sophisticated than it was in the benighted past, before these planets were discovered, and is only now able to experience new orders of emotion, thought and spirituality beggars belief; its arrogance is matched only by the blindness that could think for one moment that this age is more spiritually advanced than those which have gone before. The only thing less spiritually advanced than this age is Hell itself, and that sometimes seems a close-run thing. This view proves nothing but the truth of the adage that "Whom the gods would destroy, they first make mad." It is notable that this touching belief in human progress is shared with the scientists, who also see the last three hundred years as a dizzying ascent from utter darkness towards enlightenment. This is completely contrary to the teachings of all the revealed faiths, and fails to pass a moment's inspection at the hands of common-sense.

Complementary to this is the idea that these new planets rule things which had no existence before their discovery. So Uranus rules television and computers. It requires the splitting of the finest of hairs to claim that these things are essentially different from anything that existed before: both of these examples would be ascribed to Mercury in the traditional model, in his capacity as ruler of communication and calculation. What else a television or computer might be other than a box for performing these functions is not clear. Uranus is also held to rule divorce. We must assume, then, that the scriptural references to divorce were written only with the last two centuries in mind; the marital problems of Henry VIII are just a myth, and Milton's tract on divorce is a Victorian forgery.

The two favourite approaches to the problem of ascribing meaning to our new playfellows have utilised myth and history. It must be noted that a profound ignorance of both subjects has been consistently found more useful than any evident knowledge. The mythological approach begins with the name given to the newly found body by astronomers. The planet is invited into the consulting-room, laid down on the couch and asked to reveal whatever is going through its head; the results of which interrogation are then passed through the liquidiser of Jungian thought, reducing the doubtful connections between planet and myth to yet more tenuous levels of credibility by throwing out any aspect of the myth that fails to conform to the niceties of western middle-class existence. It is hardly necessary to say that only those parts of the myth that support the presuppositions of what the planet *ought* to be like are taken into account. About the Roman god Neptune, for example, little is known; in the classical world he became identified with the Greek Poseidon, god of the sea. But Poseidon was also god of earthquakes, which the moderns have given not to Neptune, but to Uranus (in traditional astrology, like so much of what is now considered Uranian, they came under Mercury) – and horses, which are apparently not interesting enough to be given to any outer planet. This psychomythical approach, reducing everything to the petty concerns of the twentieth-century bourgeoisie, has as its prime result the implicit assertion that the astrologer's own psychological shortcomings are an ideal to which we should all aspire. We must not wonder whether this is indeed so, and why, if the planet has existed since time immemorial, and will continue to exist for millennia yet to come, our contemporary small concerns are wide enough to span its meaning.

Nor must we wonder what this mythological approach might have dreamed up had either of the early names for Uranus stuck. *George's Star* would presumably have identified it with kings, as it would have been the only planet actually named after one, as well as agriculture, the farmer king's great interest, and insanity. It has kept a reputation for eccentricity, but this is not through association with a king who spent his time talking to trees, but through the eccentricity of its axis and orbit. Its orbital behaviour, however, is quite staid compared to that of Pluto – who has, we are told, nothing to do with eccentricity. From *Herschel* it might have developed an association with people who take all the credit for their womenfolk's work; but this would not have fitted our politically correct cosmos at all.

Having exhausted the possibilities of myth, the astrologer shakes his reader awake and turns to history, adopting a particularly bizarre method which consists of taking the date at which the planet was discovered and applying a knowledge of history learned from a children's history book with most of the pages missing to give salient events which are held to describe the nature of that planet. This history completely omits any reference to that vast majority of humanity careless enough to live outside Europe and America, whose lives are obviously of no concern to these new planets. From the late twentieth century, our noses still pressed hard against them, the chosen events seem like landmarks in the progress of the (western) world. We must wonder how significant they will appear to the historian in the distant future, and how many more planets will have to be discovered to account for all the events of similar magnitude that are yet to come. Astrology c.2,500 AD is going to be a complicated business. We may also remark on the rather partial interpretation of exactly which events are of major significance: any that fit the writer's preconceptions, it seems. We might justly ask why the French Revolution was worthy of a new planet while the births of the founders of all the great religions and the rise and fall of all the world's empires apparently passed without one.

We shall deal in some detail with the example of Neptune in a moment; let us for now glance briefly at that strange object, Chiron. Astronomical opinion on exactly what Chiron is changes every few months. Despite its utter insignificance, it fascinates those astrologers who have decided that they are spiritually evolved. On its discovery, in 1977, it was hijacked by a vociferous minority of astrologers who regard themselves as healers. Their wishful belief is that mankind is on the verge of a golden new age where each will heal his fellow. Having been discovered at the dawn of this new age, Chiron must be the planet of the healer; and as we have all had such dreadful childhoods, he is a wounded healer – the best sort, apparently.

A moment's reflection on even just our circumscribed western view of history casts doubt on this theory. Far more prominent at the time of Chiron's discovery than the dawning of a new age of healing was the rise of the yuppie, the materialist player of the markets, who produces nothing and makes himself rich. Yet the book that explains Chiron as a stockbroker, wounded or otherwise, has yet to be published. Approaching the same problem from the other end, a second moment's reflection reminds us that healing (literally 'making whole') has been going on for centuries within the established religions. The Christian Mass, for example, is a highly effective ritual of healing for both the individual and the community: "Lord, I am not worthy to receive you, but only say the word and I shall be healed". The word in question being the Word made Flesh, which the communicant is about to receive in the host. That the focus of healing has moved from the church to the bookshop does not necessarily make this healing either more widespread or more efficacious.

Thus the main role of the outer planets and their asteroid cohorts is to fuel the contemporary obsession with titillation. The basis of all the approaches to comprehending their supposed meanings is the belief that these planets, rather than being merely newly discovered, are in fact man-made objects, which we can fashion to our whim. Hard evidence for this is lacking. As we have shaped these planets ourselves, we have ensured that they all contain something to flatter the ego of each one of us in just its favourite manner. Whether an astrology built for the purpose of self-gratification is an adequate replacement for an astrology designed to lead us to God is questionable. As part of this desire for titillation, astrology itself has been given to the rulership of Uranus (astrology presumably not having existed before 1781), a planet which has developed a reputation for amiable eccentricity. In the tradition, astrology was ruled by Mercury. Where once astrologers saw themselves as thinkers, they now style themselves as eccentrics. This may fit in well with the desiderata of the New Age, but is not necessarily an improvement.

Uranus is now, we are told, the planet of astrology; but according to the historical method of assigning meaning to planets, the fact that Uranus was discovered during the Enlightenment should be of the utmost importance – and it was the Enlightenment that spelt the death of astrology. It is not, then, surprising that those moderns who choose to masquerade as astrologers should claim Uranus as their ruler.

Let us return to the great shift in the pattern of the cosmos in order to further examine these new planets. The traditional picture was this:

where * is the sphere of the fixed stars and ⊕ is the Earth. As we have seen, although the Earth is at the centre of the spheres, the Sun (the image of the manifestation of the Divine) is also at the centre, viewed in a different but not exclusive way.

The heliocentric picture is this:

The Sun and the Earth have swapped places. We find other major differences. The Moon is no longer in the line-up. From being the very image of the creation, the link and the boundary between the perfect world of the spheres and the mundane world of generation and corruption here below, she has become merely the trivial satellite of what is itself just another planet in just another solar system in just another galaxy. The historical comparison is clear: just as Our Lady was being dethroned by the Protestants, so was her celestial image, the Moon, by the scientists. And the consequence? With the Moon and all its meanings no longer of importance we have the continued rape of nature with barely a twinge of guilt. It is ironic that exactly those people who today cry out most loudly about the absence of the feminine principle in astrology, and who attempt to compensate for this by dragging various dubious-looking asteroids, hypothetical 'dark moons' or other feminist fantasies into the system are those least likely to explore the traditional model which holds the feminine principle in just that crucial position where they would wish to find it.

The fixed stars have also gone. They have lost their importance – no longer a sphere, the farthest visible marker on the road to the Divine Qualities or Names, but just a wilderness, in which oases of solar systems are sprinkled. Remembering the connections between man and stars, we might wonder if this reflects the reduction of man to nameless factory-fodder, and the reduction of all quality to a de-qualified "quantity". Most certainly the assurances of the scientists that the stars that burn brightest in our skies are not so bright at all, but are outshone by specks not even visible to the naked eye, their apparent brightness being merely an illusion created by proximity, mirrors the destruction of value in our world: we can all kid ourselves that we are as worthy or as godly as any – their apparent brightness is nothing but illusion.

So we have installed the Earth in the central position; we have made ourselves as gods. Or so we thought – for then the unexpected happened: we started to discover new planets, not in other solar systems, but in our own. With each planet that we added to the line-up, the centre shifted. With Uranus, it moved away from the Earth; then Neptune appeared.

As we have seen, when deciding what a new planet signifies, the first stop for the modern astrologer is that indispensable volume, *The History of the World in Three Paragraphs.* Looking at the era in which Uranus was discovered and the years that followed after, our astrologer plumps on the French Revolution and decides that Uranus must therefore be connected with revolutions. The intellectual forebear of the French Revolution, which took place in England and culminated in the execution of King Charles I, evidently did not merit a new planet. Nor, apparently, did the more far-reaching revolution in thought and belief of the Reformation and Renaissance. But the history text in question is so short that these events do not find a place in its pages.

The only events of note in the era of Neptune's discovery were, the modern astrologer tells us, the birth of Marxism and the introduction of ether to the operating theatre. The one proves a connection between Neptune and idealism and the other a connection with drugs and anaesthetics. The modern astrologer, as well as being eccentric, likes to think of himself as an idealist and is not keen on personal discomfort – so Neptune is strongly in favour. We shall refrain from pointing out that the contemporary picture of Neptune has more resemblance to Harpo than Karl, nor shall we wonder why the invention of a Judeo-Christian heresy is worthy of a new planet when the revelation of both these faiths was accomplished without one; we shall not wonder why idealism is accounted a thing of virtue when it has caused rather more than its share of random human suffering. Nor shall we quibble over the appropriation of anaesthesia by modern western medicine when other methods, both with and without the use of drugs, have been available throughout the world since prehistory: we shall instead turn to the suppressed fourth paragraph of the favoured history text. From this, it becomes clear that the salient developments with which Neptune might be historically connected are the refinement of the breech-loading rifle into an efficient weapon of mass slaughter; the invention of first the repeating rifle and then the machine-gun; the invention of dynamite; the age of the war of attrition, starting with the Crimean ('the first modern war') and American Civil Wars; and the explosion of a particularly bloody and exploitative colonisation. Historically, the Age of Neptune, if so we might call it, has more to do with bloodshed than anaesthetic, music, mysticism, drugs or any of the other meanings foisted onto it. The changing pattern of our model of the cosmos makes the reason clear: once Neptune enters the line-up, the centre shifts to Mars, god of war.

War, of course, is not in vogue amongst astrologers, so they prefer not to see this.

That there is more than theoretical truth to this view of Neptune is suggested by its extreme prominence in many of the mundane charts leading towards the First World War. "Aha!" exclaims the modern astrologer, "Just as I told you – gas!" But the application of a little knowledge in place of the customary woolly vagueness suggests that, awful as it was, the significance of gas in that war was minor compared to the carnage inflicted by lead. The choice of one particular weapon in a major war is hardly something that we would expect to find as the keynote of its determining astrology, especially as that weapon was of only secondary significance. Far more reason to judge that Neptune's provenance, if any, has more to do with mass slaughter than either gas or ersatz mysticism. The use of gas-lighting is commonly given as sufficient reason for associating Neptune with gases; yet gas lighting was first introduced well over 100 years before Neptune's discovery. By the criterion of historical coincidence, gas should be given to Uranus; but this doesn't fit with preconceptions about the nature of either of these planets. Historical criteria are employed only when they can be manipulated to produce convenient results: we might, for instance, wonder why Uranus is commonly associated with computers (Mercury) when their modern form appeared only long after Uranus's discovery and their proto-type, the abacus, was invented long before.

Finally, after Neptune, Pluto was added to the scheme. Pluto is much beloved by our eccentric, idealistic modern astrologer: dark, mysterious and passionate (just like him/her), the repository of all manner of anti-social but rather thrilling vices, it is the astrological equivalent of curling up with a vampire novel. The introduction of Pluto moves the centre of our planetary pattern one step further, into the space between Mars and Jupiter – a space inhabited by the myrmidon legions of asteroids. With this myriad fragments of trivial dust proclaimed as centre of our cosmos, all residual sense of value has finally vanished; the grossest immoralities are now regarded as of equal value with the highest of truths, and any nonsense can be passed off as sound thought.

One of the favourite associations of Pluto is with sexual abuse. There is a modern technique called 'local space astrology' which purports to show how the native will manage in any particular environment by projecting his birth-chart onto a map of the place. This place might be a city or a country, in which case the projection of the chart will show in which areas the native will find financial success, have fun, meet a partner, or whatever. Or it might be a house, showing how it might best be arranged and where problem areas will lie, as a kind of astrological feng shui. As every chart has Pluto in it somewhere, every house will therefore have its sexual abuse room. It makes one feel quite behind the times.

The asteroids exist in their thousands. Those first discovered were given names from classical mythology; by now, the criterion seems to be the taking of the first word that comes into the discoverer's head. Even Frank Zappa has an asteroid named after him. The sheer number of these objects is quite intoxi-cating; those astrologers who indulge in their use make their fellows in the modern astrological community seem almost rational. With so many asteroids bearing so many names, and so many minor aspects at our disposal, it is inevitable that there will always be a clutch of seemingly relevant asteroids in some sort of contact with each other at any given moment. So if I drop some spaghetti sauce on my shirt, I can confidently expect to find asteroid "Pasta" in adverse aspect with asteroid "Shirtfront" while asteroid "Being embarrassed in front of my girl-friend's parents" makes a biquintile with heliocentric Chiron in my natal chart. The reader might think this an exaggeration, an attempt at *reductio ad absurdum*, but there are no further layers of absurdity to which thought like this can be reduced. A recent account of a chart about the purchase of a car[1] tells that Mars was with asteroids "Mony" (sic) and "Pounds", while "Ernestina", the purchaser's name feminised, was prominent, along, of course, with asteroid "LeCar" and numerous others indicating the place where the event happened, the name of the astrologer involved, a close description of the local countryside and what the next-door neighbour had for breakfast. All well and good, we think – a convincing argument for the exact relevance of these tiny bodies. But what about all the hundreds of other asteroids that were also in aspect with the chart for the time, or the birth-charts of the people involved? How come our car-buyer was not being seduced by Eros, speared by Lancelot or entertained by Frank Zappa while this was happening? If I throw a large number of dice onto the floor, it should be no surprise that a good selection of them come up as six; no surprise to anyone except certain modern astrologers.

It is not unreasonable that when these new bodies were discovered, curiosity should have directed the attention of astrologers towards them. In his entertaining account of Nineteenth and early Twentieth Century English astrology, *A Confusion of Prophets*,[2] Patrick Curry tells of John Varley, the noted watercolourist and friend to Blake, who was a dedicated astrologer with a high reputation for accuracy. On the morning of June 21st, 1825, he sent his son to have his watch reset. He was, he explained, expecting some sudden and serious danger to himself or his property from an aspect of Uranus that would come into effect shortly before noon. As noon approached, Varley grew more and more worried, less from the possible danger than from the fear that his understanding of the nature of the newly discovered planet was wrong. Just before noon, however, there was a cry of "Fire!" from the street below. Varley and his son rushed outside, to find that their house was on fire. Despite his house and its contents being destroyed, Varley was delighted: his methods and his understanding of Uranus had been confirmed. If only he had had access to a modern text-book of astrology: instead of his house burning down, he might just have had a television-set delivered.

Nicholas Culpeper, author of the famous *Herbal*, had his interest in astrology awakened when the woman with whom he was eloping was struck by lightning as she waited for him to arrive at their meeting-place. Uranus is prominent in his birth-chart, closely afflicting the planet that would represent his bride-to-be. As in the chart for Varley's fire, however, the event can be clearly shown without having to involve Uranus. It is there, but gives nothing that is not told by the seven planets of the traditional cosmos. Indeed, what is shown by the outer planets can invariably be seen in the chart – given a sound knowledge of traditional method – without them.

---

[1] Pamela Crane, *Small World* (an e-mail newsletter), February 1999
[2] Collins & Brown, London, 1992, pp. 18-19.

There are occasional claims that the ancients must have known about the outer planets, as the names of these gods accord so well with the meanings that modern astrologers have given the planets that bear their names. That this circular argument is apparently stated in all seriousness says much for the standard of logical thinking among today's astrologers – evidence perhaps that Mercury no longer wishes to be associated with them. It is only thus that these planets can be afforded such importance.

Even the Caesars used to wait until someone else would elevate them to the heavens. Astrologers have seen fit to place themselves and all their dark and fascinating passions in the skies, and, like the Caesars, seem convinced that their sparkling images are far more important than the dowdy bunch of planets with which we have had to make do for so long. That these new planets should be incorporated into astrology at all is by no means a necessity: no one has found any need to place the moons of Jupiter, discovered long before Uranus, into a chart, despite the fact that several of them are significantly larger than the great majority of the asteroids with which some moderns are so obsessed, and that they are visible through a child's telescope while obscure bodies such as Neptune and Pluto are not. If one day there is "something new under the Sun" in man's soul, there may perhaps be need in the chart for Uranus, Neptune and Pluto; until then, they remain nothing but superfluities.

7

The Planets and their Essences

Crucial to the whole concept of astrology – crucial both for accurate judgement within it and for understanding how it works – yet utterly disregarded by modern astrology, is the idea of 'essence'. This idea does not fit the contemporary world-view, so modern astrologers, rather than stand firm to their knowledge – the very knowledge that is necessary to prevent their craft being truly the baseless superstition that the sceptics proclaim it – have prostrated themselves before the false idol of modern thought (we use the term 'thought' in its loosest possible sense) and cast aside the cornerstone around which the edifice of astrology, and all traditional thought, is built.

This is not the place for the technical splitting of philosophical hairs, so we shall paint with a broad brush and describe the traditional model of the world and all that is in it as looking somewhat like a fried egg. In the heart of each object is its essence; all around it is its accidental form. The classic image of essence is as the Idea in the mind of the Divine Architect, the accidental form of which Idea appears to us as an object in the world. "The essence of a thing is that which it is said to be *per se*."[1] That is, for example, that quality which would be left if I were to think of my best friend, but in doing so were to throw out every possible adjective with which I might describe him: that uncatchable 'him-ness' that would remain is his essence. Everything, even the most evanescent or intangible of things, a dream or a passing thought, has its essence; but in general (unless we be saints and have Intellection) we perceive only the accidental form.

Essence itself is imperceptible to us, at least with our external senses. The traditional science of physiognomy gives an example of how it can be seen. As physiognomy exists mainly in a corrupted state, we imagine the artist staring hard at his subject, noting every line and bump on their face and calculating the workings of their nature from this. Not so: for in the tradition, the artist will stare hard at his subject, but then turn away. That which he still sees in his mind's eye when he turns away is the essence, from which he will judge the person's nature. But this too is an image of essence, not essence itself: whatever

---

[1] Aristotle, *Metaphysics*, Z. 4.

we think we can see of it is not it but only its form on some more or less gross level of materialisation. Moreover, it is from this image – not from the person's physical beauty – that the character is shown, for it betrays the person's true inner nature.

In practice, essence becomes a relative term. It is the vision in the architect's mind's eye, which will, because of the nature of the material, be imperfectly manifested. It is also the vision in the building contractor's mind's eye, and the sub-contractor's and the brick-layer's, in each case being again imperfectly manifest in its transition from vision to material form (we are careful not to say 'from vision to reality', for it is the essence, not the material form, that is reality), though inextricably linked with it.

By the early Seventeenth Century, however, mankind had 'evolved' enough, or become 'spiritually advanced' enough to forget about essence. In the brave new world of Baconian science, essence was of no importance, primarily because of its frustrating refusal to allow itself to be weighed or measured, and all that was of concern was the matter of quantity. On this foundation is our contemporary world-view made. This is the altar at which modern astrology worships, although without the idea of essence astrology is nonsense.

Without recognising the existence of essence, we are left only with the material (and possibly not even that!). Left only with the material, we cannot possibly provide a convincing explanation for the workings of astrology. With only the material, we must follow the scientists and insist on some more-or-less tangible equivalent of a length of rope between ourselves and the planets as the only means of explaining the connection between planets and objects on Earth. As the scientists never tire of pointing out, this is nonsense (they should know – they invented the idea).

What are the options? We can posit a conscious-planetary-influence theory, with planetary 'spirits' working on mankind like a collection of (exceptionally hard-working) puppeteers. This is the favoured basis of the religious assault on astrology, even though there are precious few astrologers who would accept it. It is utterly unacceptable within the tradition. We have the physical theory, with the planets as inert masses exerting a pull something similar to gravitation as they plod along their courses. This leads to the endless and tedious debate on the relative gravitational effects of the planet Jupiter and the midwife on the new-born child. There are many modern astrologers who subscribe to some form or other of this theory, usually inventing some as yet undiscovered cosmic force to draw the link between planet and object. As many of these same astrologers are firm believers in the astrological influence of any number of half-inch conglomerations of dust floating around the asteroid belt, there is clearly an amount of work to be done on defining exactly how this force operates – and, of course, on finding that it exists. But the greater number of modern astrologers put their faith in Jung's theory of synchronicity – which is an elaborate way of saying "Let's not think about it at all."

If only we still thought in terms of essence, all would be so simple. All essence is, essentially, one. At a level further towards us, lower on the ladder of manifestation, all essence of like nature is one. In the same way that white light is split into light of seven different colours by a prism, the oneness of essence is refracted through the planetary spheres. It is as if (and I stress, *as if*) it were divided into seven different-coloured rays, with one colour for each of the seven planets of the traditional cosmos. In the same way that all things that are red have something in common (their redness), all things whose essence is coloured by the ray refracted through Venus' sphere share a certain 'Venus-ness'. That is, in their essence they all share in a certain Venus-quality. All things that share in this quality are, in a way, one, regardless of where they happen to be located. So if Venus moves, all that has this Venus-nature will move. There is no causation, in the strict sense, as they are all one; but by looking at Venus we can surmise what is happening to countless things on Earth that share its nature, and thereby save ourselves countless individual deductions. The Divine action or 'moment' that Venus's movement represents does not happen first to Venus and then to 'Venus nature things', but happens at the same time to both Venus and Venus nature things. Looking at Venus shows us what this is in a much more intelligible and palatable way than trying to deduce it from Venus things on Earth, in all their diversity and on all their different planes. This unity of essence was indeed described by the ancients as 'planetary rays'; but we are mistaken if we take this to mean something as tangible as a beam of light or energy: this would bring us back to the impossible grossness of the length-of-rope theory.

Many, many things – approximately one seventh of all that is – are in their essence predominantly of Venus-nature, as another seventh share the nature of Mars, another of Saturn, and so forth. By determining the condition of Venus at any particular time, we can determine the condition of all things that partake of her nature. Everything in life is not, of course, divided neatly into seven discrete categories, one for each of the seven planets of traditional astrology; no one thing has its essence of solely one nature: all is mixed. The modern chemical theory of the elements, which are unable to exist in an unadulterated state, is a gross representation of this. Venus rules young women: that is, 'young women' is one of the categories of being that partakes of Venus nature; but all young women do not behave in exactly the same way at exactly the same time. This individual young woman has a foul temper – she partakes strongly of Mars nature; this one is grumpy – she partakes of Saturn nature; so their movement according to the Venus-nature of their essence will be moderated, the one by what her Mars-nature is doing, the other by her Saturn-nature. This is an extremely simplified example: everything that exists is woven of an immensely complex web of all seven principles. The important point is that we are not considering a relationship of cause and effect: we are considering things moving together because they are one.

The Doctrine of Signatures, so important in traditional medicine, suggests that, for instance, a plant whose leaves are shaped like a heart will have a therapeutic effect upon the heart. In modern terms this is described as the plant having an effect because it looks like the heart. In traditional terms, it has this effect because, in its essence, it is of the same nature as the heart. The physical resemblance is an accidental (in the strict sense of the word) manifestation of this sharing of essence. In the same way, gold and the heart resemble each other, not in this instance in their shape but in their qualities, as they too both partake of the same essential nature (in planetary terms, they share in the nature of the Sun), so gold is traditionally a medicine for the heart. Modern medicine still regards gold as the most effective treatment for arthritis: this is pure 'essence medicine', in this instance by opposites rather than likes. Arthritis manifests in saturnian fashion, restricting and limiting, so the perfect balance to it is a Sun-medicine: gold.

Science, however, has abandoned the idea of essence; the emphasis on experiment in modern scientific practice has also distorted our understanding of how things happen. Modern science is essentially empirical; the nature of the experiment is to normalise all conditions except the one which the scientist wishes to test (and except, as we have seen, for time, which the scientist no longer accepts as having any influence). The scientist leaves himself only one variable to examine, and the consequent one-pointed nature of experiment has devastated our comprehension of causation. Francis Bacon, who, more than anyone, stands accused of fathering modern scientific method, himself accepted the primacy of first cause (i.e. the Divine Will); but the importance he placed on the examination of secondary causes led, owing to the nature of all things to sink to the baser, to the forgetting of first cause, and the method he fathered to the concentration on one and only one secondary cause. The ball goes into the goal; the fan cheers: the ball going into the goal has caused the fan to cheer. But there are many causes for the fan cheering: many reasons why he is there and not at work, or helping his wife with the shopping; why he supports this team and not the other; why he finds cheering an appropriate response; and so on and so on. The ball entering the goal – or whatever it is in any situation that the modern mind regards as immediate cause – hardly merits the name of cause at all; it is merely the occasion. So why are we fed with so patently superficial a view of reality? Can it be because we can then be persuaded that drinking Whizz-o-Pop will be the one cause of our catching the perfect woman, or driving a Hamster 3-litre the sole cause of our being eternally happy?

Science has abandoned the concept of essence, and modern astrologers, fawning after their scientific masters, have followed the scientific pattern. This lack of the concept of essence also enables the modern travesty of astrology to accord better with contemporary social ideas.

So much for the theory. In practical astrology, without the consideration of essence we have nothing. In immediate practical terms, the first significance of the signs of the zodiac is merely as a means of location. The signs each represent thirty degrees of celestial longitude, so to say "This planet is in Aries" means simply that it is in the first thirty-degree section of the zodiac. To say that it is at 12 degrees of Aries means that it is twelve-thirtieths of the way through this first thirty-degree section. So the placement of the planets in the various signs describes their positions relative to the Spring Equinox (0 degrees of Aries) and relative to each other. If we then ascertain which degree of which sign is rising over the eastern horizon at this time in this place, we can tell whereabouts in the sky all these planets are at that moment – that is, we can tell where all the various thirty-degree sections of the zodiac and the planets that are in them are placed relative to the observer at this location on Earth. This is what an astrological chart tells us: nothing magical, nothing arcane, just that. From this information, we can draw certain conclusions.

Imagine you are entering a village, looking for your brother. "Where's Bob?" you ask a passer-by. "He's in the bar," the passer-by replies. This is the equivalent of telling you in which zodiac sign planet Bob is located. But to find him, you still need to know where the bar is relative to your present position: "Where's that?" you ask. "It's over there," the helpful passer-by responds. We have now done the equivalent of drawing an astrological chart, except that the chart locates not only your brother Bob, but also planet Tom, planet Maggie and various others. From this piece of location-finding, we can draw certain conclusions: as we have all seen in the movies, if we know that Tom is in the bar now, he couldn't possibly have been at the scene of the crime half an hour ago. And so with astrological judgement: it is just as simple and, for things celestial, surprisingly down to earth.

As he is my brother, I am well acquainted with Bob. I understand him. I know that he is a rumbustuous, sociable, sensual man, a genial *bon viveur*. Knowing this, I know that he is in his element down in the barroom; if I had been told he was watching Uncle Ebenezer's (Saturn) slide-show in the local library, I would know that he was dying a thousand deaths waiting for it to end. We see here the judgement of essence. This is not a complicated idea, but it is rather more than modern astrology can handle. To the modern astrologer, planets are pretty much content wherever they fall: Bob is just as happy in the library as he is in the bar. The traditional world is not populated by these admirable men for all seasons, finding full contentment in whatever place and at whatever activity; we might suspect that the traditional world is somewhat closer to reality.

As we have seen, the suppression of the true awareness of time mirrors the conversion of man into cog in the corporate machine; so also with essence. The tradition in astrology teaches that a planet's essence is strong, or happy, in some signs of the zodiac and weak in others. It travels from sign to sign through time. So Planet Bob, my brother, will have his off-days – as shown by his passage through uncongenial signs. If Bob is a craftsman and feels he is not at his best, he will leave the intricate fine-work for that day and busy himself instead polishing his tools and patching the workshop roof. If Bob is the corporate cog, he will keep on pressing the lever day in day out: he is allowed no off-days.

Where once the role of astrology was to lead man to God, it is now a soporific to placate him in his daily round; as such, the retention of the idea of essence would be strongly counter-productive.

As we have seen, the nature of the creative impulse from the Divine which brought about the Creation gives different qualities to each of the signs of the zodiac. Aries, for example, the first sign of the zodiac, shows the first burning onrush of undifferentiated creative power that drives the whole of manifest creation. With this raw power, it is not a place suited to delicate little Venus, no more than a blast furnace is a suitable place for wearing a tutu. Nor is it suited to Saturn, planet of limitation, restriction and demarcation. The planets that are strong in Aries – whose essences thrive on being in those turbulent surroundings – are the Sun and Mars. So they are said to be dignified there. Venus and Saturn, on the other hand, are most unhappy there: they are debilitated.

The modern astrologer will take the planet – say Venus – and describe it as 'harmony' or some such vagary; if it falls in Aries, they will take another word to describe Aries – maybe 'assertive' or 'dynamic' – and then rhapsodise on how their victim's ideas of harmony are realised in an assertive or dynamic manner, a rhapsody which almost everybody would find gave a perfect description of themselves, like the magic suit of clothes that fits everyone. The astrologer following traditional methods would not dream of speaking on such ethereal levels, but would look to the part of that particular chart with which Venus was concerned. "Your financial prospects," they might say, if finance were the concern of Venus here, "are (because Venus is so weak owing to its placement in Aries) dismal. You are always likely to be poor. And because Mars (which rules Aries and which therefore has great influence on any planet falling in that sign) is in this particular section of the chart here, I can see that the reason for this is that you squander all your money on fast living." This is a statement which has the possibility of being either true or false, and will not be found by everybody to give an accurate assessment of their lives. The example is simplified, for many factors would be considered to build a rounded picture of even just that one area of the life; the important point is that it is only by considering essence, and therefore dignity and debility, that we are able to draw any concrete judgement about anything from the astrological chart.

The consideration of essence is the prime way in which we assess the ability of a planet to act. Modern astrology, being little concerned with anything that bears the semblance of action, fails to do this, nor has it any longer the tools by which it might be done. A planet can gain or lose strength by its placement in the chart, being greatly strengthened by a position on the Ascendant or Midheaven, for instance; this is known as *accidental* dignity or debility. The main assessment of strength, however, is by essence: its *essential* dignity. If I win the hundred metres because I am the supreme athlete, I have done it through essential dignity; if I win because all the competition have the flu, this is – in simplistic terms – as if I have done it through accidental strength: I just happened to be in the right place at the right time.

Planets gain the greatest essential dignity by falling in a sign which they themselves rule (so Mars in Aries or Venus in Taurus). This is traditionally likened to a man secure within his own house. Each planet is *exalted* in one of the signs (Sun in Aries, Moon in Taurus, for example). This is another powerful dignity, though not quite as strong as being in its own sign. A planet in its exaltation is likened to an honoured guest in someone else's home: he is treated with the greatest courtesy, but there are strict limits to his powers: he would be unwise to start rifling through the cupboards. There is always an air of unreality to exaltation, which stems from the origin of the dignity. The signs of the planets' exaltations are said to be those which they occupied before the Fall, so a planet in its exaltation gives us an almost prelapsarian view of whatever that planet represents. This is very nice – the person is greatly honoured; but in our lapsarian world we know that all is not quite as fine as it seems. As with our honoured guest: we treat him with the respect that we would like to think he deserves.

Each planet is associated with one or other of the elements, ruling the three signs of that nature either by day or by night. This is a less powerful rulership than that of the individual signs, but still gives considerable strength. The phrase 'in his element' describes it well: it is a comfortable dignity; nothing spectacular, but fully secure. If, for instance, I were starting a job and the relevant chart had shown my planet to be in a sign of its own element, I would be confident that I could cope well with all that job's demands. I would not be one of the legendary masters of the trade, but I would be quite content there.

Each sign is then sub-divided in two different ways, each planet falling always into one of each set of these divisions. The *terms* divide each sign into five sections of unequal size; the *faces* into three equal sections of ten degrees apiece. Each term and each face is ruled by one of the planets; if a planet falls into one of its own terms or faces it gains a small amount of dignity – only a little, but a good deal better than none at all. A planet in these dignities can be likened to an under-manager in an office. He has a certain amount of power, but his position is strictly subordinate. There are further, smaller sub-divisions of the signs, but these take us to a level of precision that is in practice rarely required.

The following table shows the essential dignities and debilities of the planets. The left-hand column lists the signs of the zodiac. The next column shows the planet that rules each sign (so Aries ♈ is ruled by Mars ♂ and Taurus ♉ by Venus ♀). Then comes the column showing in which sign each planet has its exaltation (so Sun ☉ in Aries and Moon ☽ in Taurus). Exaltation is more exalted yet at the particular degree given for each planet.[2] The next columns show the planets that rule the triplicity of that sign, whether by day or by night. It is simple enough to see whether any chart is a day chart or a night chart: by

---

[2] The numbers given are ordinals, not cardinals. So the exaltation degree of, for example, the Sun is the 19th degree of Aries, which is from 18.00 to 18.59, not 19.00 to 19.59.

day, the Sun is above the horizon, just as in real life; by night it is below it. Aries, then, being of the fire triplicity, has the Sun as its elemental ruler by day and Jupiter (♃) by night, while Taurus, an earth sign, has Venus by day and the Moon by night.

TABLE OF ESSENTIAL DIGNITIES

Sign	Ruler	Exalt-ation	Triplicity		Term					Face			Detri-ment	Fall
			Day	Night										
♈	♂	☉ 19	☉	♃	♃ 6	♀ 14	☿ 21	♂ 26	♄ 30	♂ 10	☉ 20	♀ 30	♀	♄
♉	♀	☽ 3	♀	☽	♀ 8	☿ 15	♃ 22	♄ 26	♂ 30	☿ 10	☽ 20	♄ 30	♂	
♊	☿		♄	☿	☿ 7	♃ 14	♀ 21	♄ 25	♂ 30	♃ 10	♂ 20	☉ 30	♃	
♋	☽	♃ 15	♂	♂	♂ 6	♃ 13	☿ 20	♀ 27	♄ 30	♀ 10	☿ 20	☽ 30	♄	♂
♌	☉		☉	♃	♄ 6	☿ 13	♀ 19	♃ 25	♂ 30	♄ 10	♃ 20	♂ 30	♄	
♍	☿	☿ 15	♀	☽	☿ 7	♀ 13	♃ 18	♄ 24	♂ 30	☉ 10	♀ 20	☿ 30	♃	♀
♎	♀	♄ 21	♄	☿	♄ 6	♀ 11	♃ 19	☿ 24	♂ 30	☽ 10	♄ 20	♃ 30	♂	☉
♏	♂		♂	♂	♂ 6	♃ 14	♀ 21	☿ 27	♄ 30	♂ 10	☉ 20	♀ 30	♀	☽
♐	♃		☉	♃	♃ 8	♀ 14	☿ 19	♄ 25	♂ 30	☿ 10	☽ 20	♄ 30	☿	
♑	♄	♂ 28	♀	☽	♀ 6	☿ 12	♃ 19	♂ 25	♄ 30	♃ 10	♂ 20	☉ 30	☽	♃
♒	♄		♄	☿	♄ 6	☿ 12	♀ 20	♃ 25	♂ 30	♀ 10	☿ 20	☽ 30	☉	
♓	♃	♀ 27	♂	♂	♀ 8	♃ 14	☿ 20	♂ 26	♄ 30	♄ 10	♃ 20	♂ 30	☿	☿

The next block of columns shows the terms of the planets. The number beside each glyph shows the limit of that planet's term rulership: so in Aries, the top row of the chart, Jupiter holds this subordinate rulership from the start of the sign until 5 degrees and 59 minutes; then Venus takes over at 6 degrees, ruling until 13 degrees and 59 minutes, when she hands over to Mercury (☿), then Mars, and finally Saturn (♄). The next block shows the faces of the signs, where the same principle applies. In Aries, then, Mars has face rulership from the start of the sign until 9 degrees and 59 minutes; then the Sun from 10 degrees until 19 degrees 59 minutes; then Venus up till the end of the sign. The last two columns show the debilities: the first shows which planet is in detriment in each of the signs; the second where each planet has its fall.

We have, then, five ways in which a planet might have essential dignity: it might be in its own sign, exaltation, triplicity, term or face, or in any combination of these. As a rule of thumb, the respective strengths of these dignities can be shown as a descending scale from five for sign down to one for face. The strengths are cumulative, so if Mars, for example, is in the first few degrees of Scorpio, where it falls in its own sign, triplicity, term and face, it is very strong indeed. A planet in none of its own dignities is said to be *peregrine,* as if it were a homeless wanderer. It has no essential strength so, unless it has considerable accidental dignity, it will have little ability to act. 'Peregrine' is commonly misunderstood by the moderns, usually being taken, even by those with one of the spurious astrological qualifications that are so common, as being a planet that makes no aspects – a feat which, with the superfluity of minor aspects which the moderns have invented, is something of an achievement. As we trust will be readily apparent to any reader with any degree of contact with the real world, the ability or inability to act is a matter of some moment; the fact that modern astrology is unable to determine it is, therefore, something of a failing. But as the moderns are concerned exclusively with the psyche, a domain in which we may all imagine ourselves Champion of the World without fear of contradiction, charting real strength is irrelevant.

This assessment of strength is vital in whichever field of astrology we work. In horary, almost all questions depend on somebody's ability or inability to perform a certain action. Their strength to act is therefore crucial. In electional astrology, choosing the moment to act, finding a time at which the appropriate planets have sufficient dignity is the main part of the art. In natal astrology, finding whether a certain characteristic is a strength or a weakness, or whether we do or do not have the ability to achieve in a particular direction tells us almost all of what we wish to know. In mundane astrology, the astrology of public affairs, the ability to determine for example whether the nation's defences are strong or weak is clearly of significance. This is done, and done solely, by the study of *dignity,* of which the key part is an understanding of essence.

Essential weakness is also shown. A planet in a sign opposite one of its own is in its *detriment,* while in the sign opposite that of its exaltation it is in its *fall.* These are serious afflictions, leaving the planet far more debilitated than even being peregrine. Our homeless wanderer might still be robust; a planet in detriment or fall can be likened to someone in the throes of an acute illness. As might be imagined, the possibility of whoever such a planet signifies in a chart achieving anything by his own efforts are slight.

One of the questions most often posed for horary judgement provides a simple illustration of the practical difference between strong and weak planets. The question "When will I meet the person I will marry?" if asked by a westerner is usually asked during a period of despondency. With the cultural expectations as they are, the querent usually feels that there is little he or she can do, other than wait hopefully for Cupid's arrow to strike. Even joining a dating agency still depends for success on the vagaries of the blind bowman. The charts reflect the situation, and as such it is common to find the planets that represent the querent in positions of considerable weakness. With querents from Asian backgrounds, however, the situation is often different. Rather than waiting on the whim of Cupid, once the decision has been made that it is time to marry, social institutions swing into action and a suitable partner is usually found quite quickly. With variations according to the eligibility of the person in question, their planets are typically strong, mirroring a situation in which they themselves have much greater power to achieve the desired result.

From the vital, now neglected, study of dignity and debility, however, we can tell not only the strength or weakness of whom or what ever that planet represents, but even what their priorities and inclinations might be. This enables us, if so we require, to conduct a detailed psychological analysis, without having to work through the empty jargon of Jungianism. In other situations, it allows us to assess how people are likely to act. If a mundane chart reveals that the neighbouring country is strengthening its army, it is important to know whether its intentions are to invade our homeland or to consolidate defences against the barbarians. This knowledge is gained through the study of *reception.*

If a planet falls in a sign or part of sign ruled by itself, it is said to have dignity. When it falls in a sign or part of a sign ruled by another planet, it is *received* by that planet. This reception shows that whatever our planet signifies in this chart is interested in whatever is signified by the planet which receives it. So if Mars signifies John and Venus signifies Jenny, Mars falling in the sign of Venus tells us that John loves Jenny. We then notice that Venus is in the sign ruled by Jupiter: Jenny loves Jupiter. What is Jupiter? We might find that it rules the section of the chart showing John's money. We see also that Jupiter itself has lots of essential dignity. So we judge that John is rich and while Jenny doesn't much care for him, she has a great affection for his bank account. This information could be of considerable help as John chooses a course of action.

The example is a simple one. The variety of different dignities in which a planet may be received allows us to conduct an analysis of great subtlety. These receptions differ in their strength, just as we have seen with the dignities; they also differ in their quality. Reception into a planet's triplicity is not only less powerful than reception into sign; it also has a different character. In most contexts, we can think of reception as showing love. If I am wondering if I will earn lots of money in my new job, the chart might show my planet received by the planet that shows the job's money: I love – in this limited context – the job's money. If the planet signifying the job's money is received by my planet, I will be delighted: my love is reciprocated! If the money loves me, it will want to be near me: this is an auspicious start to judgement. This may seem foolishly anthropomorphic, but as a working metaphor it will suffice for most situations, and it fits the underlying philosophy, in which love is the motive power of all things, exactly. It is but the darkness of our situation that makes it seem strange. On some occasions 'influence' will seem to fit the context better than love.

A planet received into another's sign truly loves what that planet represents. It sees it clearly, understands it and accepts it. It will usually be that planet's prime interest, though reception by sign can be outweighed by combinations of other dignities (I love Jenny, but although I'm not so keen on Melissa, the combination of her super-model looks and her dad being chairman of the board wins the day). A planet exalts the planet in whose exaltation it falls. This is powerful, but is never quite real. It does not see clearly. Horary charts cast in the early stages of relationships usually show receptions by exaltation: the aura of divinity has not yet been pierced by knowledge of his unsavoury personal habits. Horaries for "Is it really over?" questions frequently show significators which have just moved out of reception by exaltation.

Reception by triplicity is like friendship. There is no grand passion, but it is warm, understanding and comfortable. Terms and face are rather slighter, and, significantly, as they cover only part of a sign, they show concerns which do not last as long as the other receptions. As we saw with dignity, weak as they are, they are a good deal better than nothing. It is also possible to receive a planet into its detriment or fall. This, as we might expect, is not good. In the birth-charts of those whom absolute power has corrupted absolutely – Catherine the Great is an example – we find the ruler of the Ascendant (signifying the person himself) received into detriment or fall by the planet ruling the Midheaven (the person's career): it is the career that enables the native to indulge his vices, to his destruction.

The assessment of essential dignity and debility draws an infinitely intricate web of meaning from the chart. It tells us all that we need to know about the power and intentions of all the characters in whichever drama is unfolding before us in the chart, whether it be a simple horary or a mundane chart covering hundreds of years of political events. This is then augmented by the consideration of the accidental dignities to enable us to judge the full capacity to act. A character's essential dignities, based on his planet's placement against the signs, might reveal him as the greatest athlete of all time; if he is in prison, however, he will not win the race: such things are revealed by the placement of the planet in the chart, the accidental dignities and debilities. The study of dignity and reception is, indeed, the key to astrology, and used wisely will unravel the most complex of situations. That it is all but forgotten by the contemporary astrologer, and that having forgotten it, this astrologer still feels himself capable of judging a chart, says much for the current state of the craft.

8

Aspects

Once we have established our planets, we need to know what they are doing. In whatever form of chart we are examining, whether it be a trivial horary or a mundane chart of great moment, such as the birth of an empire, each planet will represent something specific, whether this is a fish or a tradesman as in our horary examples, or the Emperor or the rival nations in a mundane chart. As a general principle, **a planet's *position,* both by house and by its own essential dignities, shows its power, the extent of its ability to act. The *receptions,* the various combinations of its own and other planets' dignities in which it falls, shows its inclinations and priorities, and so will indicate how it might choose to apply whatever power it has. The *aspects* between the various planets show occasion: what is, has or will be going on.**

A simple example from horary illustrates this. Suppose my question is, "Will I get the job?" If my planet is strong, it shows me well qualified for the position. My planet in dignities ruled by the job's planet, and vice versa, shows that I want the job and the job wants me. But with no aspect between our two planets, nothing will happen: the occasion will not arise. No matter how friendly I might be with the Chairman, and how much he might wish to employ me, perhaps the present incumbent of the relevant position decides not to leave after all, so nothing comes of it. As this example shows, the way in which we handle aspects is of immense importance in our judgement of the chart; it is not something which can be altered at whim. Yet this is exactly what has happened during the destruction of astrology.

The tradition recognises four aspects: the trine (△) of 120°, the sextile (⚹) of 60°, the square (□) of 90° and the opposition (☍) of 180°. The conjunction (☌) is not technically an aspect, but to avoid unnecessary repetition will be treated as one from here forth. These are known as the *ptolemaic* aspects, as they are the only ones mentioned in Ptolemy's influential text-book, the *Tetrabiblos.*[1] The angle which determines the existence and nature of the aspect is nominally that formed at the Earth by lines extended from the Earth to each of the two planets in question, but the temptation to take this as literal truth has ensnared many astrologers over the centuries. The fact that the zodiac is an ellipse and not a circle results in these angles not being true: when two planets are astrologically

---

[1] Trans. F. E. Robbins; pub. Heinemann, London, 1940, pp. 73-5.

in exact square, for instance, they are quite probably not visually exactly 90° apart. The important point is the planets' places in the zodiac: if Mars is at 10 Scorpio and Venus is at 10 Aquarius, they are three signs (=90°) apart and therefore in square, no matter how this may appear from our particular position on Earth. We must always remember that the cosmos is built from the outside in: trying to remake it from the Earth up is bad philosophy and produces astrology that does not work.

Astrologers managed quite happily with these five aspects until the great astrologer/astronomer Kepler, with one foot in the tradition and one in the modern world, dreamed up a series of others, now known as *minor* aspects. Kepler is a difficult character (as indeed he seems to have been) for both scientists and astrologers. The scientists juggle unconvincingly with the conundrum of how a complete fool – for so he must have been to have devoted so much time to astrology – could discover the laws on which modern astronomy is founded. Those few astrologers who care sufficiently for their tradition to investigate Kepler marvel at his construction of astronomical laws from platonic first principles, yet are forced to admit that he was in the end rather too much of a mathematician to be a sound astrologer. It is through these minor aspects that his unfortunate intoxication with quantity is revealed.

The ptolemaic aspects are formed by dividing the circle by two (opposition – 180°), three (trine – 120°), four (square – 90°), and six (sextile – 60°). There is a certain numerological significance in this, but the numerology describes, it does not determine: to say that the square is as it is because it divides the circle in four is equivalent to saying I am ill because I'm not well. In astrological terms, the determining factor of the aspects is in the four quantities from which the universe is made: hot, cold, moist and dry. Kepler's fascination led him to divide the circle by five, eight, ten and twelve. As he explains, "These figures are knowable and constructible... they are also congruent,"[2] and so they are – mathematically; astrologically, they are irrelevant. Modern astrologers have gone still further up the garden path, dividing the circle by nine and even other numbers that fail to satisfy the qualitative demand of dividing exactly into 360°. As some degrees of latitude, or *orb*, are allowed around the point of exactitude of each aspect, it does not take many seconds of mental arithmetic to realise that once we have introduced this huge variety of minor aspects, virtually every degree forms some aspect with every other.

Strangely enough, all these new aspects produce exactly that effect which was expected of them. We might wonder whether the modern astrologers have an understanding of platonic harmony exceeding even Kepler's, or whether these supposed effects are the products of some fertile imaginations, being matters of such triviality, expressed so vaguely, that it is impossible to ascertain whether they are true or not.

---

[2] *The Harmony of the World*, p. 340; trans. Aiton, Duncan and Field; American Philosophical Society, Philadelphia, 1997

The particular significance of each of the ptolemaic aspects is indicated by the combinations of hot, cold, moist and dry in the signs between which it works. This elemental nature is what determines how the aspect will work. Surprisingly, the moderns, who are temperamentally unable to cope with the idea of benefic and malefic planets, divide aspects quite firmly into good and bad. Trine and sextile are good; square and opposition bad; conjunction variable; the myriad legions of minor aspects line up on the side of their fancy. In the tradition, trine and sextile are easy while square and opposition are hard. This is not quite the same: a nice trine aspect with a malefic planet is most unpleasant. A difficult square to benevolent Jupiter is in most circumstances preferable to a trine with malefic Saturn. Given the choice of a sextile or an opposition to Saturn, only the foolish would plump for the opposition, but that is still not enough to enable a sextile to be described as 'good' in itself.

The easiest of aspects are the trines; this is so because they bring together planets in signs of the same element: planets in air signs (eg Libra) trine only those planets that are in other air signs (Gemini and Aquarius). That is, a planet in a hot, moist sign trines others in hot, moist signs; cold and dry trines cold and dry; and so with the other two combinations. Through being in the same element, the planets understand each other well; they have a great deal in common. It is not unreasonable to expect them to get along easily. Sextiles bring together planets in signs of the same temperature (cold to cold and hot to hot); but uniting moist to dry rather than moist to moist and dry to dry shows that the planets lack the strength of understanding known by planets in trine. Square aspects take dry to dry and moist to moist, but in signs of opposing temperature. This is a weaker bond than that where the temperaments are the same. In a horary chart, for example, an event shown by two planets in trine will happen easily; shown by the same two planets in square, it may still happen, but only after delays and problems.

The opposition, like the sextile, joins planets in signs of the same temperature, but here the tension between opposing forces is too great to unite them. The nature of the opposition is to bring together and then break apart; it is the typical aspect of divorce. Quite the contrary is the conjunction, which joins planets in exactly the same place in the zodiac. The contact here is even closer than in trine, as not only are the planets in signs of the same element, but of the same quality (cardinal, fixed or mutable). Being in exactly the same planetary dignities, we can see that their priorities are exactly the same. Best of all is if they unite in a sign where they both are strong – Moon and Venus in Taurus, perhaps – so they both have power and both share great interest in each other. Conjunction is 'coniunctio', a Latin word for conjugal contact, a point made even more clearly by the other common seventeenth-century terms for conjunction: coitus and copulation. The two planets are one, which is why it is not technically an aspect,

as love in twain
Had the essence but in one:
Two distincts, division none;
Number there in love was slain.[3]

It shows clearly the traditional idea of knowledge, much different from that which is so called today, and vital for an understanding of astrology: conjunction is, literally, 'knowledge in the biblical sense', that is, to know because knower and known are become as one. It is this oneness that explains why the conjunction is not strictly an aspect: an aspect is literally (*aspectus,* Latin) a glance, and you cannot glance at yourself.[4] Conjunction brings the participating planets together easily, but as with all the aspects, how well these planets will get along together is determined by their own natures, their dignities and the receptions they share.

The fundamental importance of the four basic qualities in the understanding of aspect has been so much forgotten that the moderns now ignore all sign boundaries in deciding whether two planets are in aspect to each other. We may allow an orb around the exact point of aspect; this orb, however, stops dead at the end of a sign. If one planet were in the first degree of Taurus and another in the fifth degree of Taurus, we would recognise them as conjunct. If one planet were in the first degree of Taurus and another in the last degree of Aries, the modern astrologer would recognise them as conjunct; but without the shared element and the shared quality of sign that brings their perfect understanding, the idea of conjunction there – even though they are closer than the planets in our first example – is quite absurd. A man might try to achieve conjunction with his wife while she is in the next room, but unless one of them walks through the door, he will find it quite impossible, and probably painful. The same applies to all the other aspects: planets must be in the appropriate signs for the aspect to be formed; the flabby hanging over of aspects into the next sign to suit the astrologer's convenience is modern laxity and quite groundless.

Similarly, it must be noted that in the tradition there is only one possible aspect between any two signs. A planet in Aries and a planet in Cancer can aspect each other only by square – that is the nature of the signs in which they fall. The plethora of minor aspects in use today gives planets the remarkable ability to understand each other well at one point in a sign, yet barely at all a few degrees further on in that same sign. Yet the elemental make-up of the pair has remained unchanged.

What we see here is evidence of a determination to ensure that any two planets can be drawn into some kind of aspect. This is simply not so; yet it does allow the astrologer scope to descant upon their supposed relationship. We shall

---

[3] Shakespeare, *The Phoenix and the Turtle*

[4] It might also be mentioned that such modern 'minor aspects' as quincunx and semi-sextile are said to combine planets in signs which do not, in correct terminology, *behold* each other. If you do not behold something you cannot glance at it, so these cannot be aspects.

of course refrain from suggesting that this is in any way connected with the modern astrological practice of charging readings by the hour. 99% of our thoughts and experiences are much the same as 99% of anyone else's thoughts and experiences; that with which we are – or, at least, ought to be – concerned is the 1% that are distinctive. But the phantom glamour that attaches to our most trivial concerns when someone else starts talking about them allows the astrologer to present the 99% to us as jewels of high water. In fact, the same non-relation between the planets in our own chart that shows these concerns to be nothing but psychic wallpaper is the same non-relation that shows the same thing in someone else's chart. The points that are of interest are those shown by major aspects, and close ones at that. With the modern astrologer charging by the hour or the computer-generated 'chart-reading' of thirty or forty pages, we might compare the examples of natal judgments left by the ancient masters, which are commonly contained within a couple of paragraphs. There is no more purpose in delineating commonplace psychic ramblings than there is in informing the native that he has one head and one body.

In the tradition, each planet is held to have an orb, an area of influence radiating around it like a force-field. When the orbs of two planets touch, whether bodily as in conjunction or in any of the angles that generate the other aspects, the planets are said to be in aspect. The closer they are within those orbs, the stronger the power of the aspect. In horary and in predictive natal work, where we are usually concerned with whether or not an event will take place, we are concerned primarily with exact aspects. If we are seeking explanations, causes, colourings – description rather than action – aspects that are not exact but are still within orb also become important: they show influence from one planet to another. The size of the orb varies from planet to planet: the Sun has the largest, Mercury the smallest. They are of indeterminate size, fizzling out gradually rather than coming to a dead stop at a particular distance from the planet, for which reason authorities quote slightly differing figures for their dimensions. Lilly's list is typical: 9-10 degrees for Saturn; 9-12 for Jupiter; 7-7.30 for Mars; 15-17 for the Sun; 7-8 for Venus; 7 for Mercury; and 12-12.30 for the Moon.[5] The moderns have decided that orbs do not exist – somewhat puzzling, as the New Age end of the astrological spectrum is quite happy with the idea of people having auras, yet planets, which we might expect to be objects of some presence, have none. The orbs, having been removed from the planets, which do exist, have been given to the aspects, which do not. As an aspect is only a relationship between two bodies, a line rather than a solid, it is hard to see how it can have a force-field around it while a body cannot.

A sextile, for example, will be said to have an orb of a certain number of degrees, usually 4 or 6, while a trine will be given one slightly larger, maybe 6 or 8 degrees. This will stay the same regardless of which planets are involved, except that the Sun and Moon are sometimes allowed a degree or two extra. So

<hr>

[5] Lilly, op.cit. p. 107

a trine between Pluto and Chiron will be afforded the same degree of orb as a trine between Jupiter and Saturn. This allows everyone their fair share of dramatic outer-planet aspects, even though the newly-discovered planets will stay within orb of these aspects for months or even years, rendering their particular significance in the life of any individual trivial. But we must all have our fair share of dark and dramatic secrets, otherwise whyever should we want to consult an astrologer? The number of aspects and size of orbs which are assigned to them does mean that they tumble over each other: like a large number of overweight men squeezing into a lift, there simply is not sufficient room for them all within a circle of just 360°. But no matter – the meanings attached to all of them are so vague and capacious that there can never be any hint of contradiction.

Rather than invent large numbers of new aspects of no consequence, a feat of which we might reasonably expect our ancestors, with the fascination for complex arithmetic evinced in the ancient texts, to have been capable, should they ever have found a need, the tradition used the five major aspects, but applied them in a manner congruent with the basis on which astrology is built. The key to this is movement. That is why astrology works. That is what astrology studies. Movement. Without that, nothing. We are watching the motion of a series of spheres relative to ourselves and relative to each other. So it is surely implicit in whatever conclusions we draw from this watching that the consideration of this movement, not just of a series of apparently static points, should be of consequence. Not so, the moderns tell us, having abandoned in all but a very few limited usages any concern with this, to the extent that we find many 'qualified' graduates from astrological 'schools' who are quite unaware of even the simple fact of which planets move faster than others. The neglect of movement is probably not unconnected with the transfer of astrology from the sky to the printed page: to someone familiar with the night sky, the movement of the planets is plain to see. Such familiarity on even a basic level is now a rarity among astrologers, hence also the modern willingness to suppose invisible fragments of space-dust the equals of brilliant objects such as Jupiter or Saturn. The ignorance of how to distinguish between a major planet and the lights of a passing aircraft makes the night sky a confusing place!

Movement has particular significance in the true understanding of aspects. First, we have the question of whether an aspect has already been made and is now separating, or has yet to be made and is now applying. As we have suggested above, there is an obvious difference between two things heading towards each other and the same two things moving apart. Movement also enables planets which are not in aspect to influence each other, through the intervention of a third party. As the planets move at different speeds, a swift planet can aspect a slower one, gather up its influence and carry it on to another slow-moving planet; or two swift planets which do not aspect each other may both apply to aspect a third, slower, planet, which gathers their influence. It is as if I want to go out with Donna, belle of the tenth grade; if I can't find it in me to ask her myself, I might prevail upon one of my friends to break the ice on my behalf. Both these astrological patterns, known respectively as the *translation* and *collection of light,* show such third-party intervention, a subtlety that has been lost by the moderns. As the third party exists outside our own psyche, he or she is obviously no longer of any interest to us.

We are given the choice of a series of aspects based soundly in the structure of astrology, or an endless series of phantoms based on whim. If what we wish to do is to paint fantasy pictures of no substance, the phantom aspects serve our purpose well, as they can be manipulated at will without risk of bumping into any restrictive wall of reality. If we seek anything more from our astrology, we shall find it only by learning to use what is given: the products of our fancy will show us nothing other than our fancy. The great drawback of learning to use what is real is that is does demand a little effort, and confronts us from time to time with the inescapable realisation that we have got it wrong. Safer by far to stay with the lotus-eaters, wrapped numbly in the cotton-wool of minor aspects between asteroids.

9

Houses

The astrological chart is divided into sections known as *houses,* or, more precisely, *mundane houses,* as these are the earthly reflections of the *celestial houses,* or signs of the zodiac. Everything that exists in the world, tangible or intangible, past, present or future, real or imaginary, fits into one or other of these houses. The idea of houses in modern astrology is very different from that in traditional astrology and, indeed, this is one of the areas where we see the distortions of modern astrology most clearly.

The idea of dividing the chart into twelve seems simple enough: twelve equal slices, just as if we were portioning out a cake; but the astrologer faces the same problem as the geographer, that of representing a spherical reality on a plane, two dimensional surface. Indeed, this understates the difficulty of the task, for our 'sphere' is based on the elliptical path of the zodiac and so is not strictly spherical. We may set out to take twelve equal slices, but are soon faced with the conundrum of 'equal, but how?' Do we divide our cake equally by size, or by the number of cherries each portion contains?

There are over a hundred different solutions to this problem, each giving its different method of dividing the chart; of these, only some half-dozen have ever been widely used. The differences between the others are, as we might imagine from their number, mostly trivial. These *house systems* fall into three main groups: the chart is divided either according to time, according to space or in purely symbolic terms. In the past, different systems seemed to co-exist quite happily; in more recent times, astrologers have found it necessary to beat each other over the head in the attempt to prove that the system they are using is the one and only one that is correct. We might note that the increase in passion over house systems has proceeded hand in hand with a decrease in the ability to make any constructive use out of them, as evinced in concrete, verifiable astrology.

The house system links celestial events to the Earth. We have already seen how the position of any planet is located against the sky by noting its celestial longitude. This position is the same from wherever it is seen on Earth. If the Moon is at 4 degrees of Pisces seen from Hawaii, it is at 4 degrees of Pisces seen from London. Obviously, however, its position relative to the observer varies from place to place and according to the time of day. If this 4 Pisces Moon is high in the sky in London, it will be below the horizon of someone viewing the sky at that same moment in Hawaii. The celestial longitude tells us where the planets are relative to each other; what we are doing now is seeking to answer the question "Where is that planet relative to us – is it over there, or is it down there?" We must never forget that our astrological charts are not just pieces of paper bearing symbolic glyphs: they are plans of what we can see in the sky if we step outside our door.

There is no one 'correct' house system. Just as with geographers' cartographical projections, every solution to the problem demands compromise. In a map of the globe, if we have the countries in their correct relative places, they will be the wrong shape and size; if we demand that their relative sizes be shown correctly, we cannot put them in exactly the right places. The projection to be used in any particular situation will be chosen according to the prevailing criteria, not because one is true and the other possibilities false. One projection might be chosen because it places my country at the centre of the world; another because it makes it seem comparatively big; another because it enables the world to be shown as a coherent rectangle that pleases the eye; or perhaps I just want to see clearly which train will take me from A to B. Similarly with the astrological houses: different systems are particularly suitable for different purposes. And some are suitable for nothing at all. Some modern schools have dispensed with houses altogether, on the fashionable principle that "What I cannot understand cannot possibly be true."

Many moderns use a symbolic division of the heavens called 'Equal House'. This takes the degree of the Ascendant as its starting point and simply divides the astrological cake by cutting it at that same degree of each successive sign; so if the Ascendant falls at 10 degrees of Leo, the cusp of the second house will fall at 10 Virgo, the third at 10 Libra, and so on. Its proponents frequently claim that it is the ancient system used by Ptolemy and other astrologers of antiquity, a claim that proves nothing except their ignorance of Ptolemy and other astrologers of antiquity. It is a modern attempt to reduce astrology into terms accessible to children at first-grade level. As a purely symbolic division it no doubt tells us all sorts of fascinating things about the symbolic world so beloved of modern astrologers, but absolutely nothing about the real world which the rest of us inhabit. If all that we seek to know of our existence is what is contained within the pages of 'Janet and John and their Dog Spot', the Equal House system will serve our purpose. If not, we must look elsewhere.[1]

The system that was used by the ancients, and is still the prevalent system in Indian astrology, is known, slightly inaccurately, as 'whole-sign houses'. Here, the boundaries of sign and house coincide. So if our Ascendant is 10 degrees of Leo, Leo will be the first house, Virgo the second, Libra the third. To be exact, there are no houses as such, but only signs; all that falls within the second house is regarded as falling within the second sign. Treatment of the chart is rather different within this system, less emphasis being placed upon the degrees at

---

[1] A recent client had previously had a 'psychological' natal reading from a modern astrologer using the Equal House system. When he complained that most of what he had been told was quite untrue, the astrologer replied, "This is how you would have been if you had not been raised by your parents."!

which the various planets fall. The chart is read again and again, each time from a slightly different perspective, until a comprehensive picture is constructed. In the hands of a skilled astrologer, great accuracy can be achieved; but the western tradition, working within a different culture, adopted different house systems to deal with its different priorities.

It is within this tradition that we find the distinction between houses divided by time and by space. The prevalent examples of each are the Placidus and Regiomontanus systems. The Regiomontanus system divides the sky into equal chunks, more or less as one would do by eye; Placidus divides the sky according to the time the Sun takes to traverse it. Each Regiomontanus house covers thirty degrees of Right Ascension. Each Placidus house covers one sixth, by time, of the Sun's journey from sun-rise to sun-set or vice versa. Much passion has been vented in attempts to establish which of these systems, or of others which resemble them, is superior, rather as much passion has been vented by football supporters arguing the superiority of their favourite teams. Fortunately, like football teams, house systems can be subjected to an acid test: some work and some do not, and no amount of debate will validate a system that fails to produce results. The horary charts in this book are cast by the Regiomontanus system; all others by Placidus. These both work well for their various purposes, which is not to suggest that there are not others which are also of value.

The Regiomontanus system is named after the fifteenth-century mathematician and astrologer, Johann Muller, who used 'Regiomontanus' ('King of the Mountains') as a pseudonym; Placidus takes its name from the seventeenth-century monk Placidus de Tito. Both systems had been in use long before the time of their adoptive fathers. De Tito's astrological writing is notable mainly for reaching depths of turgidity which even the great Ptolemy failed to plumb; despite this, it succeeded in popularising this system, which is now probably the most widely used of all. This extreme elevation owes more to historical accident than any recognition of its merits, tables calculated by this method being the ones that the editor of *Raphael's Ephemeris,* the best-selling of such publications, happened to have to hand when he decided to include such tables in his annual work.

So much for the method by which the chart is divided; let us now consider what is placed in each of the divisions. Everything that there is fits in somewhere, so a complete listing would carry on indefinitely; but each house has certain main themes. Knowing which house is associated with each thing we consider is – or, at least, was – the first essential step in astrological judgment, without which nothing else can have meaning. William Lilly is typical in requiring as the first priority after the basic ability to set the chart, that his student should be 'very perfect in knowing the nature of the Houses, that he may better discover from what house to require judgment upon the question propounded.' [2] Simply put, if we do not know which house governs

---

[2] *Christian Astrology,* 'To The Reader', second page; 1647, London. Reprinted Regulus, London, 1985.

the thing we are talking about, we have only a one in twelve chance of looking in the right place in the chart to draw judgment upon it; we should not, then, be surprised if our judgments are incorrect. Tampering with this basic knowledge is akin to polluting a well; yet this the moderns most gleefully do, remaking the chart after their own ephemeral preoccupations without regard for truth.

Let us consider a typical modern list of house concerns:[3]

> 1st house: self
> 2nd: possessions
> 3rd: expression
> 4th: home
> 5th: pleasure
> 6th: service
> 7th: partners
> 8th: sex
> 9th: exploration
> 10th: career
> 11th: friends
> 12th: spirit.

Reducing the houses to just one word is an impossibility; but no matter how many words are used, there would always be room for more, thus we have no quarrel with the necessary abbreviation of this list. But even this truncated form, a mere twelve words, which we might have hoped would leave little scope for error, reveals major and decisive misconceptions about the fundamental nature of the chart. Without applying any astrological knowledge at all, we might raise an eyebrow at the divorce of sex from both pleasure and partners (let us be grateful it has not been located in the house of career); a knowledge of the astrological tradition shows that some of these house meanings have been assigned apparently at random. Unsurprisingly, it is the unpleasant houses which have been most distorted by the moderns, as in the fairy-land of contemporary astrology nothing that is not sugar-coated is allowed admittance. The sixth house has nothing to do with service; the eighth has nothing to do with sex and the twelfth has nothing to do with the spirit. Absolutely nothing. Under any circumstances. Not even in *your* chart, no matter how much you like the look of those twelfth house planets. The sixth, eighth and twelfth houses are not nice and that is the end of it. To the modern astrologer, interested in nothing other than reassuring his client that everything in the psychic garden is lovely, the idea that there are some unpleasant happenings in life is utterly unacceptable, and he has remade astrology to prove his point.

The first house is indeed the house which shows the person in question. It extends from the Ascendant, the eastern horizon, the point at which the divine

---

[3] Taken from *Astrology Source* CD Rom, Multicom Publishing, 1993-6

spark enters the material body, so by extension it is also 'the ship that you sail in', whether that ship be a means of transport or the 'earthly vehicle'. In a horary chart, it shows the person asking the question; in a birth-chart it is the person himself, and as such in a way contains all the rest of the chart; in a mundane chart it represents the general state of affairs of that country. From the first house we describe the person, both physically – even to the extent of telling where they have marks, scars or tattoos – and as a personality. It is common today to take the description of both body and nature from the Sun-sign, but this is quite fanciful. The man you meet at a party who gazes at you intently and announces "You must be a Taurus" is no more to be believed than the one who tells you "I'm sure we were lovers in a in a past life." The sign in which the Sun falls has little to do with appearance, and usually only those who are the very closest to us will be vouchsafed a glimpse of our true Sun-sign nature. But Sun-signs are so much more convenient, as everyone knows what theirs is, and in the battle between truth and convenience modern astrologers hold an honourable place in the front rank of the army of convenience.

The indicators of physical appearance are the sign on the Ascendant; the planet ruling that sign and the sign in which it falls; planets close to the Ascendant; the Moon and the sign in which that falls; all of these being coloured by planets with which they are in aspect. The Sun plays only the most minor role, unless it happens to fall into one of the above categories. Unfortunately, you are unlikely to impress anyone by leering at them and informing them sagely "Your rising-sign is Aquarius," as chances are they don't know what it is themselves. You would, however, be far more likely to be correct in your ascription than you would in guessing their Sun-sign.

The primary indication of **the second house** is resources and possessions. Astrology uses a definition of possession that is no longer current in western society, much to our loss, but otherwise this is self-explanatory. For astrological purposes, you can possess something only if it is inanimate and you can move it about. It may be quite obvious that I do not own my cat, but I don't own my dog either, whatever his opinion on this might be. Nor do I own my employees, nor even my slaves, even though they are, in a sense, 'mine'. The mobility requirement means that I do not own either land or property, no matter how many deeds of title I might possess, nor how much I have paid for it. And whatever the adverts may tell me, I can never own a star!

The third is the house of siblings, neighbours and communications. It thus includes rumours and gossip; short journeys; phone, fax and post; the native's own ability to articulate his thoughts. That cars are nowadays routinely ascribed to the third house demonstrates the lack of logical process that besets contemporary astrology, the idea that a vague feeling of benevolence towards the universe is sufficient substitute for the ability to think straight. Here, as in many other circumstances, we see a confusion between the object and what is done with that object. My car is my possession, hence second house; it is the journey I make in it that is a third house matter. The only feasible circumstance that would cause a car to be located in the third is if we were judging the birth-chart of one car and wanted to know how well it got along with its brothers and sisters. After thirty years of practice, I have yet to do this.

With **the fourth house** we enter an area of serious controversy: in the red corner, astrology; in the blue, political correctness. The fourth is the house of land, property and – through two thousand years of accurate written tradition – the father. The tenth, being the house opposite the fourth, is the father's partner, the mother. This is no longer acceptable. Modern astrologers are divided between those who reverse these two houses, giving the fourth to mum and the tenth to dad, and those who assign them according to which is the 'dominant parent'. So who is your dominant parent? It may be *en vogue* to suggest that we can dispense with the services of one or other parent, but the briefest reflection on the idea of 'dominant parent' reveals how baseless it is. So Mum brought you up single-handed; your father left before you were born and has never been seen since; this supposedly makes Mum the dominant one – yet you have your father's build, your father's temperament, your father's manner. Which of us is so subtle he can justly decide which is the 'dominant parent' of any child? The very fact of one's absence can arguably have a greater effect than the years of careful nurture from the other, regardless of what physical and temperamental legacies may have been bequeathed.

Apart from being theoretically indefensible, the reversal of houses simply does not work; hence the growing trend to assign them according to 'dominance' (a factor quantifiable only by the modern astrologer's own social ideology). Why the heavens should rearrange themselves according to prevailing concepts of social correctness is a question the answer to which can presumably be found somewhere in California. The original decision to reverse the houses comes from a strange and deformed creature of darkness known as The Alphabetical Zodiac, to which it is time our gentle reader was – with all due regard for his safety – introduced. Like some loathsome beast of fable, this creature has spawned a numberless brood of hideous offspring, who are responsible for the greater part of the nonsense that is pandered in the name of astrology today.

Being based on the repetition of a very few straightforward principles, we might have thought that astrology was simple enough, and so it has been found throughout most of its history. Not simple enough, however, for modern consumption. Having three sets of variables, planets, signs and houses, is far too confusing; so they can be rendered down into one amorphous mass by the application of a simple formula: planet = house = sign. The first house, then, is the same as Aries, is the same as Mars; the second = Taurus = Venus; and so on. The association of houses and signs in the order 1-12 and Aries – Pisces respectively does have its foundation in the tradition, but in one specific context and that alone: that of the human body and its ailments. Both Aries and the first house relate to the head, Taurus and the second to the neck and thus through the signs until Pisces and the 12th which relate to the feet. The connection is not made in any other circumstances, and with the application of a small amount of knowledge so doing can easily be seen to be wrong.

With a little sleight of mind, we can make a plausible case for connecting Aries, Taurus and Gemini with the first three houses. Cancer, however, has no connection with fathers: it is a feminine sign, ruled by the Moon. Neither does it have any connection with agriculture, property, mines, buried treasure or any other traditional fourth house concern. As is the contemporary trend, rather than seeking to understand what already exists, which necessarily involves changing ourselves, we cast that carelessly aside and impose our own foolish preconceptions of how, in our naievity, we think things ought to be. So Mum (Cancer, Moon) gets the fourth house. It is hard to understand the cries of bafflement from modern astrologers at the scientists' refusal to understand astrology, when they are behaving in exactly the same way themselves. Children of our times, indeed.

The house/sign connection becomes all the more untenable with the fifth house, the house of children. This would correspond to Leo. Leo is traditionally known as a 'barren' sign, and its appearance in the fifth house is one of the strongest indications that the native shall not have children.

The second part of the equation, that which ties planets to houses, is – if possible – even more baseless. We start with Mars in the first house, for the sole reason that it happens to rule Aries. So it does; yet throughout the tradition this has never seemed a reason for placing it in the first house, for Mars does not start anything. In whatever scheme of the cosmos, geocentric or heliocentric, Mars sits in the middle. The tradition associates Saturn with the first house, as the outermost of the planets, and thence works through the cosmic spheres in their natural order, which, as we shall see, equates exactly with the meanings of the houses.

The simple one-to-one formulation of the Alphabetical Zodiac has, on the neat democratic principle of one planet – one sign (it is reassuring to see the heavens pulling themselves together and adopting modern political creeds), caused the recently discovered planets Uranus, Neptune and Pluto to be roped in to serve their turn as house-rulers, becoming associated with Aquarius, Pisces and Scorpio respectively, signs with whose traditional meanings the arbitrary significations assigned to these planets have not the slightest connection. Even with their assistance, poor Venus and Mercury still have each two signs/houses with which to deal; the state of fatigue to which this has reduced them, as they race from one to other in desperate attempt to keep up, perhaps explains the palpable shortage of love and reason in the modern world.

Apart from the absence of any true justification, the Alphabetical Zodiac simply does not work, as evidence of which we may note the inability of modern astrology to make accurate, specific prediction. While there are serious ethical reasons why we should not predict, the demonstrable ability to do so should we so wish remains the acid test by which astrological theory stands or falls.

The fifth is the house of children, pleasure and, according to William Lilly, 'ale-houses and taverns'.[4] Here again we find confusion. The seventh house, both ancients and moderns agree, is the house of the 'significant other'; but where do we locate the insignificant other, the brief romance, the mistress, the one night stand? The heavens, which we might have supposed fully occupied reorganising themselves to keep up with changing social and political trends, seem able to adapt themselves at will to the personal morality of whichever astrologer happens to be writing about them. There is an immensely flexible dividing-line between the 'serious' relationships in the seventh and what goes on in the fifth, while even the most libertine astrologers neuter all these relationships, long-term or fleeting, by locking sex safely away in the eighth house. None of that in my zodiac, if you please!

The more straitlaced the astrologer, the more restrictive becomes the seventh house, the more capacious the fifth. But the true distinction between the two has nothing whatever to do with morals and everything to do with the division between object and function that we have seen causing problems before. The person belongs to the seventh house, the activity to the fifth. So whether she be wife or blind date, she is seventh house; while the ale-house or tavern to which I may take her are fifth: the one is the person, the other what I do when with this person. These activities include sex, which belongs naturally to the house of children – and of pleasure, though evidently not in astrological circles.

The sixth is the first of the unpleasant houses that modern astrologers have found necessary to whitewash to avoid any trace of unpleasantness polluting the toyland in which they dwell. It is now known as the House of Service, which is a revealing attribution, as in our narcissistic world the idea that we might be of service to anyone is evidently deeply unpleasant and belongs in this unfortunate house. It is also known as the House of Health; throughout the tradition it has been the House of Illness, a different thing altogether.

The sixth is the house of the slings and arrows of outrageous fortune; of all the nasty things life does to us without our in the slightest deserving them; the general problems of life, significantly located next to the seventh, the house of other people, as it is usually they who are responsible for them. It contrasts with the twelfth house of self-undoing, which, situated next to the first house, shows the foolish things we manage to inflict upon ourselves. The most important of the many monsters who dwell here is Ill-health. The tradition sees illness as a trial of strength between the sixth house and the first, house of the vital spirits of the nature. The sixth is the house of service, but only in one specific sense: it shows our slaves and servants – so if I have recurrent problems with tradesmen, I should expect to identify the underlying cause of these from the study of my sixth house. But if I am a servant, my job is located in the same house of career as anyone else's: the tenth. After all, everyone who works is in service to someone, or we should never be paid.

---

[4] op. cit. p. 53

The seventh house the moderns have left unchanged. This is the house of 'the other person', particularly someone with whom we are closely bound, whether through love, business partnership or enmity; but it is also the house of any other, anyone who does not fit into one of the specific categories elsewhere in the chart.

The eighth is traditionally the house of death. Our modern brethren inform us that since the birth of the true Messiah, Carl Jung, death is no more. Modern text-books of astrology tell the student in no uncertain terms that under no circumstances should they ever suggest to their client that they might not be immortal. Speaking of death is the sin greater than all others. Yet in the past, the prediction of death was an essential preliminary to the judging of the natal chart: there is little point in promising true love, fame and happiness for Wednesday if the native will die on Tuesday. Ptolemy writes, "The consideration of the length of life takes the leading place among inquiries about events following birth, for, as the ancient says, it is ridiculous to attach particular predictions to one who, by the constitution of the years of his life, will never attain at all to the time of the predicted events."[5] Death is, indeed, the one prediction that an astrologer can make with a reasonable certainty of being correct: the timing may be out, but they will at least get the event right. But as the judgement of birth-charts today involves little more than the intense mutual contemplation of the client's navel, it is not difficult to understand why death should be rigorously excluded, introducing as it does a harsh chill of reality into the benign numbness of the consultation.

Our ancestors, blinded by ignorance and superstition, held the opinion that people do die, and that, as this is an event of considerable significance in the life, it is only reasonable that the astrologer should direct some attention towards it. Being of some importance, it is not unreasonable that it should warrant a house in the astrological chart. Now that death has been abolished, however, the modern astrologer finds a gaping hole in the chart where the eighth house stands. To fill this void, sex has been transformed into an eighth house matter; somehow the human race managed to procreate through several millennia of misunderstanding. The propagators of this relocation make much of the Elizabethan poets' usage of 'die' as a euphemism for orgasm to point a connection between sex and death. This emphasis and the conclusions drawn from it suggest a rather shaky understanding of the concept of metaphor: in case our gentle reader is in any doubt, the bedrooms of Elizabethan England were not filled with the corpses of decaying poets.

For most modern astrologers, all sex belongs in the eighth house. Some, however, limit the eighth to 'orgasmic' sex, apparently having invented some other kind which they consign to the fifth house. Yet strangely this presumably non-orgasmic sex manages to produce children (the main topic of the fifth house) while the orgasmic variety does not. Some distinguish between

[5] Claudius Ptolemy, *Tetrabiblos*, tr. Robbins, Heinemann, 1940, p 271.

'orgasmic' (eighth) and 'recreational' sex (fifth), evidently on the understanding that sex is recreational only if something goes wrong. But let us draw a discreet veil over whatever this confusion might reveal about the world of the modern astrologer.

The ninth, we are told by our representative modern, is 'exploration'. It is known traditionally as the House of God, as it concerns those activities which most obviously draw us close to Him: religion in all its forms; knowledge and learning; dreams and visions. As such it is the most important house in the chart, as from there we draw much of our information about the quality of faith the native possesses. The purpose of judging the natal chart is to assess the strengths and weaknesses of the nature in the light of the potentials revealed by this house: all else is just decoration. It is also concerned with long journeys: the third, as we have seen, covers the mundane trivial journeys of our daily round (at an extreme, the trip to the bathroom would be included there); the ninth concerns the longer journeys, each one of which is an image of that one journey to the Divine.

Apart from being, as we have seen, the house of the mother, **the tenth** is, in both modern and traditional astrology, the house of the king, of the boss in whatever situation we are considering, of the native's career. This is a significant point, as these few words rubbish the great majority of all the supposed scientific tests of astrology. The career, in traditional astrology, is judged by weighing the tenth house, the planet that rules it, planets that happen to fall in it, and Mercury, Venus and Mars. This is a fine selection, but in most charts will not involve the Sun. Scientists – such as the astronomer Paul Couderc, to whose so-called research we have previously referred – commonly take a list of birth-dates from which they conclude that there is no correlation between sun-sign and profession. As nowhere in the tradition and only at the newspaper end of the modern spectrum do astrologers claim that there is any such connection, whatever foolishness this research reveals is not within astrology.

The eleventh house the moderns have left largely untouched, continuing to see it as the house of friends and friendship. In the tradition, it is also the house of hopes and wishes, as one's hopes are, whether on real or metaphoric level, the gift (second house) of the king (tenth house), that is, they are located in the king's house of possessions, or the eleventh.

The third of the unfortunate houses is **the twelfth**, so here too the moderns have found it necessary to subject truth to major cosmetic surgery in order to avoid any dirty footprints in their squeaky-clean Walt Disney world. According to William Lilly, the twelfth is the house of "private Enemies, of Witches, great Cattle, as Horses, Oxen, Elephants, &c. Sorrow, Tribulation, Imprisonments, all manner of affliction, self-undoing, &c. and of such men as maliciously undermine their neighbours, or inform secretly against them."[6] We have nothing against Horses, Oxen, Elephants, &c, – nor, perhaps it must be

---

[6] op. cit. p 56

pointed out, did Lilly or the tradition in which he was working – but otherwise the contents of this house are Not Nice. Lilly has made no mention of things spiritual, having treated of them in the house where they belong: the ninth. The moderns, however, have remade the twelfth as the house of the spirit. We might suspect that it is only this relocation of spiritual matters into what is the most unredeemedly difficult and negative of the houses of the horoscope that enables modern astrologers to maintain the almost pathological level of delusion that leads them to claim – apparently in all seriousness – that the modern world is growing ever more spiritual at a great and constant pace.

Unless there are some specific circumstances (close aspect or strong reception) that enable them to do otherwise, planets falling in the twelfth house find the greatest difficulty in acting. It is like a dark well into which planets fall – we hear the distant echo of their voices calling from deep within, but can do little to help them get out. Explaining this to audiences of modern astrologers is, we have found, productive of vehement and lasting hostility. In the assignment of bodily parts to the astrological houses, the twelfth rules the feet, and any discussion of it in real terms is guaranteed to tread hard on someone's corns. It is a delicate spot, for it reveals the fatuity of the prevailing modern belief that "I am hopeless at life, so I must be deeply spiritual". With many planets in the twelfth, there is every likelihood (with the above rider) that the native is hopeless at life; the second part of the equation does not, however, follow. As can be seen from its true position within the chart, spirituality is a part of life, not a consolation prize for those who drop out of it. The twelfth "can also" a modern informs us, "indicate a deep service for Humanity;"[7] for modern astrologers are all psychic warriors battling selflessly on mankind's behalf. This service is 'deep' because it is conducted while sitting at home in isolation with no noticeable effect on anyone. As the house of secrets and self-undoing, the twelfth is also the house of masturbation – psychic or otherwise.

This distortion of the meanings of the houses has at root the determination of modern astrologers to keep everything in their world sugary-sweet, to ensure that their confection offers a wholly pleasurable experience for both client and astrologer, regardless of its lack of any nutritional content. The true relationship between planets and houses has been suppressed in order to perpetuate the parody of astrology that is the Alphabetical Zodiac.

As the first of the planets, Saturn's association with the first house – now usurped by Mars – should be obvious. The first shows the incarnation, the entry of spirit into flesh, which very act is symbolised by Saturn. Saturn is the ruler of material nature *per se* and of the significant parts of the body in particular: the bones that support it, the skin that is its external boundary, and the joints that are its points of articulation. Jupiter is second planet, and so associated with the second house. As planet of prosperity and fortune, this is not inappropriate. Mars, rather than with the first, is associated with the third

[7] Tybol, op. cit. p. 23

house; Mars is natural ruler of brothers, one of the main meanings of the third, and is the impulse behind communication. Mercury has its obvious connection with the actual voicing of any message, but Mars is the impulse behind it, the desire that makes the communication happen.

In complete reversal of the groundless modern association of the Moon and Cancer with the fourth, the tradition gives the Sun. The Sun is the archetypal father, and so the fourth is the house of father. Maybe the moderns doubt that the Sun is the dominant planet. After the Sun comes cuddly little Venus, a most appropriate planet for the fifth house of 'Pleasure, Delight and Meriment',[8] and then Mercury, natural ruler of servants, who holds the sixth, the house of servants. The Moon, eternal symbol of the heavenly marriage, is associated with the seventh house of close relationships. When we consider that the Ascendant, directly opposite the seventh cusp, is above all else the point of sun-rise, we begin to see the beauty of this natural pattern, poising Sun and Moon, the masculine and feminine, the divine and the created, in their perfect harmony. The distinction is the same as confused the moderns in trying to separate seventh and fifth houses: they give Venus to the seventh; but it is the Moon that gives the principle of partnership (seventh house). Venus (fifth house) is the lovey-dovey we do within that principle.

Unlike the moderns, when the tradition ran out of planets it found no need to invent new ones, but simply ran through the pattern again. So Saturn, which saw us into life in the first house, sees us out of it in the eighth; Saturn, Lord of boundaries, of beginnings and endings, of death and the grave. As Saturn is also ruler of all dark and unpleasant places, it is no surprise to find that the eighth house is, on the house by house ascription of body parts, associated with the excretory system. The reproductive system, reasonably enough, belongs to the seventh, house of marriage, saving us from the manifold perversions the moderns suggest with their fanciful confusion of eighth house, Pluto and Scorpio.

The ninth is the house of faith, and so is naturally associated with the next planet, Jupiter, natural ruler of religion, priests, teachers and the like. In Indian astrology, Jupiter is known as 'Guru', which makes the point exactly. The tenth is the house of career, and belongs to Mars. As with the third, the important point is the energetic impulse that makes us go out and conquer, for our career is our conquering of our own little empire. The eleventh house is nowadays held to take its nature from Uranus and Aquarius, so shows the native's altruistic desire to help the community. Rather than delving into the realms of fiction with the newly-discovered planets, we might content ourselves with giving the Sun its rightful place in this house, through which we find astrology within itself asserting its own limitations; for the eleventh is the house of the servants to the king – so if the Sun, mightiest of planets, 'Lord of Life', is but the servant, how mighty indeed and splendid must be He who Rules.

---

[8] Lilly, op. cit. p 53

Finally, the twelfth house: Neptune, according to moderns, for it fits well their strange understanding of spirituality. The house of self-undoing, according to the tradition, and as such ruled of course by Venus, the cuddly bundle of fun that we found in the fifth house being transformed into the seductive temptations of the twelfth.

This pattern of relation between planets and houses, the root of which leads back to the distinction and connection between the potential of the twelve and the articulation through time of the seven, makes plain the true meanings of the houses, which are thus seen to be connected unalterably with the structure of the cosmos. This is not some random attribution of meaning in which things have been dumped at whim into one or other of a collection of twelve baskets. Also laden with significance is the second scheme of association between planets and houses, which gives the now neglected system of the *joys* of the planets, in which each planet is said to joy in finding itself in one particular house.

The joys of the planets are these: Mercury joys in the first house, the Moon in the third, Venus in the fifth, Mars in the sixth, the Sun in the ninth, Jupiter in the eleventh and Saturn in the twelfth. In practical terms, when judging the chart any planet falling in the house of its joy gains in strength. If in the house opposite, it is weakened. It gains in strength because this house is the appropriate place for it to be; it is there that it can best display its true nature. Again, this takes us back to the basic meanings of the planets and houses.

Mercury joys in the first house because its nature is as the articulation through time: discursive reason. In a way, it thus contains the function of the whole of creation – the articulation of potential into form that is carried out by the movements of the seven planets, for which reason it is the symbol of Man, the Crown of Creation. Mercury is thus a reflection, on a 'lower' plane, of the Word, through which all was created. In the first, the house of the body, we have the Word made flesh that is creation. In practical terms, the first house is the initiating point of whatever action has inspired the casting of the chart, which action is one example of the articulation of potential into material form.

The Sun, the light of truth, presides over the chart from the ninth house, the house of religious faith, vision and knowledge. Its partner, the Moon, is at home in the opposite house, the third, from where it reflects the light of truth into our daily round, as shown in the house of short, trivial journeys. When both Sun and Moon are in their favoured places they are opposite each other, so the Moon is at full, and thus reflects all that it is able of the light of the Sun. It is filled with the light of Heaven, and as such has no room left for anything of its own: it is become 'the handmaid of the Lord', fulfilling its role perfectly.

Venus, the spirit of love, joys in the fifth. At one level we find love working here in its most obvious form as sex and procreation; but the fifth is also the house of messengers and ambassadors, which display the basic drive to conciliation with one's fellow man. The other benefic, Jupiter, holds the opposite, eleventh, house. This is the house of hope, where Jupiter's presence demonstrates the soundness of our hope in the Divine. In material terms, we see the eleventh as the house of 'gifts from the king' on which we depend – the pennies from heaven which shower upon us, even in the most usual sense of the eleventh as (second house from the tenth) our boss's money and so our wages. Midway between the houses of the Divine and of the articulated moment – or the 'Now' of the chart – this is where we see the immediate practical intervention of the Almighty to constantly uplift and sustain us.

Our comprehension of the malefic planets, Mars and Saturn, and their placement in the chart is seriously hampered by our innate conviction that their effects have nothing whatever to do with us, but are the result of some malign conspiracy to deprive us of our just deserts. In this sense, they are indeed quite at home in the unfortunate sixth and twelfth houses. But to think thus is to miss the point. The twelfth is the house of sin, of our own misdoings; Saturn, the planet of restraint, is the most useful tool which we might find there. The sixth is the apparently random unpleasantness and nastiness of others and the world. Mars is the sword which we may take up to fight against it, and thus provides the will to do good. Mars can be either the disease, or the surgical intervention that rids us of the disease; so also with Saturn: either the burden of sin that imprisons us, or the discipline that restrains the sin and frees us from it. The choice is ours. Whichever planet it is, if it is in its joy, we are most easily able to avail ourselves of its working at its best.

As Lilly said, a clear understanding of the houses is vital if correct judgement is to be made; knowledge cannot be replaced by ignorance and preconceptions. Or, rather, as the existence of the modern forms of astrology proves, it can; but they cannot fulfil the same role. Not only do they not work, but they also destroy the connections between houses, planets and signs that provide a profound understanding of the wonders of creation and its connection with the Creator.

10

Electional Astrology

From horary, the next step in our astrological hierarchy is the art of elections, of choosing the best moment to act. "Oh goody," we think; "Can you elect the moment for me to buy a winning lottery ticket?" "Probably not," is the disappointing answer; for we can elect nothing the possibilities of which are not shown in the birth-chart, so if the potential for acquiring sudden wealth is not in your nativity, no elected chart will bring you a winning lottery ticket. This response invariably brings disparagement upon the astrologer's head, as if it were a failing in astrology. But none of us would quibble if told that the lack of a body capable of running exceptionally fast excluded us from the possibility of breaking the world 100 metres record, at no matter what moment we chose to make the attempt. If some shyster were to tempt us, "Buy a ticket, enter the race – you too could break the record," we would rightly ignore him; that we misplace our hopes is a failing in ourselves, not in astrology, and a prime purpose of the art is to reveal such illusions to us for what they are.

Electional astrology would be well described in the same terms as politics: it is 'the art of the possible'. What is not possible cannot be done, no matter how much attention the astrologer might devote to his calculations. Any action I wish to undertake brings together two groups of things: my potentials and the realities of the situation; only insofar as they accord with each other can anything be achieved. Electional astrology aims to bring these two groups together in the most productive way. My potential cannot necessarily be realised. My nativity may indicate that I am potentially the greatest general who has ever lived, yet if there is no war to fight this potential will rust unused; similarly, if my country's army consists of two men and a dog I cannot elect a moment at which to display my talents by winning the battle.

Consider an attempt to build a house. I have a pile of materials: this is the potential contained within my birth-chart. Some of these materials are of the very best; some are shoddy; some of finest are of excellent quality but of no use whatever in building a house. I also have a variety of sites from which to choose: this is the reality of the situation. If I build on the hilltop, the views are wonderful but it's a long way to the shops; if I build in the valley, I'll be close to the shops but the materials I have don't accord with the local building regulations. Then there are constraints of time: if I start work in winter, the ground will be too hard to dig my foundations; but if I don't start before March, the house will not be ready when my baby is born. Juggling these various factors to produce the optimum situation is exactly the challenge of electional astrology.

When selecting the materials I am to use for my house, however, I must exercise caution. If I build my house of sticks, it will not transform itself into a house of bricks when the Big Bad Wolf appears; and so with electing a chart. The upwardly mobile young couple may be adamant that they do not want children; if the astrologer who elects the time for their marriage is foolish enough to build this desire into the chosen chart, he has a good chance of seeing them again in ten years time, requesting an election for the commencement of fertility treatment. As in the fairy stories, if we have our wishes granted we are apt to be left desperately begging that the sausage might be removed from the end of our nose and circumstances put back as they were. The cold, clear light that horary astrology casts on our wishes makes it quite plain that most of the time we are far better off without whatever it is that we are convinced that we want; by electing a chart we have the real danger of building these ephemeral intoxications into our lives and having to live with their consequences. This alone is a compelling reason for adhering to the traditional hierarchy of astro-logical practice, by allowing ones eyes to be opened to the random nature of human whim through the practice of horary before advancing to the practice of elections. It is also a persuasive argument for trusting our actions to God in confidence that He will provide what we need rather than electing the moment in an attempt to create what we think we want. We cannot, of course, remove ourselves from the sphere of God's providence by electing a chart; we can, however, remove the protective layer of incompetence that usually shields us from the results of our desires.

But act we must, and in any action we will elect a time, although rarely astro-logically. If I want to sun-bathe, I will not do it when the Sun is below the horizon, though I will not usually figure this in astrological terms. I may be naive enough to think that I can comprehend all the qualities of the situation through my own clear thinking; if I feel this is beyond me, I might choose to avail myself of the wider viewpoint offered by the stars. If I do elect a chart, however, the result is likely always to be somehow unsatisfactory, leaving nagging doubts that the election was of no avail. I do not have a spare life that I can run as a control group. I cannot marry Judy at a random moment in this life and at an astrologically elected moment in that one, so I may compare the outcomes. There are rare occasions when we are dealing with a specific goal that is either achieved or not: buying a jackpot-winning lottery ticket, for example. The majority of elected events, however, have no such clear-cut outcome. No matter how happy my marriage or successful my business, maybe it would have been even better had it started at a different moment; no matter how disastrous, maybe it would have been even worse.

For all the reservations about its use, electional astrology has been widely employed to determine the optimum moment for an immense variety of activi-ties, from major events such as founding cities or crowning emperors, to trivia such as cutting one's hair (depending on whether it was required to grow back quickly or stay short) or putting on new clothes for the first time. Henry Coley gives an anecdote of the great astrologer William Lilly, who failed to check the position of the Moon before putting on a new suit, 'the Moon being in Leo, and ill dignified, and tore many holes in the Suit going a Nutting, within a fortnight after; not did that Suit ever do him any service.' 'Yet,' as Coley continues, 'We must not be superstitious, but modest in our Elections, only use them as natural helps.'[1] Matters of particular importance were the investing of cities to ensure they were quickly captured, the timing of surgery, and 'venerial sports' to ensure the maximum delight for both parties, with or without conception as required. Nowadays, it is a rare client who requests advice on besieging cities – and a foolish one who asks a modern astrologer to choose a time for sex: with the modern ascription of sex to the eighth house, the traditional house of death, following such advice could have the direst of consequences.

Rough and ready elections can be taken just from a knowledge of the planetary rulership of the hour, or of the phase of the Moon, as is still practised by gardeners around the world. Proposing marriage in a Venus hour is likely to be more successful than in a Saturn hour; for founding a city, just the opposite would be the case. Even the scientists grudgingly admit that surgery is more bloody at full Moon, though this has, of course, nothing to do with astrology. But a full election is a more detailed process, as it demands attention to the birth chart of the person or people involved. The Moon or hour-ruler method is the equivalent of thinking "Red sky at night: shepherd's delight," while the full election would compare to a careful analysis of all the meteorological variables. The ideal situation for electing a chart was that of the royal astrologer. With nothing else to do other than study every tiny nuance of the royal family's birth-charts, he would be totally familiar with all the possibilities contained within their nativities; he would have found electing a chart comparatively straightforward.

From the birth-chart we will determine which planets must be particularly well-placed in the chart of the moment chosen for the election. These will vary depending on what the desired action is, and the exact nature of the outcome required. It is important to know what this outcome should be: just saying "I want to start a business," is not enough. What do you want from that business? To make a fortune? To enjoy your work? To change the world? To employ all your cousins? As the emphasis varies, so will the points that the astrologer must bring out in the chart he is electing. From the birth-chart, we will determine which planets are thus involved. We will always want to have the ruler of the Ascendant in the birth-chart (ie the person himself) as strong as possible, together with both the luminaries, as they are the conduits of energy into the chart: with both luminaries weak, there is unlikely to be enough oomph to make anything happen. Then we would look to other planets depending on the subject at hand. If electing a wedding, we would strengthen the ruler of the

---

[1] *Key to the Whole Art of Astrology*, p. 318, London, 1676; reprinted Ascella, Nottingham.

seventh house (the partner), as we would also in choosing the moment for the start of a business partnership, though then we would be careful to make the seventh house ruler strong, but still slightly weaker than the Ascendant ruler: we want our man on top. For a business, we would strengthen the rulers of the tenth and second houses (career and money); to build a house or sink a mine, the ruler of the fourth; to throw a party, the ruler of the fifth (fun). Finally, we must strengthen the planets naturally associated with the task at hand: Venus for a wedding, for example, Saturn for founding a city.

This will give us a list of usually five or six out of the possible seven planets that we want strong in our elected chart. On top of that, we would also like the Ascendant ruler of the elected chart, and the relevant house rulers, to be strong. Achieving all of this is an impossible task. Invariably, if we take the time when this planet is strong, that one will be weak; if we wait until that one is stronger, a third will have lost what power it had. The task usually boils down to avoiding the most unfortunate possibilities and making the best out of what is left, for although we conventionally speak of 'making planets strong' or 'putting them in a powerful position' we can do no such thing – we can merely watch as the planets arrange themselves, as if we were looking through a kaleidoscope, our only power being to seize the moment when the picture is at its prettiest.

The need to strengthen the planets ruling the appropriate areas of the native's life – that is, those ruling particular houses of his birth-chart – shows why an election cannot be done without reference to the birth-chart, and why modern attempts at electional astrology are usually so misguided. We must know which planet rules which area of the life, which is something that cannot be known without studying the nativity, and is beyond the ken of the moderns, who regard planets only as innate principles and disregard or, at best, diminish, their importance as house rulers. If we do not know this, we are fighting in the dark. Suppose we are electing a chart to start a business. Other things being equal, one of our main priorities is to ensure that the malefic planets, Mars and Saturn, are safely out of the way. So we would gratefully seize an opportunity of putting Saturn in the twelfth house, from where it will find it hard to act. But if Saturn happens to rule the tenth house of the birth-chart, the native's career, sticking it into the twelfth is the worst thing we can do. By not judging the nativity first, we have done more harm than good.

Other factors with which we can work include the selection of appropriate signs. For things that we hope will last, we would choose fixed signs on the Ascendant and other appropriate places. If our aim were, for instance, to start a business which would make a quick million and then be liquidated, cardinal signs would be more appropriate. Similarly, if we were starting a farm, earth signs would be best; a television company, air signs.

We are not limited to strengthening planets by essential dignity, but can manoeuvre them into helpful places in the chart. As we have seen, it is always of benefit to have the Sun strong, but by essential dignity this is usually not possible; placing it on an angle, usually the Midheaven, will do just as well.

What we cannot achieve by juggling planets, we may well be able to make up by the judicious placement of fixed stars. Each fixed star partakes of the nature of one or two of the planets, so if we must choose a time for marriage when Venus is weak, stars of Venus nature on the angles will work as well. Regulus, the Heart of the Lion, a brilliant star of worldly success, is prominent in many charts elected for affairs of state: the birth of Alexander the Great is said to have been artificially delayed until Regulus was appropriately placed. Spica, the bright star in the constellation of Virgo, is often emphasised in charts where happiness rather than success is the goal desired.

Although we might wish to keep the malefics out of the way, we are often impelled to incorporate them as they rule one of other of our required houses. Even if they do not, they may on occasion be useful: the Centiloquium, or Hundred Aphorisms, attributed to Ptolemy advises that we "make use of the Malevolent Planets, Saturn and Mars; for even so doth the expert Physician use poison moderately for cure of man."[2] Within these words lies the great possibility of electing a chart, that we might choose the time wisely to balance our innate imperfections. Perhaps our client wishes to start a business, but our assessment of his birth-chart has revealed a strongly phlegmatic (watery, emotion-centred) temperament; other indications show that, while a charming individual, he lacks any of the qualities needed to maintain a competitive edge in the market-place. If he is determined to go ahead with his plans, we must make the best of what we are given: placing Saturn strongly in the elected chart will give him some backbone, bracing him to endure the difficulties that will come; placing Mars strongly will make up for the vim that he by nature lacks, giving him the ability to wield the knife when necessary. Were our elected chart to be dominated by benefics, the business would flounder on his good intentions. Similarly, a chart elected for an operation should not resemble that elected for a party: the operation chart will be bloody and unpleasant, no matter how successful the outcome might be. In our election we are providing, from the limited array at our disposal, the tools with which the enterprise must be carried out; we must be sure that the ones we provide are those that are most appropriate for both user and function. Electional astrology will not work miracles: no chart will make a success of a marriage between two fundamentally incompatible people, or of a business selling ice-cream at the North Pole. But if there is potential there, a well-timed electional chart will bring out its best qualities and smooth over the faults.

Good Queen Bess

Showing what can be achieved with only 'the body of a weak and feeble woman' and some smart astrology is John Dee's election for the timing of Elizabeth I's

---

[2] The *Centiloquium,* one of the most influential texts in astrology's history, can be found in Coley, op. cit. pp. 315-328. This quotation from p. 316.

coronation.[3] Dee did not leave us his rough papers, but following the traditional principles of electing a chart enables us to come close to the path his thinking must have taken. As always with an election, his two constraints are the possibilities of the natal chart with which he has to work and the practical time-frame within which the event must take place. Had Elizabeth's birth-chart shown an early death, no election could have given her a long and glorious reign; had he waited for the ideal moment for the coronation, he would be waiting yet.

As the Sun is the natural ruler of kingship, his first thought would have been to make it strong. He would no doubt have liked to have the Sun in Aries or Leo, in which signs it has powerful essential dignities; even the spring sign of Aries, however, would have demanded too long a wait. Constraints of time gave him the choice of the Sun in either Capricorn or Aquarius. In the last ten degrees of Capricorn the Sun has some very minor dignity; in Aquarius it is badly debilitated: this must have tempted Dee to hurry the coronation, holding it during the first ten days of January, before the Sun left Capricorn. But although the Sun is weak there, Aquarius does have one appropriate virtue: it is a fixed sign. As Dee's overriding aim was evidently for a long period of stability, Aquarius, despite the Sun's debility in that sign, was to be preferred. It is also the most humane of the signs, and other indications suggest that the furtherance of the humane graces was an important secondary consideration, in which he most gloriously succeeded. By placing the Sun in the Midheaven – holding the coronation at noon – it could be strengthened by position if not in essence. If other variables refused to fall into place, he might have to think again and revert to Sun in Capricorn; but so far, he no doubt thought, so good: "Sun in Aquarius on the Midheaven – OK, let's see what options that gives us."

Looking at the relative positions of the planets during the time available, he would have been deeply concerned by the opposition between Saturn and Mars. This is one of the most malign indications in the heavens and would have to be handled with the greatest care to avoid building insurmountable difficulties into the elected chart. Both Mars and, most particularly, Saturn move slowly, so this was not a configuration that would go away if he waited a couple of days: it had to be dealt with, turned to his advantage if at all possible, or neutralised if not. He would immediately have ruled out all dates after around 22nd January, as by then the Sun (symbol of the new monarch) would itself have entered a difficult square aspect to the two malefics. By the time it was free from their influence, it would probably have been too late for the coronation and would certainly have meant losing the stability of an Aquarius Sun. So he has now reduced his window of opportunity to January 10-22.

Later versions of Elizabeth's birth-chart, attempting to idealise her as "a most Masculine spirited Princess"[4] adjust the time of her birth to give her a

---

[3] January 15th, 1559, 12.14 pm, London gives a close match to Dee's chart. He would also have paid much attention to the appropriate mundane charts.

[4] John Gadbury, *Collection of Nativities*, p. 13; London, 1662. Reprinted by Ascella, Nottingham

Sagittarius Ascendant. Dee was almost certainly working from a chart showing a Capricorn Ascendant; this means that Saturn, ruler of Capricorn, has particular importance, signifying Elizabeth herself. He would have found it imperative, then, to ensure that the warlike malefic Mars was not applying to this difficult aspect with Saturn, but that it was safely past it. The effects of the opposition would still linger: the reign would not be a quiet one (as it would have been unrealistic to have expected); but holding the coronation after January 14th would divert the worst of the troubles onto other heads. The necessity of avoiding this applying opposition to Saturn would have confirmed that he was right in waiting until the Sun had left Capricorn.

By now, Dee had determined that the coronation should be held at noon on a day between January 14th and, at the very latest to keep the Sun safely away from difficult aspect to Saturn, January 22nd. He would then have noticed two fortunate occurrences. With the Sun on the Midheaven, as he wanted it, the two troublesome malefics would have been confined to the twelfth and sixth houses, the houses of their joy and by far the best places for them. Also, the Sun on the Midheaven in the dates available gave a Gemini Ascendant and Sagittarius Descendant for the coronation chart. With Sagittarius on the Descendant, its ruler, Jupiter, would signify the country's open enemies. During these dates Mars was separating from Saturn, the great malefic, and applying to a difficult square aspect with Jupiter: Mars, planet of war, picks up all the unpleasantness of Saturn and throws it straight at Jupiter, the open enemy. With Jupiter falling in a sign ruled by Saturn, this can only be to the great discomfiture of England's foes. How delighted Dee must have been to find this.

He now needed just to fine-tune the date. The 14th or 15th placed Jupiter, the enemy, in minor dignity of Mercury, Ascendant ruler and therefore significator of England, slightly strengthening England's position. More importantly, the earlier the coronation was held the closer was Mercury to the Sun, keeping the country (Mercury) under the power of the monarch (Sun). Dee would probably have wished it closer still, but that was not possible without falling foul of the Mars/Saturn opposition. Choosing the 15th would place the powerful fixed star Rigel (the brighter of the two stars at the base of Orion), on the Ascendant. Suitable fixed stars in prominent places are of the utmost importance in an elected chart for any long-term matter; Dee would have liked to have been able to place his Midheaven on one, but this was not possible in the time available. Rigel, a strong benefic, on the Ascendant was a very acceptable alternative.

Following simple astrological logic, making the most of the predominant celestial configurations of the time, had suggested noon on the 15th as the best of the available times for Elizabeth's coronation. So far, Dee had been working largely by constraint; he would now have checked to see what possibilities this chart offered, and to make sure there was nothing untoward that he had overlooked. He would have noted other helpful fixed stars on Mars, the Moon and, most importantly, the Part of Fortune. This fell conjunct Regulus, one of the strongest of the stars. It would have been preferable, he no doubt thought,

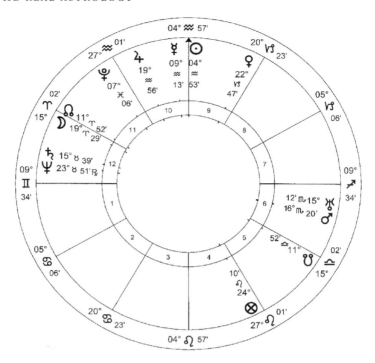

Chart 6: Coronation of Elizabeth I.

to have this conjunction above the horizon, especially in the tenth house; but its position here would do quite nicely and would ensure the nation kept tolerably solvent.

He would have been particularly pleased to notice the favourable connections between his elected chart and Elizabeth's nativity. The Sun and Moon in his chart fall in close favourable aspect to the two benefics, Jupiter and Venus, in Elizabeth's. The luminaries are, in the chart as well as in the sky, the source of light; so looking back years later Dee may have seen this as the source of the prominent artistic cult of the Queen's virtues. In the election, benefic Venus is closely bound to Saturn (because each rules the sign in which the other falls); it is exactly opposed to the position of Saturn (Elizabeth herself) in the nativity; this natal Saturn, being in Cancer, is very weak. Venus rules the ninth house of piety and learning in the natal chart, and is placed in that same house in the election. Dee would have seen this as a useful way of curbing Elizabeth's more unsavoury personal habits; as the court's resident sage, he probably saw this Venus, apart from its general fortunate significance, as signifying himself and so built his own influence over the new queen into the chart. As the preceding eclipse was a solar eclipse in Libra, Venus's sign, Venus was lord of that eclipse. By placing Venus in the elected chart in a close trine to its position at the eclipse, Dee, as it were, 'plugged in' the elected chart to the power-source provided by the eclipse, allowing Elizabeth to catch, and indeed embody, the spirit of the time in a way her predecessor, Mary, never could.

The history of Elizabeth's reign is, at least in outline, well enough known to suggest that Dee's electional work was not wasted. He did not create anything of what followed, but by choosing an inceptional moment to take advantage of the prevailing conditions he enabled certain possibilities to flourish while other less desirable ones withered away. Elizabeth's reign was not a story of uninterrupted success and happiness for queen and country; the astrologer cannot choose a perfect moment, for the perfect moment is not there to be chosen. As a trivial, but nonetheless true, example, Dee's chart promises great artistic achievement; he could not have elected a chart showing great breakthroughs in the development of nuclear power: the one was there to be elected, the other was not. The inherent limitations of electional astrology reflect nothing other than the inherent limitations of life; for all that this means we may fall short of our aims, he who wishes to set sail is foolish to do so against the tide.

11

Natal Astrology

In a world where the individual becomes ever more insignificant, the vain desire to convince ourselves otherwise grows ever stronger. So it is that the natal branch of astrology has come to dominate the craft to such an extent that the great majority of the public, and more than a few astrologers, are quite unaware that there is any other. The desire to admire ourselves is insatiable, so every astrological bookshop has several rain-forests devoted to the endless ways of holding the mirror in order to obtain a more flattering view. So yes, dear reader, let us get this over and done with and then we can discuss something more serious: you are quite wonderful, no one understands you and none of it is your fault. Now let us move on.

We have seen how both the practical techniques and underlying ethos of astrology have been changed, most markedly over the past hundred years, to remove all objectivity and render it solely an instrument of narcissism. The keynote is now 'psychological delineation'. An attempt to criticise such an attitude crystallises a quite erroneous view of the past, as if our forebears had no mental world, and no concern whatever with the inner man. Like any science, psychology depends for its validity on correct orientation: there is no point at all in just going – we need to be going somewhere. Traditional astrology contained a profound and subtle understanding of psychology implicit in the traditional, normal, world from which we are now so helplessly adrift: a psychology oriented towards the knowledge of the Divine. It would not be incorrect to say that without such orientation we have no psychology, only error, as if we were trying to work with the lights turned out.

Let us consider first the modern approach to the natal reading. It is evident that people rarely ask for a birth-chart reading because it is a wet afternoon and they have some spare cash burning a hole in their pockets. They ask usually because they are emotionally lost: feeling down, confused or directionless. They are, then, in a vulnerable state of mind, open to suggestion. We might compare the literature of 'self-help' to which modern astrology bears so close a kinship: people do not buy self-help books unless they feel they are unable to cope alone. What is being sought is primarily comfort and reassurance. Most modern astrologers make it quite clear that the one thing they do not, under any circumstances, offer is definite information (that is, anything that might actually be of practical use to the client). If our client has, as it were, fallen overboard, let us not do anything so vulgar as throw him a life-belt; much better to debate the circumstances of his falling and the temperature of the water.

"Can you read my birth-chart?" we are asked. By which is meant: "Can you talk exclusively about me for an hour." It does not greatly matter what we might say during that hour, for as long as we speak in the cotton-wool tongue of modern psychology, we shall never say anything capable of contradiction. We are all made up of the same characteristics, just in slightly differing proportions, so no matter what is said the client can always feel, "Yes – that's me to a T: however did you know that, oh Wise and Mighty One?" And let us not deny it – obtaining someone's undivided attention for an hour or more is a fine and rare thing: even in close relationships it does not happen often once past the infatuated early stages. Anyone offering total attention on a plate will find a long queue of eager customers, who sit enthralled, regardless of what is being said so long as it contains the word 'you' on sufficient occasions.

Being listened to open-mouthed, one's words received as if they were gold, is another fine and rare thing, so between the two of them client and astrologer stoke the fires of mutual admiration like a couple of gibbons in a grooming session, filled with all delight. The seductive witchcraft of the consultation seems, in our hedonistic age, harmless enough – it no longer makes you go blind, we are told – but such intimacy is properly reserved for emotional relationships, for sound reasons. It engenders an opening of psychic doorways which is most unwise unless we have good knowledge of exactly who or what is about to walk through them. The great majority of astrologers are undoubtedly well-meaning; but good intentions are not enough: it would be foolish to infer that it is safe to have them wandering around in our psyches – they know not what they do. It is an unfortunate fact that a good proportion of those who claim to be astrologers today drift into astrology because they are unable to cope with life and find dealing with symbols on pieces of paper a good deal easier than dealing with the real world. We have the bizarre circumstance of leading astrologers being in daily therapy – which we might suspect implies a certain degree of mental imbalance – and yet still judging themselves worthy of trampling their muddy footsteps around the inside of their clients' heads. Caveat emptor indeed.

Modern astrologers will frequently comment on how "the charts I get reflect my own problems." This is hardly a surprise. The whole function of true astrology is to provide an objective means of analysis; the tools by which the astrologer can do this have been abandoned, so the poor client is now merely submerged in a sea of the astrologer's mental refuse. "It's my therapy," as more than one professional astrologer has remarked. Whether the unsuspecting client sees his function as aiding the astrologer's own therapy might be open to question. There is often no longer even any pretence of striving for objectivity, and many an astrologer will find far more significance in what meaning the client's presenting issues have in his own life, and in how the client's birth-chart connects with his own, than in any concern for the client. The level of competence among these astrologers is such that we might well think that the less involvement they have with the client's chart the better, but exactly the opposite happens: what we have is a mess where the astrologer's own unresolved issues flood into the client's and are judged as if part of his birth-chart, made part of his own problems. Far from finding things clarified, the client walks away bearing a collection of problems that he didn't have when he arrived. All is justified by appeal to the 'Law of Synchronicity' – that is, if this client is here now, he must have bearing on whatever mental sewage I am currently wading through: like it or not, he is going to have his head stuck into it.

This is not to suggest, of course, that every astrologer in the past was an enlightened and well-balanced being; but the practice of astrology by traditional methods maintains a strict barrier between astrologer and client. There is no scope for subjectivity on the astrologer's part – however determinedly even many practitioners of a pretended traditionalism today may try to justify its introduction. The astrology is in black and white on the paper before you: there is no more scope for subjectivity here than there is in repairing a car: it is purely objective, and either right or wrong – either the mechanic gets the car to work or he doesn't. Such an approach is as different as can be from the stated aims of so many contemporary astrologers, who style themselves 'astrological counsellors' or the like. It is clear that they are as hungry for the emotional connection as are their clients. This is not a healthy state of affairs. Practitioners who would be horrified at the suggestion that they might sexually molest a client will work through a karma sutra of psychological ravishment and come away convinced they have done a good and ethical day's work.

In its worst cases, the psychic vulnerability engendered by the consultation is open to far graver abuse, albeit still usually unwittingly on the part of the practitioner. Particularly among those who deliberately work with 'psychic powers' (which are far more real and sinister than is nowadays commonly allowed) or the anti-spiritual and therefore anti-human initiations of psychoanalysis, which initiations are woefully common and even regarded as a badge of rank among certain sections of the astrological community, the powers summoned or unleashed can be of far more toxic quality, having the potential to result in possession of various kinds, whether by 'spirits' (such as genii, fairies or sylphs: in short, *jinn*), 'ghosts' (that is, 'psychic remains' of people whose eternal souls have passed on to their final destinations, yet leaving certain lower animic elements, unappeased by 'death rites', thrashing around in the World Soul, usually because of a violent death), or outright (and often multiple) demonic possession. The soul is a vulnerable creature; it must be treated with care. Yet people who would not dream of walking in off the street to an unknown person with qualification of unknown validity and inviting him to operate on their eyes, will do just that with a part of themselves yet more precious and yet more delicate, and on top of all that, eternal.

The key to the modern natal reading for the modern client is now validation. Having someone talk about about Me is a validating experience: I am important.

What this person actually says, although of rather slighter import, is geared to the same end. The astrologer's job is to show me that I am not just one more of the faceless masses, but that I am unique and important and exciting. As is common today, we are validated best by our sins. We see the extreme example on day-time TV: my vices make me interesting enough to deserve the attention of the nation for my fifteen minutes of fame. So with astrology – and so the reason for the great importance placed upon the outer planets, Uranus, Neptune and Pluto. These are become the repository of any number of interesting but not too horrific vices – the kind of things that would cause an acceptable level of gossip but are not going to result in a petrol-bomb through my letter-box. These vices, of course, are carefully chosen: sexual peccadilloes are fine; kicking the cat is most definitely not. The astrologer picks out a few of these – not too hard a feat, as we all have our fair share of ills not far below the surface – and we respond with a strangely pleasurable feeling of embarrassment as we blush gently. He has displayed his Great Wisdom by the remarkable feat of knowing what we have beneath our clothes. He does not judge us for our vices, but rather lets us nurture them; for we enjoy the feeling that they make us slightly dangerous, in a rather thrilling fashion. We have been entranced by the illusion of intimacy, the illusion of understanding: but all that has been understood is that which is common to us all.

We will then be given the Secret of the Universe, the words of power that kiss it all better and make it all alright: *none of it is our fault*. The astrologer, who shares Philip Larkin's view of parenthood, will first explain how specific people have conspired against us. First candidate is usually Mum, closely followed by Dad. It is not surprising our life is such a mess having been brought up by these two – we deserve some kind of public recognition merely for grittily battling on in the face of such handicaps. We have all had such 'difficult childhoods' we may rightly feel aggrieved that our parents did not abandon us to be brought up by wolves. It is notable that in ages when the majority of children died during infancy, the excuse 'you had a difficult childhood' was not part of the astrologer's repertoire. Suggesting, however, that your childhood was tolerably content reveals a serious level of denial and will be greeted with dogged attempts to prove that your chart shows quite the opposite, you poor trauma-tised thing, you. Your partner is probably not quite as reprehensible as your parents, but is undoubtedly part of the conspiracy, as shown by his inability to realise how endearing your bad characteristics really are. And after your parents, your partner and the whole world have been dragged into court and summarily found guilty, the next stage is to understand that the the real villains are the planets. They have it in for you. You personally. For no reason whatsoever.

It started with your birth-chart. Look at all those problems! How can you expect anything from me? You can't expect me to be on time – I'm a Gemini. And you certainly can't expect me to pay my way – look at that Saturn in my second house! With a Moon like mine – I'm bound to be unfaithful. Pluto in Scorpio – I've got to play dirty games. The birth-chart is indeed a wonderful invention: the failing of your choice justified by the astrological configuration of your choice. Now no need even to pin it to specific people – no more of those awkward conversations: "My mum ruined my life;" "But your mother's a lovely woman." It is the planets, who take a strong and perverse delight in making you fail.

But they didn't stop with the birth-chart: so determined are they to mess your life that, rather than occupying themselves in elevated planetary pastimes, they are forever manoeuvring themselves into unfavourable transits to your nativity. As there is always at least one of them doing something unpleasant – by some more or less trivial aspect to some more or less sensitive part of your natal chart – you have always an excuse for being miserable or failing in whatever you do. This also provides a guaranteed ice-breaker at any gathering of astrologers: "I've got Saturn transiting my Moon;" "Oh, you poor dear – I know just how you feel: Pluto's going over my natal Chiron."

This is quite contrary to true astrology. Astrology is not a means by which we may give up all responsibility: "Saturn went over my Midheaven so my business failed." No – your business failed because you rented fancy offices and bought a fleet of cars and didn't spend money on cultivating your client-base. Saturn had nothing to do with it: it was your responsibility and your action. Saturn just marked the moment when these pigeons come home to roost. The challenge of any real astrology is that it faces us with the possibility of accepting total responsibility; but this is possible only within the spiritual orientation of the traditional world, so we are returned yet once more to the same crossroads: no faith, no astrology.

None of what we have seen, of course, means that the client's conscious thought when consulting an astrologer – whether this be the flesh-and-blood variety, or the computer print-out – is "I want someone to talk about me." This is what happens, what makes the experience seem worthwhile, what lures him back when the effects wear off. What is wanted, however, is change. Somehow the astrologer is going gather up the cards the client was dealt at birth, shuffle them and deal them out in more acceptable pattern (preferably without parents/partner/Saturn or anyone else who is messing things up). Somehow, the astrologer will press a magic button that will transform the life, perhaps not dramatically, but significantly. The myth of the astrological reading is that it is somehow outside the life; a distinct vantage point, from which all may be rearranged as easily as we might move the characters in a toy theatre. This is, of course, not so; but the client is purchasing the forlorn hope that it is. He is indulging the same dream of change through which he buys a lottery ticket. But in this lottery nobody ever wins.

The reading of the natal chart was not always thus. Aims, methods and results were far different before the corruption of astrology into that which we have today. To begin, the aim, whether dealing with external events or the native's psychology, was to provide concrete information. Apportioning blame, whether to parents or planets, was not part of the package. Method was clear and straightforward. Much debate takes place in modern astrology over the correct method of 'synthesis', or the drawing together of all the varied indications of the chart. What is the key? Which is the way in? The traditional astrologer follows the outdated but effective method of starting at the beginning and working towards the end by way of the middle.

We have seen something of the nature of the traditional natal judgment during our blind examination of Hitler's nativity. First, the temperament, manner and qualities of mind would be assessed, giving an understanding of, as it were, the material from which the man is made. That done, the reading was a simple process of working through the chart one house at a time, dealing with the affairs of that house. As everything is contained within one or other of the houses, by the time we have reached the end, we have found all we need to know about the character and the basic trends of the life. In practice, the reading would usually be confined to whichever houses were of particular interest at that time: a robust twenty-year old would be more likely to want information about his marital, financial or vocational prospects than about the illnesses from which he was likely to suffer in old age. Much of the immediate secular usefulness of the nativity is found in this light, as it allows an understanding of particular situations. Why do my business ventures never come off? Am I better advised to seek my fortune at home or abroad? The answers given by the traditional method of judgment will be clear and specific: your businesses fail because you are gullible and persistently choose dishonest partners, for example.

The chart is then *progressed* or *directed.* That is, we let it move in order to find out what is actually going to come to pass and what will remain as unfulfilled potential. Modern astrology does the same, but in a quite different way. In both traditional and modern method, the houses of the chart and the planets within it move in various interlocking cycles of real and (what appears to us as) symbolic time. That is, we concern ourselves both with the relationship that planets in the sky Now (real time) hold to the birth-chart, and also to those shown by certain other measures, such as taking the position of the planets *x* days after the birth to show events *x* years or months after the birth. The former positions are known as *transits,* the latter, *directions* or *progressions.* There are various refinements of technique for the exact determining of directions, but the underlying principle is the same. By the time we have involved other means of relating passing time to the fixed time of the birth, such as the technique of *Solar* or *Lunar Revolutions,* whereby we cast a chart for the moment at the which the Sun or Moon returns to its place in the birth-chart (hence the phrase 'many happy returns' on one's birthday, or Solar Return), we have a large number of apparently unconnected cycles. There is no apparent reason why the position of the planets thirty-six days after the birth should show the same events as the Solar Return taking place that many years later and the Lunar Returns taking place each month during that same year. Yet they do, for in His infinite wisdom, the Almighty has shaped a universe that fits together in coherent fashion. Not the least of the many delights of the study of astrology is the chance to marvel at the precision and intricacy of this construction as it turns.

Although the traditional and modern astrologer both use many of the same techniques of direction – some extra ones here, some extra ones there – the manner in which they are applied is quite different. If we liken the planets in their cycles to the guests circulating at a cocktail party, we can compare. To the modern astrologer, every trivial conversation between any two guests is a matter of great importance. If Miss Directed Venus happens to bump into Mr Natal Mars, we must attend to the result. The traditional astrologer, however, knows that the significance of this party is the presence of the royal family, who are moving among the guests and selecting some here and some there to dispatch on errands. What Miss Venus happens to be whispering to Mr Mars is of little interest.

The tradition sees the natal chart as a series of promises, or potentials. If we lived for ever, all these promises would eventually be fulfilled; but we do not. Many of them, even perhaps some of the most glittering, will be frustrated by the prior fulfilment of the promise of death. That which we seek by progressing the chart is to find which of these promises will happen, and when these events will take place. What shows us this is the movement of the five main points of the chart against the others: these are our 'royal family', who move through the party giving orders. The other guests mix as they may, but this signifies little. Events are set off by directions of the Sun, Moon, Ascendant, Midheaven and Part of Fortune. It is when one of these meets young Miss Venus or Mr Mars that something of significance will happen. Meetings between the other planets can show events – especially those concerning other people such as parents or partners – if the chart is interpreted correctly; but it is, as it were, the royal family that gives these planets permission to act.

As these five points progress, we watch for the times when they hit other planets in the natal chart, or house-cusps, or fixed stars, or when they move from one term (sub-division of a sign) to another. These directions are the signs that an event is in the offing – the gun, as it were, is loaded. Once loaded, we need to pull the trigger: this, and this alone, is the role of the transit, the position of a planet *now* relative to the birth-chart. Transits are much over-valued in modern astrology. As a working astrologer, I find it a rare week in which I do not have to assure someone who has read too many modern astrology books that the world, or at least their world, is not going to end because Pluto/Chiron/Saturn happens to be transiting something or other in their birth-chart. Transits pull the trigger: the gun, once loaded, will not go off until the trigger is pulled; but pulling the trigger, no matter how hard or how often, while the gun is empty will do nothing. Most transits pass harmlessly, with no effect other than a change of mood.

We watch for the times when our progressing points hit other planets, house-cusps, fixed stars, or change terms. Modern astrology has forgotten the terms and woefully neglects the fixed stars. Having thrown away most of the tools, it is no wonder that it fails to work.

The charts for the Solar and Lunar Returns show outstanding events in themselves, but are read mainly in the light of the birth-chart. That is, for example, if a marriage is to take place in the year following a Solar or the month following a Lunar Return, we may well see the planets ruling the first and seventh houses of the return chart applying to conjunction; more often, however, we shall find the planets that rule the first and seventh houses in the radical chart applying to conjunction in the chart for the return. Planets emphasised in the return chart, whether by close aspect or by placement within a degree or two of a house cusp, can be judged alone; but we are looking mainly for connections from chart to chart. Jupiter strongly placed in the return, casting an exact trine to the ruler of our natal second house, for instance, would be a testimony of financial good fortune during that month. Saturn in its detriment opposing that same planet would indicate just the reverse. The exact way in which these testimonies might manifest could be traced in the house-placement, receptions and other aspects of this Jupiter or Saturn in the return chart, always qualifying all these indications by whatever signification the planet we are considering holds in the radical chart. So if the Jupiter that offers us such good fortune is placed in the ninth house (foreign countries) of the return chart and is conjunct the planet that rules the eleventh house (friends) of the radix, the money might come from a friend who is abroad.

Most return charts, no matter how disappointing this might be for the dramatically inclined among us, show nothing of any great significance. Most months and even most years of most lives pass without any momentous events. The chart has various ways of demanding our attention when something important is about to happen. Finding the degrees on the angles of the return chart repeating or exactly mirroring those of the radix is a strong indication that we should sit up and pay attention. The Nodes falling on the angles, or powerful planetary aspects close to the angles are other typical indicators of moment. If all the planets in a Lunar Return chart are tucked away in the middle of cadent houses, we can safely stay in bed all month without fear of missing anything interesting.

It is important to remember that, as with progressions and transits, the return charts cannot show anything that is not promised by the nativity. I may spend a month dreaming of winning the lottery, but no matter what my Lunar Return suggests, if there is no indication of the acquisition of sudden wealth in my radix, this dream will not come true. This is the touchstone that enables us to do what the moderns claim is impossible: to differentiate between events in the world and subjective moods.

Those astrological indications that will manifest as events are the ones that build in a continuous, traceable chain from the radical chart through the various progressed and return charts to the transits. Those that exist on one level only, such as an unsupported transit or indication in a Lunar Return, pass over us as the shadows of clouds on a sunny hillside.

To comprehend the way in which these apparently unconnected systems connect is not easy; it does not accord well with our common linear thinking. We might say that they each offer a different method of measurement: as we can measure the distance to a point in both inches and centimetres, each of which will determine the same point in its different way, so we can measure the distance from the birth to an event in the life by progressions, returns and transits. But this does not fully explain the interconnectedness of the astrological patterns.

We might see the life as similar in structure to the human body, within which various systems – the skeletal, the venous, the nervous, and so forth – unfold according to their individual natures and entwine to fill out the same space. When all these systems do something significant at the same point – at a finger's end, for instance – we have an 'event' in the human body in a way that we do not have an 'event' half-way along the shin. Similarly, when the separate systems of progressions, returns and transits all do something significant at the same point, we have an event in the life.

While this metaphor has its limitations, the image of several systems combining to weave the structure of the life is a valid one. The anchor of this structure, the skeleton, as it were, that holds the body upright and provides the frame on which the patterns are spun is the progressions, with the strange telescoping of time that they imply by finding the events of one year in the planetary movements of one day. While this may seem arbitrary to the Twentieth-Century mind, we are given this measure on the highest of authorities: that of the scriptures. In the book of Numbers, after explaining who it is that shall proceed out of the wilderness into the Promised Land, God continues: *As for you, your dead bodies will fall in this wilderness, and your sons will be nomads in the wilderness for forty years, bearing the weight of your faithlessness, until the last of you lies dead in the desert. For forty days you reconnoitred the land. Each day shall count for a year: for forty years you shall bear the burden of your sins, and you shall learn what it means to reject me.*[1] This same measure of one day to one year is repeated when Ezekiel is told to prophesy against Jerusalem.[2]

We certainly do not mean to reduce the significance of these verses to that of a guide to astrological practice; but they do say something of immense significance with regard to the nature of time and of life lived in that time. The linear conception of time by which we live may be convenient for daily life; it must, however, be set aside as soon as we begin to look at time itself or any its products, as we do continually in astrology. We cannot hold this 'telescoping' time against our conception of time as straight line and find it wanting because it fails to match it. When we look at the planets, we are looking into higher

[1] Numbers 14:32–34
[2] Ezekiel 4:4–8

worlds, looking back as far as we can see towards that true 'Big Bang' of Divine Creation; if we forget this, we cannot hope to understand the nature of time within astrology. Rather than clinging to the picture of time as a straight line running from Start to Finish, we are better to replace it with an image such as that of a stone thrown into water: the model of time that we are offered in astrology has our life as the outermost of the rings radiating from that inceptional act. There is an obvious, mathematically definable, 'telescoping' relationship between the various radiating rings. Our progressions are an example of this. Whatever it may look like from here, as we peer into higher worlds we see a time-scale that is not our own.

The manner in which progressions, returns and transits unfold from the birth-chart challenges our model of life just as it challenges our model of time. Our common perception of the life as a sequence of more or less random happenings that befall the person as he wanders a line from birth to death is not congruent with the way in which the life is seen to grow from the birth-chart according to regular organic patterns. The chart and the nature of progressions from it suggest that person and life are entwined far more intimately than is our common perception. The life is not a series of accidents. It is, rather, as if the person were a cross-section of the life, a snap-shot of the life at one particular moment; or as if the life were the person extended through time. This model fits well with the account of the soul's choice of life given by Plato.[3] He explains that, before becoming incarnate, the soul chooses the life that it wishes to lead. "There was no choice of quality or character since of necessity each soul must assume a character appropriate to its choice (of life)". Having chosen the life, and therefore the character consequent upon it, the soul is led first to Clotho, the Fate of the present, who chooses the necessary birth-chart for that life, and then to Atropos, the Fate of the future, who checks the progressions, "so making the threads of its destiny irreversible."

A soul who carelessly grabbed a life with dreadful fate "beat his breast and bewailed his choice... and forgot that his misfortunes were his own fault, blaming fate and heaven and anything but himself." For the intimate, indissoluble connection between the person and the life demonstrated by the progressions, returns and transits, all of which in their different ways are determined by the birth-chart, argues most strongly against the common accusation laid against astrology, that it is an abdication of one's personal responsibility. Although it cannot be denied that a good proportion of those who consult astrologers do seek exactly that, it is not given them. On the contrary, astrology underlines the absolute responsibility of the person for the life they live, and for the whole of that life, past present and future.

We have not yet approached the real meaning of the nativity, however. If astrology was originally revealed knowledge, or, at least, a knowledge having its origin in Inspiration (in the true sense of the word), it was not revealed or

---

[3] *Republic* 616b-621d; translations from Desmond Lee, Penguin, Harmondsworth, revised edn. 1987.

inspired without purpose, and that purpose was not just to inform us when we are likely to marry or whether we shall ever be rich – nor even what dreadful people our parents might have been. The true purpose is indeed, as the moderns would have it, 'psychological'; but 'psychological' in a manner as utterly distinct and opposed from the modern distortion of the term as it is possible to be. This is a true, directed psychology, elucidating our position 'here', which can be done only in relation to our direction 'there'.

Any request for a birth-chart reading is, although only on the rarest occasions overtly so, an attempt to grapple with the mystery of incarnation: what is this divine spark within me doing amid this heap of lusts and confusions? The natal reading can elucidate just his point. The birth-chart deals with the Lesser Mysteries – the art of becoming truly human, recovering the lost dignity and integrity that are necessary before embarking on the Greater Mysteries or the life of the spirit. Thus in it we see the possibilities for the formation and nurture of the soul.

The soul comes into the world through the Ascendant; what we see in the chart is the accoutrements it picks up when it gets here. Some of these are more helpful than others. Generally, the stronger the planet is, the more serviceable it can be, if well directed. Indications in the chart, mainly around the ninth house, will show whether such sound direction is likely, although here above all it must be remembered that the Almighty is never bound by astrology and will intervene as He in His wisdom sees fit. Weak and afflicted planets usually show the particular difficulties with which the native must wrestle. Even the strong planets must be used with caution, however: excess is just as harmful as shortage, although easier to remedy. It is easier to redirect an ardour that is aimed in the wrong direction than to conjure up an ardour which is not there.

As always, we must begin with the assessment of temperament. The gift of the choleric, fiery, temperament is desire; the challenge, to direct that desire rightly. The sanguine, airy, temperament has its mental powers (not necessarily the same as what is now called intelligence); its common problem that of knowing everything and understanding nothing. The melancholic, earthy, temperament is prone to bitterness and inertia, but once moved has a practicality and solidity of approach. The phlegmatic, watery, complexion is traditionally that most beset with emotional difficulties, usually manifesting as self-indulgence and apathy.

Against this background the planets can be judged: Mars powerfully placed in Aries, for instance, will vivify a phlegmatic temperament. It is a sorry chart indeed that has no strong point anywhere with which to work. Saturn offers wisdom and discrimination, abstention from evil; its sin is avarice. Jupiter gives faith and right judgement; its sin is gluttony, which, as with all the sins, should be understood in its widest sense: the greed for experience is gluttony too, needing the discrimination of Saturn as a curb. Mars, perhaps the most unfashionable of the planets, gives greatness of soul, the ardour for both the lesser and greater *jihad* – the outer and the inner holy war – the power to do the good; its sin, of course, is wrath. The Sun gives life, dignity and clarity – literally eluci-dating – and thence prophecy; its sin is pride. Venus offers love and the urge for conciliation; its sin, lust, loses this right desire in the flesh. Mercury gives articu-lation and mental understanding, its sin being envy, which is misunder-standing, and thus its product is lies. The Moon gives procreation – again, in its widest sense; as the fastest of the planets, its failing, as with the hare in the fable of the hare and the tortoise, is sloth.

In the individual chart, the exact placement of each of these planets, their dignities, their receptions and their aspects, will display clearly and in the greatest of detail the truth of the native's position. This is of the greatest impor-tance. It is always easy to paint our own vices in the most positive colours: I'm a romantic hell-raiser; you're a drunken slob. The chart gives a clear, objective (remembering that we are working with the tools of the tradition) picture which we may choose to ignore but which we cannot truthfully deny. As the mores of society become ever more corrupt, the value of such a picture grows ever the greater. I may be assured by all around me that certain behaviour is the mark of a questing spirit; I may look to figures widely held in high esteem, and see they did the same; but if my chart shows this behaviour by, for instance, the ruler of the twelfth house of self-undoing receiving the ruler of the Ascendant (me) into its detriment, I cannot pretend that I have not been warned. Moreover, the chart not only provides us with a clear and indisputable assess-ment of where our weaknesses lie, but also shows just as clearly what tools we have at our disposal to remedy these faults.

Pointing out the appropriate tools for such remedial action is the most important advice that the astrologer can offer his client. The chart will make such advice absolutely specific to the individual, avoiding the well-meaning but irrelevant suggestions that can be proffered by those without such specific knowledge. The study of the receptions within the chart shows us which attrib-utes can ride to the rescue of those that are not functioning correctly. Suppose our subject is doing badly at college, with parents and teachers nagging him to apply himself to his studies. If Mars (energy) and Saturn (discipline) are helpfully connected with his Mercury (mind), there is potential for such advice to bear fruit. If not, there is little point in continuing to offer it. The chart may show an affliction that is easily removed: Mercury is afflicted by the Sun and Moon, both of which fall on nebulous fixed stars, indicating that his eyesight is poor (the Sun and Moon rule the eyes) – so we stop shouting at him and buy him some glasses. Or we may, perhaps, find Venus in favourable contact with Mercury, so we allow him to drop maths and enrol in the art class where the particular qualities of his mind can excel.

The same principles apply to the inner life. One man's badly placed Venus might be in helpful reception with Saturn: fasting could be the way to keep his lusts in check. For someone without such a contact, however, asceticism might be pointless misery, while the suggestion of a positive contact from the ruler of his seventh house, that he look for a wife, could be just what is required. We can either view the planets in the chart as functions of the outside world, and suffer their consequences, or see them as attributes of our own soul and work to integrate them.

This directed perspective offers us a profounder schema for approaching the birth-chart. First, the religious inclination is assessed, as this is the only framework that makes sense of all that follows. After all, without that, there is no reason for the life to exist in the first place. So we start by studying Jupiter, the natural planet of religion; the ninth and third houses (the ninth being the house of religion, the third the bringing of that religion into daily life); the Ascendant (the ego); and the Moon (the psychic substance of the soul), considering these in their dignities, aspects and placements. We can then look to the spiritual background, without which support even a promising chart is likely to amount to little. If the picture so far is sound, we can turn to the Sun, significator of the Spirit, to see what connection there is with that. The consideration of these points gives us that elusive quality which the moderns assure us cannot be judged from the chart: the 'level' at which the person is operating. The Arabian Parts, which we shall discuss later, and certain of the fixed stars – notably those which mark the four quarters of the sky: Aldebaran, Regulus, Antares and Fomalhaut – are also of great importance here.

We can then examine the life in which the being has found himself: the temperament and manner, knowledge of which enables him to understand not only himself, but also the fact that others are not as he; and the potentials, the strengths and the weaknesses, as indicated by the planets, and the possibilities for change as suggested by receptions. This possibility of change, the 'way out' from whatever problems are inherent, shows where human freedom lies. Then we have the life around him, as shown by the various houses of the chart: immediate family, wider circles of acquaintance, work, learning, the family he may acquire, and so forth. Finally, although we may wisely choose to follow the traditional proscriptions against doing so, we have the capacity to see how the life is likely to proceed by examining the progressions, revolutions and transits.

For all our astrology, however, our picture of the person and the life can be drawn only within the scope of a sound knowledge of man: it is all very well having the tools; we must also have the understanding necessary to apply them. Once again we are returned to the same point: we can have an astrology only within the revealed faiths. Applying even these fine tools within a concept of life dreamed up on some Californian beach will give us nothing except a fleeting amusement. Astrology is not an end in itself: it must be directed, and as a true science its direction is given within the spiritual traditions. Take away the faith and, as history has shown, astrology dies; what seemed so glorious a jewel is revealed as so much dust. But keep the two combined and the benefits of the study of the natal chart outweigh even the most unredeemable promises of the modern psychobabble.

12

Mundane Astrology

Despite the contemporary obsession with the goings-on inside our own heads, the crown and the flower of astrology has traditionally been regarded as mundane: the study of events in the world. With the hierarchical nature of astrology it is implicit that the lesser is always contained within the greater. The minor events of my life are contained within the promise of my nativity, so if it is not in my nativity that I shall win either the lottery or the Olympics, no passing transit will contradict this and indicate that I shall; just so, all the possibilities of my natal chart are contained within the possibilities of the larger cycles within which that nativity took place. This statement says nothing which is not obvious to common-sense, yet never fails to produce extreme opposition. To give examples: I am born in mid-Twentieth-Century England; no matter what might be indicated in my nativity, I shall neither be burned as a witch nor lead a victorious cavalry charge. Similarly with the larger cycles with which mundane astrology deals: the King of Fiji, no matter no glorious his nativity, will not rule an empire on which the Sun never sets.

If it is the scale on which these cycles work that gives them their place at the top of the astrological hierarchy, the sheer complexity of the judgments involved should warn off those who have not attained mastery of the lesser grades from trying their hand here. The lives of each one of us tend to proceed on their way rarely touched by the larger cycles within which we live. The fate of our nation may provide the backdrop against which our lives are played, but we bump into it only on infrequent – and usually unpleasant – occasions. How different the life of the king, whose nativity is entwined from birth with that of his country. So while we may safely judge the individual's chart as a thing alone, the king's, and still more, his country's, can be judged only with reference to a series of others.

Mundane astrology deals with events comparatively vast in both scale and time. It deals with the rise and fall of empire, yet even this is but the flicker of an eyelid within the larger cycles that are included within its broad domain. These large cycles of time are commonly regarded as the exclusive possession of Indian philosophies, but are alive and well, if gravely neglected, within the western astrological tradition. That they are so neglected demonstrates the egocentricity that keeps our astrological interests tied to our own trivial concerns. There is not much consolation to be gained from studying the next World-Year of

360,000 years in the hope that our love-life might perk up a little when it begins.

It is notable that the greater has been society's concentration on the significance of the individual, the less has been its interest in mundane astrology. Part of the illusion with which modern astrology deals is our thinking ourselves free from these larger cycles; but if we are not free from the automatic responses which determine almost all of the lives of almost all of us, how much the less are we free from the history – as shown by the grand astrological cycles – that determines our surroundings. The particular unfashionability of mundane astrology in the contemporary world is surely not unconnected with the predominance of generations of astrologers most of whom lack the experience of people dropping bombs on their head for no other reason than their nationality. The illusion that mundane astrology does not exist, or that we are free from its grasp, is the illusion that the world stops at the door of the play-room.

It pleases us to think of our own lives as susceptible to astrology, played out against a background of reality that is not. Astrology and reality thus become two separate things, leaving astrology as an add-on extra, which we may admit into our lives or not as we desire. As astrology carries the promise of change, we can realign our fate by waiting for that nice Venus transit, acting on the Jupiter aspect, or just by going to a different astrologer – the one who tells us what we want to hear. But the astrology of our lives proceeds within larger cycles: rulers, nations, empires and the like. No matter what possibilities are in my chart, much of what happens to me is determined at a higher level. I may have the capacity to become the greatest general of all time; I may join the army and work my way to the top; but if the larger cycles fail to provide me with a war to fight, I shall not be remembered by history. Similarly, one person may have the nativity of an expert businessman; another of a mediocre one: it is the turning of the mundane cycles producing a period of economic depression that will reveal the difference between the two. For this reason, the tradition has always stressed that notability can be found in the birth-chart only by comparison with the larger wheels that determine the time.

An obvious example of this is the person of no apparent talent who achieves fame by riding the spirit of the age. Astrology suggests that anyone who achieves fame or notable success in the world will be doing just the same. There will be many people with similar qualities: one catches the wave while the others do not. This ability to catch the wave will be shown by connections between the person's nativity and the *lunation* (New or Full Moon) or *eclipse* (a lunation at which Earth, Moon and Sun are aligned in such a way that either the Sun is wholly or partially obscured by the body of the Moon, or the Moon is wholly or partially obscured by the shadow of the Earth) immediately before or after the birth. Just as each sphere of the traditional cosmos is contained within a larger, so all that is possible within one cycle of time is contained within the limits of what is possible within a larger cycle. Expressed in astrological terms, this sounds debatable; expressed in common-sense terms, it is obvious. The world does not proceed in random fashion. What is possible in a small cycle (the small cycle that is today, for example) is enclosed within the possibilities of a slightly larger cycle (this year); if this were not so, there would be a small but nonetheless real danger of my being eaten by dinosaurs if I set foot outside my house. This does not accord with the modern dream, where all things can be achieved if only we drink the right cola; but its failure to do so does not necessarily expose it as false: a boy *can* grow up and move from log-cabin to White House, but only a particular boy *will*.

The delineation of the cycles varies from the conjunction of all seven planets in the first degree of Aries, occurring every 360,000 years, to the simple revolution of all the planets around the Earth. The latter is, of course, our familiar day; the former is the World-Year, which is itself but 'one day among the days of the macrocosm'. The world-year is subdivided by the mighty *qisma,* which moves 1° along the celestial equator every 1000 solar years, and further defined by the big, middle and small *qismas* which move 1° every 100, 10 and 1 solar years respectively. There are many other cycles of varying extents, the overlapping of which defines the particular quality of any period of time, no matter how large or small. Most, such as the *intiha'at* and *fardarat,* are little known; some, such as the movement of the sphere of the fixed stars, which produces the fabled 'Age of Aquarius', have in garbled form become common knowledge. For practical purposes, those with which we are most concerned are the cycles of the two outermost planets, Jupiter and Saturn, known as the Great Chronocrators, the timekeepers of the cosmos.

Jupiter and Saturn conjunct every twenty years. These *grand conjunctions* take place in signs of the same element (earth, air, fire or water) for periods of 240 years. After 960 years (4 elements at 240 years each = 960) the cycle recurs. As the Arab Neoplatonists the Brothers of Purity (Ikhwân al-Safâ') explain, "for faiths and empires, we seek the indications from the grand conjunctions which recur approximately every thousand years; the passage of rulership from one nation to another, or from one country to another, or from one dynasty to another, are things which follow from events the indications of which we seek in the conjunctions which recur every two hundred and forty years; for the accession of individual rulers and the things which cause this, such as wars and dissensions, we seek the indications of the conjunctions which follow every twenty years." [1] Here we have the three highest levels of our astrological hierarchy: kings and potentates; dynasties and families; and, at the peak, states and great nations. The grand conjunctions are judged both from the time at which they occur and from the start of the preceding *revolution of the world,* that is, the moment at which the Sun enters Aries in that year. The charts are cast for the place with whose events we are concerned. Against the background of these conjunctions are interpreted the charts for eclipses and both New and Full Moons. Other conjunctions, especially those of Mars with Jupiter or

---

[1] *Les Révolutions et les Cycles,* pp. 104–5, trans. from Arabic by G. de Callataÿ, Academia-Bruylant, Louvain-la-Neuve, 1996. Author's translation.

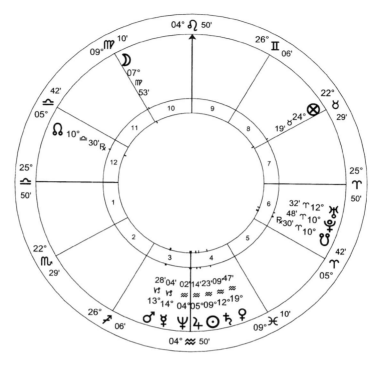

Chart 7: Coventry, foundation chart.

Saturn, are not without their significance, but are generally much less impor-tant. These astronomically determined charts will be considered in the light of charts for relevant events, such as the founding of a city or the independence of a country. As with each of these charts we must consider the charts for the preceding eclipse and grand conjunction, it is easy to see the extreme complexity of the mundane branch of astrology. We have come a long way from the simplicity of horary judgment, where we watched the movements of just two or three planets in just one chart: here, we have a sheaf of charts, each of which must be considered in the light of each and all of the others. Without mastery of the lower degrees, the would-be mundane astrologer is doomed to flounder.

This necessary complexity does not make it easy to present mundane judge-ment in simple fashion: either we ask our reader to toil through dozens of associated charts, carrying relevant points in their head from one to another, or we present an image of judgement so truncated as to appear trivial, losing not only the complexity but the sheer awesome grandeur of the movement of these cycles, wheel within wheel, against each other. Our example necessarily gives but the faintest flavour of mundane astrology.

Cities, like people, have their horoscopes. Unlike personal horoscopes, however, these are only rarely set for the moment at which the city was born, as most cities just accumulated without having an official start-time. There are some exceptions: al-Biruni gives the chart which the caliph al-Mansur had elected to time the foundation of his splendid new city of Baghdad; but for the most part, our city charts are timed from some significant event, most often the granting of the city charter. We shall consider the chart for Coventry.[2] With its Ascendant ruled by Venus, which falls in the fixed air sign of Aquarius, the chart shows immediately its appropriateness for a city most noted for a woman riding naked through its centre in order to prove a point.

On the night of 14/15th November 1940, the centre of the city was destroyed by German bombers in the most devastating single attack of the blitz. Astrology does not partake of our simplistic modern ascriptions of cause: "plane crashes, who is to blame?" as if there were one reason and one reason only why things happen as they do. In accordance with traditional philosophy, we have cause within cause, all being contained within the prime cause of all things that is the Will of God. So for any action we can point to causes at any number of levels of immediacy: my teeth fall out because I eat too many sweets, which is because I am self-indulgent, which is because of certain bodily imbalances, and because my parents compensated for their own hard upbringing, and so on. So with astrology, we can always go one step further back on the path of causation, a feat represented by looking ever further back along the series of connected charts, until we have no more charts and must face the Prime Cause. For practical purposes, we may start our investigation with the Grand Conjunction of 1921.[3]

There was another Grand Conjunction shortly before the night of the raid, on August 8th and October 20th 1940 (although these conjunctions occur only every twenty years, the retrograde motion of the planets sometimes results in one conjunction being twice repeated within the space of a few months). The raid, however, grew from seeds sown during the period covered by the 1921 conjunction, so that is the one with which we must concern ourselves. The conjunction occurs at the same time, no matter where we are on Earth; we set our chart for this time by the longitude and latitude of the place we wish to investigate. Setting the chart for the conjunction for Coventry places the eighth cusp of Coventry's birth-chart – the eighth being the house of death – exactly on the Midheaven. This is not good. It is all the worse as Caput Algol, the most malefic of all fixed stars, known to the Chinese as 'piled-up bodies', falls on this point. Mars rules Coventry's seventh house (open enemies) and afflicts the Midheaven of the conjunction chart by a close square aspect. Coventry might expect to suffer at the hands of its enemies. The Moon's South Node shows where the native will be hurt. In the conjunction chart, set for Coventry, it falls

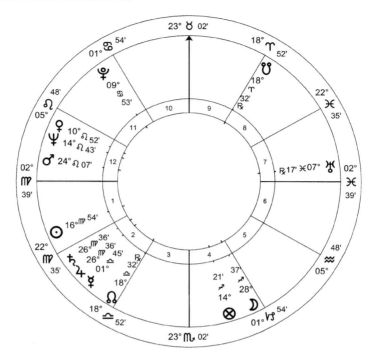

Chart 8: 1921 Grand Conjunction

exactly on the cusp of the ninth house: Coventry will be hurt through foreigners.

Together with the chart for the moment of the Grand Conjunction, we must consider that for the moment of the Sun's entry into Aries immediately before it.[4] Again, we set this chart for Coventry. At the 1921 Aries ingress, Mars was conjunct the Moon's South Node. This is a most unfortunate combination, but it was the same the world over. At 27 degrees of Aries, however, this conjunction fell just on Coventry's natal Descendant, cusp of the seventh house of open enemies. Once again, violent (Mars) suffering (South Node) through the enemies is strongly indicated. By virtue of its strength, its applying aspect from the Moon and its rulership of both Midheaven and (by exaltation) Ascendant, Mars is Lord of this ingress chart. The timing at which these astrological chickens will come home to roost is shown through its progression onto the Ascendant.

As these wheels turn within wheels, we find the chart for the eclipse immediately before the outbreak of war confirming the forthcoming problems for Coventry, notably by the Lord of the Eclipse, Venus, falling exactly on the city's

---

[4] March 21st, 1921. 3.51 am GMT

Chart 9: 1921 Aries Ingress

natal South Node.[5] Both the hierarchy of astrology and common-sense tell us that Coventry's fate is subject to the fate of the larger bodies of which it is a part. No matter how grim the charts for any of the preceding conjunctions or eclipses might have been, they would not have resulted in Coventry being bombed by the Luftwaffe unless Great Britain were at war with Germany. This, of course, brings a further ream of charts into consideration, which we shall not do here. The relevant charts for Germany do, however, show an inbuilt propensity towards the demolition of Coventry. The birthchart of the Third Reich, for example, has its Mars falling by antiscion exactly on Coventry's South Node, the point of vulnerability, through which it will suffer. There are cities around the globe for which we could say the same thing; their containing larger wheels did not grind in such a way that this propensity was brought into play. The fate of nations meant that Coventry's was; and in this same German chart we find the fatal date: if we progress the Third Reich birth-chart to November 15th 1940, we find that the Part of Fortune – its 'treasure' – is exactly conjunct the Part of Death in Coventry's chart. That is, the Third Reich's treasure at that time was congruent with the death of Coventry – as became apparent.

[5] May 3rd, 1939. 3.11 pm GMT

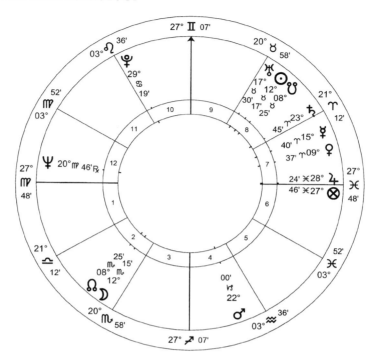

Chart 10: Eclipse prior to outbreak of war

If we consider the Solar and Lunar Returns for the period concerned, we can watch the clouds gathering.[6] Coventry's Solar Return for 1940 – its birthday chart, as it were – is as black as could be. We find that Aries, the sign on the seventh house of the birth-chart, falls on the Ascendant of the Return. According to William Lilly, "the Native will then receive loss and detriment in that year according to the nature of that house which the ascendant of the Revolution did signify in the radix";[7] so in this case, as it was the seventh house in the radix, the loss will be through open enemies, or in Lilly's words "contentions and brawlings".[8]

As the actual degree on the Revolution Ascendant is so close to that of the radix, what is indicated will be that much the sharper. Lilly also tells us that "when the Ascendant of the Revolution comes to the hostile Beams of the Infortunes... the native may expect great peril that year".[9] The Revolution Ascendant is immediately conjunct all three of the infortunes: Mars, Saturn and

---

[6] January 30th, 1940; 10.07 am GMT and October 26th, 1940; 10.24 pm GMT respectively.
[7] op. cit. p. 737
[8] ibid.
[9] ibid.

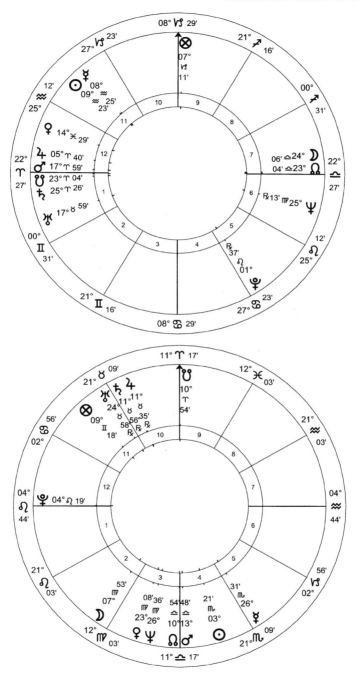

Charts 11 and 12: Coventry's Solar and Lunar Returns prior to the raid

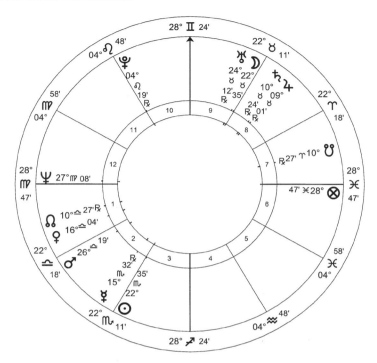

Chart 13: Full Moon on the night of the raid.

the South Node cluster around it at a maximum distance of only four degrees. The dire state of being pinned between two malefics is known as besiegement; here, the Ascendant is trapped between all three. The Nodes lie conjunct the Ascendant/Descendant axis: with the South Node just inside the first house, this repeats the strong indication we have already seen of suffering at the hands of the enemy. Mars, ruler of the natal seventh, bearing down on the Ascendant, confirms this. The Lunar Revolution, with the South Node in a fire sign exactly on the Midheaven paints a graphic picture: how will Coventry be hurt? By fire up in the air.

Finally, we look at the Full or New Moon before the event. The Full Moon was on the actual night of the raid.[10] At 22 Taurus, it falls just on the cusp of Coventry's natal house of death and takes us back to Grand Conjunction chart, where this same degree is conjunct the Midheaven, showing that we now have the fulfilment of the potential of that conjunction in this particular place. At the time of the full Moon – during the raid, that is – Mars, whose recurrent malignity we have traced through these charts, fell exactly on the Ascendant of the Coventry birth-chart. We might note also that Neptune lies just on the

---

[10]   Full Moon at 2.23 am GMT, November 15th, 1940.

Ascendant of the Full Moon chart: modern astrology will tell us that the bombing was a deeply mystical experience.

These are just the salient points from a series of charts the full delineation of which, even if limited to this single event, would demand an extensive book of its own. The 1921 Grand Conjunction had effects around the world: they were not limited to the events of just one night in one city nineteen years later. By a continual process of scaling down, moving from wheel to wheel on ever more specific levels of time and location, the mundane astrologer selects from the mass of potential of the great charts that which will come to pass in the particular locality with which he is concerned. If the judgement of a human nativity, with all the tangled concerns of a personality throughout a life, is a demanding task, the judgement of the mundane cycles is awesome indeed. But to have a true understanding of the man without understanding the environment within which he lives is impossible, even if only because the environment has a habit of sweeping him up and making away with him. That mundane astrology is so neglected leaves us with nothing but the facile explanations of the political commentators. These explanations for the behaviour of such complex creatures as nations and societies would be laughed to scorn if they were applied to an individual person; yet for want of any better, we take them seriously and so find ourselves living within them. This is not to our advantage. Our fond illusion is that we can cultivate our individuality regardless of what proceeds in the world outside our door; but when the soul enters the flesh it takes on a place in society as surely as it takes on a human form. The outside world has a far greater effect upon us than it is fashionable to admit; as such, the current neglect of mundane astrology is most seriously to our detriment.

Comets

It is in mundane astrology that the comets, those awesome harbingers of 'the sterility of the earth, Pestilence, Famine, War, alterations of Kingdoms, States and Empires, Laws and Customs, Winds, Earthquakes, Inundations, extreme heat and drought, grievous diseases and infirmities, and suchlike horrid evils',[11] have their greatest influence. These 'hairy stars', as is the derivation of their name, appear as if from nowhere, their shape, movement and, often, brilliance marking them out from other celestial objects. Although some comets travel in orbits allowing prediction of their return, the intrinsic nature of the creature is as something that is, from our limited human perspective, beyond all law, a spanner thrown into the regular clockwork of the spheres, signifying, therefore, turmoil and disruption. As what is above mirrors that below, these unwonted manifestations in the skies cannot but mark dire happenings on Earth.

The nature of the events that a comet portends are seen primarily from its colour and position in the heavens. A reddish hue displays its connection with

[11] William Ramesay, *Astrologia Restaurata,* London, 1653; reprinted Ascella, Nottingham, n.d.

Mars, for example; blue with Venus. Extreme brightness relates it again to Venus, the brightest object in the sky after the Sun and Moon; visibility only around sunrise or sunset with Venus or Mercury, which two planets behave likewise. Its effects will be felt in those sections of creation governed by the signs through which it passes, the greatest significance being accorded to that in which it is first seen: soldiers might suffer if it appears in Aries; the seas and their denizens if in Cancer; kings and leaders if in Leo. Conjunctions with planets and fixed stars will add further information according to their natures.

As an example, we may consider the comet Hale-Bopp, whose appearance in the Spring of 1997 had not been anticipated. Its silvery-blue colour identified it as being of Venus/Mercury nature, as did its appearing only around sunset. Its brightness confirmed the primacy of its Venus-nature, indicating that the afflictions it presaged would primarily concern the feminine, and thus childbirth and procreation. Its secondary Mercury-nature meant that it would also concern the mind and thus invention. It appeared in Taurus, so its effects would be felt among four-footed beasts, and then progressed into the humane sign of Gemini, carrying this turmoil to humankind. Its first appearance was conjunct that most malefic of all fixed stars, Caput Algol, traditionally associated with losing one's head. With this clear sign of the losing of heads affecting four-footed beasts through vanity of reason (Venus/Mercury) it was no surprise that this comet's appearance was soon followed by the announcement of the cloning of Dolly the sheep. We await with trepidation the consequences of this action as indicated by the comet's passage into Gemini.

13

Astro-meteorology

The branch of mundane astrology in most common use in the past, and that most neglected today, is that which has perhaps the most immediate practical use: the forecasting of the weather. This neglect is all the more surprising as the direct relevance of certain astrological indicators is obvious to anyone: as the Sun moves through the zodiac the seasons change; as it rises to the Midheaven the temperature increases; and as it sinks below the Descendant (the western horizon) the temperature drops rapidly.

In principle, the astrological forecasting of the weather is simple; there are, however, so many variables to be considered that the simple principles occur in patterns of the utmost complexity. As with any branch of mundane astrology, the practitioner is faced with an indefinitely extendible array of charts, each of which works within the bounds laid down by another chart, which is in its turn limited by another. With political matters there is usually a cut-off point beyond which we need not look: the chart for the foundation of a dynasty, perhaps, or the independence of a nation. But with astro-meteorology there is no such cut-off point. We do not have a chart for the moment at which our country came into existence as a geographical entity. Much, though, can still be done.

The key to weather forecasting lies in the fundamental divisions of signs and planets into the various combinations of hot or cold and moist or dry. These carry the obvious implications for the weather.

The simplest way of forecasting the weather for any specific occasion is by use of horary: the question itself limits the chart to that particular time, saving us the necessity of overlaying a series of mundane charts and comparing their various testimonies. Indeed, questions of weather are usually among the easiest horaries to judge. Suppose I ask about the weather on the holiday I am planning: finding the Sun (hot and dry) in Leo (hot and dry) just on the cusp of the ninth house (long journeys) in the horary chart would – if there were no contrary testimonies – assure me of the ideal weather for basking on the beach. If, however, I were planning a barbecue and found Jupiter, the planet of rain, in Pisces, where it is strong and also wet (if in its other sign of Sagittarius it would be equally strong, but drier) opposing the cusp of the fifth house (parties), I would be well advised to change my plans. If a general question about the weather is asked – "Will it be a fine summer?" for instance – we would look to the first house of the chart, as indicator of the general situation in that place.

The limitation with horary is that it does not work mechanically. If the question about my barbecue or the weather over the summer wanders into my head of its own volition, a horary chart will give accurate judgment. I cannot ask as a matter of routine each morning "What will the weather be like today?" and expect any degree of accuracy – any more than I can work my way through a lottery ticket asking "Will number 1 come up?" "Will number 2?" So for forecasting when there is no specific event in mind, we must resort to mundane charts.

We can cast a chart for the whole year, perhaps to ascertain some general information such as the amount of rainfall; but the longest period for which we shall probably enquire will be a season, as the natural variations from season to season render any enquiry into the weather for a year less productive than might be expected: there is little point in exercising our astrology to decide that summer will be hotter than winter. For the seasons, we cast a chart for the moment of the Sun's entry into each of the four cardinal signs: Aries for the spring, Cancer for the summer, Libra for autumn and Capricorn for the winter. These charts, however, are not judged alone, but together with that for the new or full Moon immediately preceding the Sun's ingress into that sign. The positions of the planets with regard to both the zodiac and each other will, of course, be the same the world over; the difference in weather from place to place is seen by casting the chart for the location in which we are interested. House positions, especially aspects to the angles, are crucial. A wet Jupiter on the Midheaven will bring rain in abundance, while if he is tucked away in the twelfth house he will have little effect.

Such variations from place to place will allow us to see the broad outlines of the weather patterns; but there is little appreciable difference between our Jupiter exactly on the Midheaven in one place and two degrees away from it in another. The fine detail of local conditions is provided by the fixed stars. Each star has the nature of either one planet or two – or occasionally three – in combination, and, most significantly, it operates over only a small orb. There is a great deal of difference between a star of Jupiter nature exactly on the Midheaven and the same star just a degree or two away. Particular attention must be paid to the celestial latitude of the stars. We are usually concerned only with celestial longitude: movement around the ecliptic, more or less from side to side of the viewer's horizon. The planets also have an up and down motion within the limits of the band of the ecliptic; this is measured by latitude. Occultation, which occurs only if planet conjuncts star by both longitude and latitude, is of the utmost significance in weather-forecasting. Planets return to the same degree of longitude at regular intervals; they aspect each other regularly; any particular planet occults any particular star only rarely. We see here one of the major variables in our judgement, reflecting the fact that weather does not recur in a precise regular pattern.

Once we have determined the broad outlook for the season, we can look in more detail at its component months by casting the ingress and lunation charts for the Sun's entry into each zodiacal sign. Further detail is provided by casting new charts for each phase of the Moon. The lunation before the ingress is taken as our starting point; charts cast at the exact moment of each quarter (that is, when the Moon squares, opposes or conjuncts the Sun) will break the month down into weeks. The weather day by day can be determined by the distance between aspecting planets in these charts, by the rising and setting of the fixed stars and by casting a chart for sunrise on the day in question. It is important to remember, however, that these more detailed charts cannot be judged alone: no stage in the gradual refinement of precision from chart to chart can be omitted; the testimonies of each chart operate only within the bounds laid down by the next level in the 'hierarchy' of charts. The information we draw from all of these charts must be judged against the overall climate (we are compensating here for our lack of geographical foundation charts): what is cold and moist for Scotland is not what is cold and moist for Algeria.

In judgment, the signs follow their elemental natures: the fire signs are hot and dry; air hot and moist; water cold and moist; earth cold and dry. These basic natures are qualified by the season of the sign, whether or not that is the season for which the chart is cast. Leo, being a summer sign, is hotter and drier than autumnal Sagittarius; wintry Pisces is colder and wetter than summery Cancer. Saturn brings cold, and if moistened by position or aspect, cloud. His is the east wind. Jupiter gives good weather, although astrology's conception of good weather is that of the farmer rather than the holidaymaker: as the Great Benefic it brings weather fine, mild and clear – but any hint of moisture attaching itself will bring rain in plenty. His is the north or north-east wind.

Mars, as might be expected, brings violent weather: the thunderstorm that breaks a spell of sultry days; the intensification of any testimonies with which he is connected. His is the west wind – the 'wild west wind' of Shelley's poem, stripping the leaves from the trees. The Sun's indications change with the seasons: moist showers in Spring; heat in Summer; mist in Autumn; drizzle in winter. It indicates the east wind.

Venus is much like Jupiter, on smaller scale: fine weather, unless moistened, when she then shows rain. Hers is the south wind. Mercury's main signification is of wind and turbulence – even as far as earthquakes. As ever, it adapts its nature to that of whichever of the planets it is in contact; the particular direction of wind he provokes will be that of the planet to which he applies. The Moon is itself moist, but works mainly as a catalyst, bringing the other planets into action as she forms aspects with them. Like Mercury, she provokes the wind of the planet to which she next applies. So if our lunation chart showed Mercury in Virgo (cold and dry) exactly on the Midheaven, we should expect cold wind. If it were applying immediately to oppose Jupiter in Pisces, the wind would take its direction from Jupiter (northerly) and bring rain.

Attention must also be given to some Arabian Parts: the Part of Weather, which shows the weather in general and the winds in particular (Ascendant +

Dispositor of Mercury – Mercury); the Part of Fire and Heat (Asc + Mars – Sun); the Part of Clouds (Asc + Saturn – Mars); the Part of Rains (Asc + Venus – Moon); and the Part of Cold (Asc + Saturn – Mercury). In the daily chart, cast for sunrise, the Part of the Day can be used: Moon + Sun – Saturn. As always, the condition of that planet that rules the sign in which a Part falls is of equal significance with the condition of the Part itself.

Finally, recourse must be made to that long-forgotten astrological technique of switching off the computer, stepping outside and looking to see what is happening in the sky: sub-lunar indications have their own important place in astro-meteorology. Alterations in the appearance of the planets, especially the luminaries, owing to atmospheric changes will, if wisely combined with information from the charts, give the finishing touches to an accurate forecast.

The astrological indicators which we consider when predicting the weather are, of course, exactly those which we consider when examining any aspect of human life. It may be that here we find the reason why astro-meteorology has fallen from favour. As it suits post-Enlightenment man to consider himself a machine, capable of grinding in daily toil hour by hour regardless of time or season, the idea that the weather and his state of well-being are so intimately connected that they can both be deduced from study of the same indicators is not a convenient one. But what is convenient for his current obsessions and what is for the benefit of his body, mind and soul are not necessarily the same.

Farmers and gardeners around the world still plant by the phase of the Moon, often without for one moment considering that they are doing anything astrological, although they are practising a simple form of electional astrology.

The ground will have been turned, an action preferably started during an hour ruled by Saturn, ruler of the soil. Manuring will ideally have been started during a Jupiter hour on a Saturn day, or *vice versa,* bringing nourishment and fertility to the soil. The Moon should be strong (in Taurus, an earth sign, if possible), increasing in light and applying to either a fortune or, at least, a planet with some strong essential dignity. For sowing, a Jupiter hour should be chosen, with the Moon increasing in light and with a minimum of thirty-six hours having elapsed since New, to make sure it is free of the debilitating rays of the Sun. Similarly, there should be at least thirty-six hours before the Full Moon, for the same reason. First quarter, when the Moon squares the Sun, is also best avoided.

Unless some slow-growing plant, such as a tree, is being planted, the Moon should not be in a fixed sign. Cancer would be the ideal, as the Moon is strong and the sign is cardinal, giving quick growth. If the Moon itself is not in a water sign, it should be aspected by another planet that is, in order to promote succulence. Fortunate aspect from the Moon to the natural ruler of the plant in question is helpful, as is contact with Jupiter, the ruler of growth. There are exceptions to these simple rules, notably with legumes, which should be sown when the Moon is decreasing in light to stop them producing flowers at the expense of fruit. Any plant with a tendency to bolt will benefit from adaption of these principles, by avoiding the speed given by cardinal signs and moderating the strength of the Moon. Contact between the Moon and Mars, which gives undue speed of growth, in such circumstances must be scrupulously avoided.

Again, the Arabian Parts are most helpful, there being Parts for any number of crops, from onions (Asc + Mars – Saturn) and maize (Asc + Saturn – Jupiter) to water-melons (Asc + Mercury – Jupiter). But always, no matter how subtle our astrology, the first step in the choice of moment to plant is to find out what the weather will be like, whether this is done by astrological or more mundane means. No choice of lunar phase or careful placement of Jupiter carries a magic that will override lack of sun or water.

14

Medical Astrology

The purveyors of modern medicine, determined to establish a monopoly on all medical knowledge, not merely today but through all time, would have us believe that our ancestors were incurably disease-ridden. When feeling more than usually rough, they would visit the local charlatan, who would sever a vein or two and dose them with whatever wild plant was handy, then send them away having convinced them they were cured, despite the buboes that still sprouted from their every limb. What silly folk our ancestors were to fall for such chicanery!

The charlatan in question would probably, but not invariably, have used astrology as the basis for his treatment, both diagnosis and prescription, following Hippocrates, who emphasised the importance of astrology in medicine. He would have cast a chart for the illness, taking either the time at which the patient took to his bed – known as a *decumbiture,* or 'lying down' chart – the time at which a sample of the patent's urine was delivered to him, or just the time at which a question about the course of the illness was asked. Common practice would have been to judge the astrological chart and the patient's urine, if available, together.

The chart would have been judged as a battle between the patient's vital spirits and the illness; if necessary, the physician and his medicaments would weigh in on the side of the patient. The patient and his vital spirits were shown by the first house of the chart, the illness by the sixth, the physician by the seventh and the medicine by the tenth. Also relevant would be the Arabian Parts of Sickness and of Surgery. The course of short-term illnesses, lasting up to a month, was shown largely by the movement of the Moon; that of longer illnesses by the movement of the Sun, though the Sun, as Lord of Life and therefore image of vital spirits *per se,* was of great importance in any medical chart.

Having both the patient and the illness shown in the chart indicates that the method is essentially – in modern terms – 'holistic': it is looking at a particular disarrangement of a particular person. The idea of illness X being treated with medicine Y is quite alien; *patient* X is treated with whichever medicine his current condition might require: it is the patient who is treated, not the illness. A consequence of this is that traditional diagnosis can look terribly crude when seen from a modern perspective. We are used to the finer and finer categorisation of disease, as if the disease were a chess opening: "Oh yes, you've got Ruy Lopez' Disease, exchange variation;" and just as with a chess opening, the doctor has a certain set response, regardless of whom he might be playing: "Antibiotic to King's Bishop 4." The traditional physician is less concerned with putting a label on the illness than in determining exactly what is happening and, most importantly, what is the cause of it. So a diagnosis such as "There lodged in the Brest or Stomack some melanchollick Obstruction, the cause of all his disease and Misery,"[1] is perfectly clear. The principle is that causes are but few, symptoms are manifold, so chasing symptoms is a waste of time; best just deal with the cause.

The cause will be an imbalance in the temperament. As we have seen, everyone is made up of hot, cold, moist and dry, which are usually in a manageable balance, though always with one or two of these humours in greater proportion than the others. Each person will have his or her typical illnesses, which will fall into two categories: those caused by a bubbling up into excess of the dominant humour, and those caused by an unusual short-fall in the weakest humour. A simple example occurs in the teenage years. Teenagers, particularly boys, become more choleric, with fire running through their veins; this finds typical outlets in sexual obsession and hitting each other – and also in outbreaks of spots, which are, like volcanoes, symptoms of excess of choler. They are most predominant in those whose temperamental balance is most heavily choleric by nature, or those in whom it is most lacking and whose system lacks the ability to deal with it.

So, far from the modern idea of illness as an alien life-form which has invaded an unsuspecting victim who would otherwise live forever in unblemished good health – and far from the modern obsession with the futile attempt to eradicate all diseases – the illness is an integral part of the person, an imbalance that will, when it becomes gross enough, assume physical form. We see something of this in common parlance, where words such as 'gouty' or 'sclerotic' describe personality traits as much as illnesses. So too, there is a far closer relationship between symptom and cause than is allowed by modern allopathic medicine. The symptom is not the body's attempt to deal with this alien invader; rather, it is the cause itself appearing under different guise. The example of Aids makes this plain. Aids, in modern terms, is a breakdown in the body's immune system; that is, it is a lack of barriers or boundaries. Its cause is exactly this: the lack of boundaries, hence its common manifestation among promiscuous homosexuals, what might be termed promiscuous drug users – who lack the requisite boundaries between mine and thine in their use of needles – and haemophiliacs, bearers of an illness which is itself a manifestation of lack of barriers – the body lacks the barriers to stop itself bleeding. In astrological terms, each of these groups displays in its different fashion a desperate shortage of Saturn, the planet connected with barriers and boundaries. And

[1] Lilly, op. cit. p. 287

what is the main weapon in the 'fight against Aids'? Use of the condom, providing just that barrier (Saturn) which the being itself is not providing.

Once the imbalance that is the root cause of the illness has been identified, treatment will aim to restore the equilibrium that has been lost. This is done either by draining off the excess humour, through methods such as bleeding or purging, or by strengthening the opposing humour. The traditional English public school remedies for the excess of fire in teenage veins demonstrate these principles: the poor lad is either given a cold shower, balancing the excess of heat by the application of cold; or he is packed off on a cross-country run, draining off the excess of heat through physical exertion. Cross-country running is nowadays a more socially acceptable form of balancing treatment than bleeding, though best not applied to the seriously ill. An excess of any humour could be treated by bleeding, the part of the body and time at which the bleeding was done determining which humour would be drawn off. Evidence for ancient surgeons wading through blood as their patients expired exists only in the minds of modern medical apologists; unless our ancestors were very foolish, we must suspect that it was at least as effective a treatment as the modern practice of bleeding the patient's wallet.

If the imbalance were particularly extreme, however, it could be treated by sympathy rather than antipathy. So suppose the illness were shown in the astrological chart by a powerful Mars, while the patient's vital spirits were shown by a badly debilitated Venus. This would indicate an severe excess of heat, while there is precious little resource within the patient on which the doctor can build to restore a balance. In this case, rather than join a hopeless fight to strengthen the cold humours, more heat can be applied. Unlikely as it might sound, this will draw off some of the excess heat within the system. If we remember that an Englishman will drink a cup of hot tea to warm himself on a cold winter's day, while an Indian will drink a cup of hot tea to cool himself in the heat of the summer, and make our standard assumption that neither of them has taken leave of his senses, we can see that this might work. Rather than puzzling his head, we suggest that the sceptical reader might try it.

Most treatment would have been done with diet and the internal or external application of herbs and minerals. Dietary treatment was considered preferable, as being less traumatic; medicines and the physical treatments should be used only when the condition necessitated a quick intervention. In an age when the aim of altering diet is almost always for the trivial purpose of adjusting physical appearance, it is forgotten how powerful an effect dietary regime can have on the being. Much can be done for the general well-being of the individual, whether that individual is well or ill, simply by altering the diet in the light of the birth-chart – though we must stress that attempting this with a knowledge only of Twentieth-Century astrology is likely to cause more harm than good.

The medicaments are chosen according to their nature, whether the remedy required is hot or cold and moist or dry. Different medicines have differing degrees of heat, cold, moisture and dryness. Those which have these properties in the first degree are the mildest; those which have them in the fourth are usually very harmful or even fatal, though having medical uses when applied with caution in extreme circumstances. The knowledge of the properties of plants, like astrology itself, comes from Inspiration, as is shown by the hadith related by As-Suyuti:

"when Sulayman, peace be upon him, had finished constructing the Temple, he entered the place of prayer, and suddenly there before him was a bush. When he had finished his prayers, the bush said, 'Are you not going to ask me who I am?' And he replied, 'Yes, who are you?' And the bush said, 'I am a such-and-such bush, and a remedy for so-and-so, and this and that come from such and so.' Then Sulayman ordered that the bush be cut down. And when this had been done, then suddenly another one, similar to it, grew up. And so every day, when he entered the place of prayer, he would meet another of these bushes. In this way he acquired a complete knowledge of all of them, and then wrote his book on Medicine about them, describing the remedies from them."[2]

Within the basic humoral framework, each plant or mineral falls under the rulership of one of the planets, or of two of them in combination. To allow it to work with the maximum efficacy, the plant should be picked in an hour ruled by its own planet, and preferably when that planet is strong either essentially or by position (so much for store-bought herbs!). The medicine should be prepared under similar circumstances, and, most importantly, it must be administered at an appropriate moment, which will be determined from the chart for the decumbiture. This allows considerable scope for fine adjusting of the medicine: suppose we wish to strengthen our patient's Saturn while also perking up his Mars; we might then pick our Saturn herb in a Saturn hour on a Mars day, or in a Saturn hour when Mars is powerfully placed in the sky; or when a fixed star of Mars nature is in a prominent position; or pick our Saturn herb in a Saturn hour and then prepare it in a Mars hour. Any one of these will allow us to give the patient's Mars the tweak it needs while concentrating on boosting the Saturn. Herbs can also, of course, be straight mixed, and we are advised "in all cures whatsoever to use a select number of herbs which are under the Sun, in regard he is Fountain of Life, and sole Monarch of the Heavens."[3] This needs a knowledgeable hand, else, as with mixing colours on a palette, what is intended as a delicate tint will emerge as a neutral splodge, of no use to anyone.

Why is my daughter ill?

This is a horary chart on a medical theme.[4] The querent's daughter had for some months been suffering from headaches of gradually increasing severity. Medical treatment was of no avail: the headaches continued to get worse.

---

[2] Jalalu'd-Din Abd'ur-Rahman As-Suyuti, *Medicine of the Prophet*, p. 33, Ta-Ha, London 1994.

[3] Joseph Blagrave, *Astrological Practice of Physick,* p. B3. 1671; reprinted Ascella Publications, Nottingham.

[4] February 25th, 1999. 9.36 am GMT, London

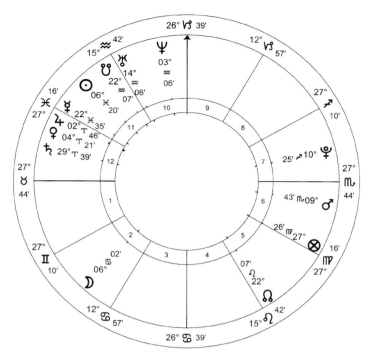

Chart 14: Why is my daughter ill?

Doctors had tested for various possible causes, including her eyes, her motor responses and her chronic constipation. The parents, baffled by the inability of the doctors to treat the ailment, understandably feared the worst.

What we have here is something at several removes from the conventional idea of reality. There is, we are told by modern doctors, no possible connection between the stars and human life. This chart, however, is even more distant from the usually envisaged connection, as it is a horary – a question asked at an apparently random moment. What is more, the question was not even asked by the person concerned, but by her mother. Superstitious nonsense of a high order.

As the question is asked by the mother, we look not to the Ascendant but to the fifth house for our main significator. This is the part of the chart concerned with children, so its ruling planet will represent the querent's daughter. Here, it is the Sun (☉). We immediately notice the Moon's North Node (☊) just inside the fifth house. This is an indication that all will be well.

Our first step in any medical chart is to check that the person is actually ill, that they have not perhaps been studying a medical dictionary too avidly. The Sun (the daughter) is hot and dry by nature; in this chart, it is in Pisces (♓), which is a cold, moist sign. Our main significator in a sign of nature uncongenial to its own confirms that our patient is ill.

Then we must determine the seriousness of the situation: will the patient recover or not? With the parents worrying about a possible brain tumour, the prospect of death was one that had to be considered. The houses representing death are the eighth and the eighth house from the house of the patient, in this case the eighth from the fifth, which is the twelfth. Both of these houses are ruled by Jupiter (♃). The lack of any aspect between the Sun and Jupiter (the daughter and death) is a strong testimony that there is nothing to fear. The greater part of a judgement that the patient will not die rests in the absence of compelling testimonies that she will; here, however, there are two strong indications for life and recovery: the Sun and Jupiter are in each other's dignities, and, stronger still, there is a close trine aspect (120°) between the Sun and Moon. This is the most fortunate aspect possible, all the more so as the Moon is so powerfully placed in its own sign of Cancer (☽ in ♋). Our patient will not die.

The illness is shown by both the sixth house of the chart and the sixth from the house of the person concerned (so the tenth in this instance). It is common among the moderns to call the sixth the 'house of health', but this is quite wrong: the sixth is the house of illness, a different matter altogether. The house of health is the first, which is where the vital spirits are shown. The sixth here is ruled by Mercury, the tenth by Saturn. As the Ascendant and both the sixth and turned sixth houses have late degrees on their cusps (26 or 27 out of a possible 30), we can judge that there will soon be a major alteration in the state of the illness, either for better or for worse. That none of our relevant planets falls in a fixed sign confirms this. With the benevolent testimonies of the Moon/Sun trine and the North Node in the daughter's house, supported by the absence of anything particularly unpleasant happening to her planet, the Sun, we can judge that the alteration will be for the better.

So far, so good; but what is actually wrong with her? The first thing to examine must be the planet ruling the sixth house. Mercury (☿) is the planet naturally associated with the brain, and falling in Pisces it is in poor condition; but it is doing nothing untoward. It is not afflicting either the Sun or the daughter's house, and it is not afflicted itself. If it were, concerns about a possible tumour would lead us to look at it in more depth; but there is no cause to do so. A much more plausible culprit is Jupiter. The Sun is ruled by Jupiter (because it falls in Pisces, Jupiter's sign), which reflects the situation: we would expect there to be evidence of the illness having power over the child. Jupiter rules things that are big; it is in Aries (♈), which rules the head: if she suffers with big headaches, Jupiter in Aries would paint an acceptable picture of the ailment. Conclusively, the technique of antiscion, by which we reflect a planet's position in a line between the two solstice points (0 Cancer/0 Capricorn) takes Jupiter at 2°46 of Aries to 27°14 of Virgo (♍). This is exactly on the cusp of the sixth house of illness. We have sufficient grounds for taking Jupiter as the illness.

We have as yet seen nothing to suggest any problem with the brain; we can now make a little diversion to rule out the possibility that eyes are the cause of the trouble. The eyes are signified by the Sun and the Moon, the two lights, by natural association. The usual indications of eye problems are affliction to these planets and, most commonly, their placement on particular fixed stars. Several stars, mainly clusters or nebulae, which appear fuzzy to the naked eye, are associated with poor eyesight. The chart gives no indication that there is anything wrong with her eyes.

Back to Jupiter, which we have identified as the source of the problem. Jupiter is the planet associated with the blood (Mars only when the blood is outside the body) and the liver. As Jupiter is the seat of the illness, we can see that it must be caused by – in the loose modern phrase – 'bad blood'. Jupiter (the illness) stands exactly half-way between the Sun (the patient) and Saturn. Saturn rules the fifth house from the girl's own house, that is, the ninth. The fifth house shows the liver, so Saturn particularly signifies the girl's liver and Jupiter (the illness) then as it were joins the liver and the girl. With Saturn in Aries, where it is very weak, we can see that her liver is in a bad way. Both Jupiter and Saturn are in the eighth house from the girl's own house; this is the house ruling the anus and associated functions, so we see the connection with her constipation. In technical terms, the chart indicates an excess of yellow choler mixed with the blood.

Even without adopting the language of traditional medicine, we can see that the headaches are caused by a liver malfunction. The close conjunction of Venus to Jupiter, allied with the girl's age, would show an association with menarche. The constipation does not cause the headaches, but is another symptom of the underlying problem. The traditional physician would have treated the liver; his prescriptions (such as rhubarb) would have had the secondary effect of clearing the constipation, though it must be stressed that his prime concern would have been to treat the seat of the problem, while providing immediate relief of discomfort. Long-term treatment to avoid recurrence would have been by regulation of diet. Any prescription would have involved a more detailed judgement than the brief outlines above, which are drawn only to show the identification of the ailment.

After several weeks of tests, conventional medical specialists arrived at the same conclusion as the astrological chart.

15

Synastry

A basic form of synastry is one of the most common uses of astrology today, the question "Where is your Moon?" being the mating cry of anyone with the merest smattering of astrological knowledge. All you need do on being told the whereabouts of this person's Moon – no matter whether it is in Pisces, Leo or under the cat – is keep silent, while giving an expression as if something of the utmost significance has just been said, and you are well on the way to a happy relationship.

Synastry is the art of comparing two birth-charts to assess the potential for whatever form of interaction is desired between the people in question. Although this usually concerns emotional relationships, synastry can also be of great use in business partnerships and the relationships between teacher and pupil or employer and employee. It is all very well hiring the person with the glittering qualifications, but if there is a fundamental problem in communication between the two of you, as though your respective mental radios were tuned to different frequencies, it might be wiser to look elsewhere. This is exactly the kind of problem that can be identified by synastry, using astrology to cut through the subjective reactions of "He's stupid," He's being awkward," or "He's not paying attention," and cast a dispassionate light revealing the true source of the difficulty, which can then be tackled or circumvented.

Traditionally, synastry would have been used while arranging a marriage. This simple fact points to a major problem with the modern use of the art: if you are assessing two people's potential for marriage, it is necessary to have a sound idea of what marriage is. Emotional and sexual compatibility would play their important role – the things of this world, as it were – but more significant would be the facilitating of each partner's spiritual development, for if the relationship does not have a direction, which need not necessarily be overt, beyond that of the satisfaction of material needs, it will necessarily wither. We recall Socrates, deliberately choosing the infuriating Xantippe as a wife: this is not a marriage that would have been advised by any astrologer without this deeper view of the significance of human relationship. Yet without this understanding, any amount of emotional, physical or mental compatibility is so much dust. The necessity of the astrologer having a sound outlook is paramount, else he simply does not for know what he is looking; so, once again, we are confronted with the absolute necessity of astrology being oriented within the spiritual framework that has been normal within human society throughout history. Perhaps even more obviously than in the study of the individual birth-chart, synastry points the narcissistic emptiness of the so-called 'humanistic' astrology.

We must also doubt whether any meaningful work can be done with the crabbed and distorted tools of modern astrology, no matter how many asteroids are dragged in to bolster the argument. The first step in synastry (a step which is often ignored by the moderns) is to carry out a detailed assessment of each of the natal charts individually. Only from here do contacts and comparisons between the two charts have any significance. To return to our amorous astrologer with his cry of "Where's your Moon?" – with the plethora of planets, planetoids, bits of space-dust, trivial aspects and other paraphernalia with which the modern chart is cluttered, he would have to be singularly unfortu-nate if his victim's Moon were to fall somewhere where it did not make some kind of contact with something or other in his own chart. "Aha!" he then thinks, "We're made for each other!" But, irresistible as our astrologer of course is, we might venture to suggest that this is not necessarily so. What is forgotten is that an impressive list can be made of 'significant contacts' between his chart and that of almost anybody who has ever lived – all the more so if we are using the catch-all methods of the moderns. While on the one hand this reflects the truth that if she were the only girl in the world and I were the only boy, we would probably find a way of getting along together, it shows that it does need something more than just a few planetary contacts to form a working relation-ship in the real world. For all the Sun/Chiron and Mars/Pluto contacts between your charts, you may well be left with no more than a feeling of puzzlement when she makes it quite clear that the two minutes she has so far spent in your company is at least three minutes too long.

The text-books commonly fall into exactly this trap, presenting the chart of Romeo and the chart of Juliet and listing the planetary contacts between them to prove their love. This is all very well, until we wonder what contacts there might be between the charts of Romeo and Flavia, Claudia, Rosalind, or any one of ten thousand others. Edward VIII and Wallis Simpson and Freud and Jung are the favoured examples; but the contacts listed prove absolutely nothing. Indeed, with the examples given, which are always those of intense relationships, the question must arise "Why aren't there more connections? If this handful of contacts gives the intensity that I know existed between these people, what is wrong with me that the many contacts I have observed between my own chart and so many others have produced nothing similar?"

The answer is that these planetary contacts, even if judged well, are compara-tively trivial in import; if judged according to the contemporary rules, they are more or less meaningless. They show the superficialities, the kind of points we see listed in the lonely-hearts ads: "Vegetarian cyclist seeks similar for boring relationship". Vegetarian cyclist – Mars sesquiquadrate Pluto: much the same kind of thing. But this does not true love make. That for which we are really searching is exactly what we do not find in the shopping-list expectations of the lonely-hearts ads: "Vegetarian cyclist seeks bad-tempered womaniser whom I can just about refrain from murdering but whom I will love dearly for the rest of my life." We can find any number of charts with any number of planetary contacts (anyone versed in astrology will have done exactly this with the birth-chart of every vaguely tolerable member of the opposite sex that he has ever met, and contacts there are in plenty – this game is the astrological equivalent of writing her name all over your school books, and about as productive); but if the more fundamental building-blocks of the chart do not mesh, nothing will happen. There must be a bond at the level of temperament, or she will not wish to know me, even if she does find my jokes amusing.

Let us take a theoretical example. Suppose Romeo has the Sun at 15 degrees of Aries in his birth-chart. An aspect between the Sun of one chart and the Moon of the other is regarded as one of the most significant indicators of compatibility. We should regard a conjunction between Juliet's Moon and Romeo's Sun as of the utmost importance. Being modern astrologers, with our urgent desire to drag significance into absolutely anything, we shall allow an orb of ± 10 degrees; so if Juliet's Moon falls anywhere between 5 and 25 degrees of Aries, we have a strong testimony of love. Similarly if her Moon is in trine (120°) aspect, again ± 10 degrees, giving a strong testimony of love if her Moon falls at either 5-25° Leo or 5-25° Sagittarius. So far, we have sixty degrees out of a possible 360 which would give us a strong indication of love between Romeo and Juliet. We must also consider the sextile (60°) aspect, perhaps with a slightly smaller orb, say ±8°. Juliet's Moon at 7-23° of either Aquarius or Gemini would form a sextile to Romeo's Sun. Even the square or opposition must be taken into account, as although these are less favourable aspects "they involve an element of fascination even when stress is present at the same time".[1] Here we are back with ±10°, so anywhere between 5-25° of Cancer, Libra or Capricorn will give us another strong indication of love. We now have Juliet's Moon in any one of 136 degrees out of a possible 360. Being modern astrologers, we can now involve any number of minor aspects, all at rather smaller orbs: 150, 135, 45, 30 degrees, all ± perhaps 4°, giving another 64 significant degrees. We have now accounted for 200 out of the possible 360 – and we have not yet considered aspects of 36°, 72°, 144° and so on and so on. Based on this important Sun/Moon contact, we can see that from Romeo's point of view at least two out of any three women will fit the bill quite nicely. But we must remember that any of the above aspects between Juliet's Moon and Romeo's own Moon is also sign of a powerful bond. Or with his Ascendant. Or his Mars, Venus, Jupiter, Pluto and quite possibly Neptune, Uranus, Saturn or Mercury as well. To say nothing of Chiron, the Dark Moon Lilith and 4000 asteroids. Placed almost anywhere in the chart, Juliet's Moon will strike some significant chord in Romeo's birth-chart. He is obviously not fussy. But should by some oversight she have secreted her Moon

[1] Ron Davison, *Synastry*, p.103, Aurora, New York, 1983

in whatever stray degree makes no contact with the significant points in Romeo's chart, all is by no means lost: her Ascendant, Sun, Venus, Mars, Jupiter or Pluto will do the trick just as well. Romeo is, of course, an adolescent male; so we might see this inevitability of meaningful contact as reflecting the fact that providing the girl has approximately the conventional number of heads, he will find her attractive. Both his and her birth-charts, however, remain the same throughout the life, even when the hormones have quietened down, a fact which does not bode so well for their future life together.

To be fair, the modern astrologer would expect to find significant contacts between several pairs of planets before judging in favour of true and undying love; but as we have seen, significant contacts are less of a rarity than seems at first the case. We should be hard put to it to track down two charts which did *not* have some reasonably powerful planetary connections. Marooned on a desert island, maybe we could get along; but what interests us, and what modern synastry, despite its claims, fails to tell us is not that we could get along if there were no prospect of any alternative, but whether we will forge a relationship while surrounded by alternatives in plenty.

Let us now consider a practical example, following the usual custom of discussing notable relationships about which the writer knows very little. Contrary to the evident belief of many of the popular astrological journals, the sacred science is not a means for peering through locked doors, and we shall not treat it as if it were. But we may perhaps glance briefly and, we hope, unobtrusively, at one of the few lasting marriages in the Hollywood Babylon, to see if we might find some traces of the glue that binds it so fast.

The mere comparison of aspects between the birth-charts of Paul Newman and Joanne Woodward leaves nothing but a sense of puzzlement.[2] Close aspects there are, but hardly more than we might expect from a random scattering of planets. Woodward's Saturn, particularly important because it rules her Ascendant, falls conjunct Newman's Jupiter. His Mercury/Venus conjunction lies close to her Ascendant and sextile her Venus. Her Sun and Venus sextile his Ascendant and Jupiter. This is all well and good; but why, we might reasonably ask, did not Loretta Young, whose Sun and Moon make powerful contacts with Newman's Jupiter, Ascendant and Venus, or Doris Day, whose Sun and Moon hit the same points, or Jane Russell, whose Moon, Venus and Jupiter tie in nicely with Newman's chart (to say nothing of many other contacts in all three cases) snap their fingers and whisk him away, while Woodward in turn disappeared with Jack Lemmon, Robert Wagner or any one of dozens of others whose charts provide close aspects to her own? The contacts we see are impressive, but only for as long as we do not compare them to those of possible rivals.

The key lies at deeper levels. If there is no bond there, no number of aspects between planets will substitute. The aspects are important, but it is the deeper

[2] Woodward: February 27th, 1930, 4.00 am EST, 30N50 83W59; Newman: January 26th, 1925, 6.30 am EST, 41N28 81W43

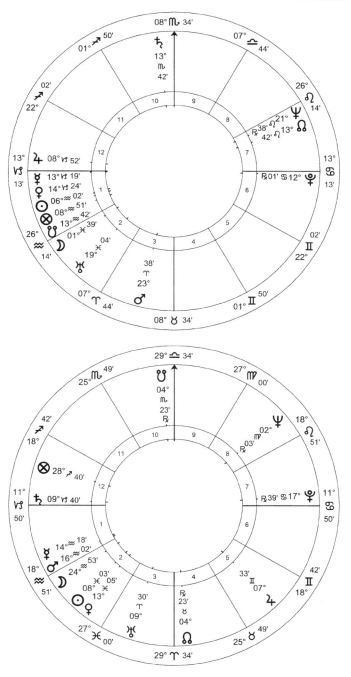

Charts 15 and 16: Paul Newman and Joanne Woodward

levels of contact that are vital: without them, nothing. The aspects show the manner of relating; if they were not there, we might have two ideally compatible people quite incapable of connecting with each other – as if they were the tenants of a flop-house, one using the room by day and the other by night, but never meeting. In synastry, the aspects provide the 'how' of the relationship; we must first have a 'why'.

The root of the why is found at the level of temperament. The temperaments of our examples are comparatively well-balanced, with Newman's of slightly sanguine (airy) complexion and Woodward's slightly melancholic (earthy). Sanguine is hot and moist; melancholic, cold and dry: between the two we have a perfect balance, reminiscent of the platonic half-soul seeking its lost twin. There is no stronger bond than this: opposites do indeed attract; so do similars, but the similars grow bored with each other. That both charts are only slightly weighted in their respective directions is significant: we are looking for the right combination of the complementary and the similar between the two people, so that they may each complete and yet identify with the other.[3] If the temperaments were strongly sanguine and strongly melancholic, much as they might need each other, each would find the other incomprehensible and probably insufferable.

The shared Ascendant is part of a matrix of similarity welding the temperamental attraction of opposites, as a carpenter's brace holds a glued joint until it is set. Both having almost all the traditional planets below the horizon and on the eastern (Ascendant) side of the chart we have two fundamentally private people who are to a large extent emotionally self-sufficient. On first meeting, we might expect them to have found a shared outlook, seen through their opposing temperaments, and to each have found a sense of emotional integrity in the other that they could respect. Also significant is the taking up in each chart of the weaknesses in the other. In both natal charts, the main points of weakness are the Sun and the Moon; both partner's Moon falls in the sign of the other's Sun (and, of course, *vice versa*), giving if not a remedy at least an understanding and empathy with the other's major frailties. We might note that their Suns fall in adjacent signs, an indication, as any magazine article will tell us, of total incompatibility. If all we seek in a partner is ourselves in different clothes, this sweeping statement is surely true; in fact, given other indications to bind the relationship, this very dissimilarity can be a major point of strength.

We have looked as hard at these charts as discretion permits – the common use of astrology as substitute for a paparazzo's zoom lens is to be utterly abhorred – but in sufficient depth to show that there is more to synastry than mixing and matching aspects in search of similarities. Even what we see here, however, would not allow us to judge that these two people would form a lasting relationship: so much depends on the nature of the time at which they meet. No matter how ideally compatible they might be, there are any number

---

[3] This necessity is perhaps easier to see when considering business partnerships: there is no point in choosing a partner whose skills duplicate our own; we want the partner who can do the things that we cannot. Yet there must be sufficient shared ground for us to want to work together.

of possible circumstances that might have kept them apart. In the first place, they have to meet; this is in itself a remarkable occurrence. This meeting or meetings, however, must happen in suitable circumstances: boy may meet perfect girl, but if he is currently infatuated with femme fatale, he will fail to notice her, to cite but one of an endless array of possibilities that might cause the most promising of relationships to die before it ever begins.

The fundamental difference between aspects and temperamental proclivities in the chart is that the temperamental balance shows the possibilities of growth in the relationship. The concentration on the aspects, although not construed as such, is typical of a society that treats relationships as if they were different varieties of breakfast cereal: buy the one in the fancy box and either eat it or throw it away. This emphasis on the possibility of growth is crucial, revealing the most common use of synastry – as answer to the question "Is this Mr Right?" – as misjudged. The usefulness of this branch of the art is, at least in western culture where marriages are not customarily arranged, not to catch a mate, but to provide concrete evidence of the weaknesses with which an existing relationship must deal, and the strengths which it has available to deal with them.

The great snare with synastry as device for selecting a partner is the necessity of incorporating a time-factor into the judgment. This is rarely, if ever done. The astrologer will take the two birth-charts and judge them as if they were the charts of a couple of may-flies, whose lives are over in hours. There is every possibility that my chart and Tammy's chart show the most powerful of bonds, even at the temperamental level of which we have seen the importance. The astrologer will give the match her blessing. But I am still wet behind the ears, with no idea of how to treat my perfect mate. Had we met a few years later, I might have matured and all could have been well; but we did not, and so it ends in tears. We might liken matching two people to docking a space capsule; judging synastry without the consideration of time is akin to trying to dock the craft knowing the design of the mother-ship, but with no idea of where it might be in its orbit. It has about as much chance of succeeding.

Synastry is susceptible to some very dubious uses. There is a common belief that it gives some kind of power over the other person, or that it will make something happen: many a lovelorn astrologer passes his time gazing at Ms Perfect's birth-chart and assuring himself that the Sun/Moon contact (or whatever) between her chart and his promises lasting bliss – and will even tell her as much, with the underlying compulsion "This is written in the stars, so lie back and enjoy it." Ms Perfect, meanwhile, is displaying the good sense to cultivate a relationship with someone who is interested in her, rather than her birth-chart. Correctly employed, synastry works as an extended form of natal reading, analysing and clarifying with the tools of dignity, reception and aspect that we have seen at work elsewhere. Without these tools, it is nothing but pointless titillation, catching us by what our modern culture has rendered our most vulnerable point, the endless desire to be loved, which of course now holds us utterly entranced.

16

Astrological Magic

Closely connected with both electional and medical astrology is the art of astro-logical magic. It is this magical practice which has called down the fiercest anathemas onto astrology; yet it is just this practice which astrology's public most requires, and the absence of which it most regrets. When client asks astrologer for information, there is usually a more or less overt wish for not only information, but also action. The desired response to "When will I marry?" is not a prediction, but a wave of the wand and the appearance of an Officer and a Gentleman out of a cloud of smoke; the desired response to "When will I get a better job?" is "Blodgett and Sons, start 9 o'clock on Monday." Astrology's refusal to even attempt to perform these feats has much to do with the public's rejection of astrology: "You can't make me rich; you can't match me with Julia Roberts; so I'm not going to believe in you."

There are those astrologers who promise magic. Advertisements entice the gullible with claims that "I will bring your loved one back to you," or "You cannot find your soul-mate without my help." Exactly why we should want to bind our loved ones with the unreliable ties of magic, when we would not dream of physically locking them up in our home is hard to understand; but these charlatans presumably find a clientele. In non-Western cultures, astrolog-ical magic is still commonplace: the astrologer will sell talismans or gems, often, but by no means exclusively, in cases of illness.

Much of the problem with our understanding of this is our society's prevalent attitude to magic: we have not taken it totally seriously since grown-ups stopped reading us fairy stories. However much some may claim to be involved with the 'occult' (which is now apparently something of a misnomer, as anyone who so wishes seems to be able to find it), we are indelibly stained by the thinking of our age. It is a commonplace that one man's science is another man's magic: to the man rubbing two sticks together, a cigarette-lighter is a magical device; but this is not quite true. Magic is not only science of which the speaker is ignorant, but also science of which the speaker does not approve, usually because its basis does not accord with his view of the world. In the arrogance typical of our Age of Enlightenment, what I do not understand cannot possibly be true. This definition of magic as lack of knowledge is 'scientist-friendly', as it implies that these powers are strictly mechanical, and the remorseless march of science will sooner or later tame them and make them its own. It disposes of the problem of magic by reducing it to a question of semantics. The possible explanations for any magical display are just two-fold: it is either fraud, or a curable lack of knowledge in the beholder.

Our rational world claims to have swept magic quite away; but it is not, however, such a stranger to us as we may think. Our days are filled with what we believe are magical actions. I drink this brand of cola to make myself sexy; drive that marque of car to fill my life with glamour and adventure. If I think of my true love and burn a candle in front of a statue of Venus, I am performing an overtly magical action; if I present my true love with a bunch of roses (ruled by Venus) or a box of chocolates (ruled by Venus) my action is none the less magical for being apparently ordinary. I am plying her with Venus, as it were, seeking by sympathetic magic to raise her "Venus-levels" to a point where she finds me irresistible. The scientific sceptic may deny the efficacy of magic, but he still does not arrive on his girl-friend's front porch carrying a cabbage.

The object of my desire, meanwhile, has performed a long and painstaking ritual in front of her magic mirror, with an array of condiments each one of which contains the latest equivalent of eye of newt or toe of bat, guaranteed to effect some fortunate transformation in her appearance and thence her life. She has dabbed essence of skunk behind her ears and plies me with Mars by painting her lips bright red. The apparent distinction between what is magic and what is 'real' action is illusory. Burning the candle, for instance, has an effect in the world: changing the operator's own psychology, at the very least (quite apart from any planetary influence that may be invoked, just as my girl-friend's make-up ritual puts her in the right mood for the evening; but unless we stretch scepticism to the point of wilful obtuseness, we cannot deny a magical content in what has been done).

There are *three broad strands to astrological magic. We may elect the appropriate moment* to perform a ritual, which although itself magical has no overt astrological content. *We may regard planetary influence as a substance* which may, given the requisite knowledge, be tapped at will, or *we may regard the planetary influence as something which can be either dispensed or withheld* at the whim of the planets' 'presiding angels', who must therefore be cajoled into cooperating with our wishes. Let us consider these in turn. For reasons which will become clear, our consideration will be restricted to an overview of the subject, omitting all technical detail.

The best-known example of the first of these strands is the incident Geoffrey Chaucer relates in his *Franklin's Tale*. Chaucer had a sophisticated knowledge of astrology, and assumed the same in his audience: he expects, for instance, it to be able to distinguish the soundness of astrological knowledge in his characters by the way in which they employ technical terms in their speech; this is a feat beyond most members of modern astrological societies. In his *Chaucer's Universe*, J. D. North plausibly argues that the story the Franklin relates is structured on the horoscope for a particular moment, with the appropriate astrological features built into the tale.[1] North's reasoning seems strained, but only because he is tracing the path backwards, picking up clues in the text and seeking to match them to astronomical patterns of the time. For Chaucer, it would have been no more difficult to structure his poetry on an astrological chart than for Dante or Spenser to build theirs on complex numerological structures.

The plot revolves around an act of magic. The squire has fallen for the wife of his knight, who is currently away overseas. To put an end to the lad's tiresome importuning, the lady sets him an impossible task: to remove the fiersome black rocks that line the coast of Brittany, threatening her husband's safe return. His ardour preventing him from seeing that the woman's only concern is for her husband's safety, the squire sets out to perform this feat. He finds an astrologer who asks £1000 to create the illusion that the rocks have gone. This is duly done. It is unclear whether direct planetary invocation is involved in the magic, although the time of the operation is certainly elected: the squire has a long wait until the astrologer 'hath his tyme y-founde' for working the magic that renders the rocks invisible. Similarly, it is not clear whether the moment chosen was just a propitious one for magic, or whether there was an actual working with planetary influence to make the event. This is not so hair-splitting a distinction as it might seem; in the one case the prime factor would be the weakness of Saturn, the planet which rules 'grisly rokkes blake'; in the other it would be the strength of the planet ruling whatever were being used to obscure these rocks (the specific choice of horoscope in North's argument is based on the rather mundane premise that this was achieved by a unusually high tide). If we accept the idea that we may consider astrological factors in selecting a suitable time for any action, we might elect a time as well for the performance of magic as for the performance of anything else; the astrological involvement says nothing about the reality or otherwise of the magic, nor does the dubious nature of magical art reflect upon astrology. It is only when astrology and magic blend that these problems arise.

Our second form of magic treats planetary influence as a natural resource, which he who has sufficient knowledge may apply as he wishes. We need only look around at the consequences of natural resources being applied as people wish to see the dangers of treating planetary influence in the same way. Yet the same magic, technological or astrological, may be applied with wisdom for our benefit. Much as we may deplore many of the developments in the modern world, it is not the technology *per se*, but the way in which it is applied that is to be lamented; so also with this understanding of astrological magic.

The action in this type of magic is purely *mechanical;* it is in this instance that 'magic' becomes truly nothing but a pejorative term for technology that is not understood. It must be stressed, however, that the association with astrology is not in itself sufficient to redeem much that this practised under this guise

---

[1] Chapter 13; Oxford University Press, 1988

from being superstitious nonsense. Most astrologically-based medical treatment is 'magic' of this straightforward kind; the physician applies a herb of Venus or of Mars, which will have been picked and prepared at the appropriate planetary hour to ensure that it is brim-full of the correct planetary influence. To the scientist, the application of the herb, while probably deluded, is not magical; it is the idea that the timing of the herb's picking, preparation and application might be significant that changes what we are doing from mistaken technology to magic. Similarly with the distinction between grinding a healing gemstone to powder and swallowing it, or hanging it around one's neck: one is just odd, the other is magic. The next step, which takes us to the preparation of talismans, leaves comprehensible if eccentric technology behind and becomes purely magical.

A talisman would typically be – and in some cultures today still is – a small metal disc figured with a particular design and possibly set with particular gems. The design and, most importantly, the time at which the talisman was made would be chosen carefully to catch and channel the influence of a particular planet or planets. The idea is similar to that behind medical treatment: a weak planetary energy might need to be bolstered; one overly strong balanced by an opposing force. The talisman would work over a rather longer period than medical treatment, and its use would be by no means confined to questions of physical health. We hear of Elias Ashmole, the semi-official court astrologer to Charles II, labouring hard while Saturn was well-placed to produce the large number of leaden talismans his clients required to ward off rats. The young woman seeking marriage might wear a talisman of Venus kind; the young man off to war, one made under Mars to strengthen his courage. The great problem with the talisman is that it might actually work: our young woman finds herself with a tarnished reputation; our young bravo gets killed in a brawl long before he reaches the front. When using herbs to treat an illness, we can start with a mild preparation and strengthen it if required; but *pure planetary force is powerful and hard, if not impossible, to regulate.* These mechanical forms of magic can, just like the application of herbs, apparently be done by anyone with the requisite knowledge. Al-Kindi, the great theoretician of magical astrology, says they will work even if the operator doesn't believe in what he is doing.[2] Just as with the Sorcerer's Apprentice, *the ability to work the magic does not necessarily imply the wisdom to use it well.* As with electional astrology, we are protected largely by our own ignorance; given the power to achieve what we think we want, we would wreak our own destruction – as the consequences of modern science make quite clear. The possibility of mechanically manipulable planetary influence is the same invitation into a technological wonderland that the world of the Enlightenment has so gleefully embraced. As inevitably as the concentration on the ability to manipulate nature led to a totally secular society devoid of true values, so the ability to wield planetary influence at will would do the same.

[2] Al-Kindi, *On the Stellar Rays,* trans. Robert Zoller, p.48, Golden Hind Press, Berkeley Springs, 1993

As the tradition has always made clear, science, laudable as it is, must never be more than the handmaid to faith, no matter whether this science be celestial or mundane.

The invocation of planetary 'spirits' is when we start getting, from the modern perspective, seriously weird. Current attitudes can cope with the idea of mechanical planetary influence: they deny its existence, but it is at least feasible. The idea of an influence that can be turned on or off at the whim of some planetary spirit is quite out of bounds. Yet the invocation of these spirits has been practised throughout history and survives in some astrological societies, those of 'Theosophical descent', for instance, today. From the perspective of traditional astrology it is both blasphemous and pointless; in both Islam and Christianity it is strictly forbidden and regarded as heretical.

As we have seen, the seven traditional planets can be equated with the archangels, or with the 'gods' of the Greek pantheon; these are three different ways of describing the same phenomenon. A melange of these ideas gave the common picture of the planets in their spheres being pushed along by their several 'tutelary spirits'. So far, we are still just describing the same phenomenon in slightly different terms. But we are specifically forbidden from worshipping anything other than the Almighty, as is frequently regarded as necessary if we are to cajole these spirits into doing our will; while if we choose to ignore this injunction, or to pray but not worship, we shall find our prayers unanswered. We may pray to the Almighty; we do not pray to His angels. The angels exist only as a function of God; they are there to serve His purpose, not ours, informing us of His will, not Him of ours. They have no scope to serve our turn. In astrological terms, this is shown by the simple fact that no amount of pleading – and no amount of dressing in silly costumes – is going to shift Saturn around the zodiac to suit our desires. It will move as it will move; our duty is to get used to it. As S.H. Nasr has written, "The important part (of astrology) was the cosmological role of astrology, which tried to show the dominance of 'heaven' over 'earth', the unfolding of all creation from a unique principle, and the helplessness and passivity of earthly creatures before the angles, or divine agents, who are symbolised by the planets."[3] This role is not furthered by man's attempts to rise above his station.

Much though the prospect of possessing the magical powers of fairy tale may appeal to our baser nature, there is a catch with invocatory magic: while the purely mechanical forms will work for anyone, sources agree that the operator must raise himself to a suitable level of being before he is able to win the favours of the planetary spirits. By the time he has done this, he presumably no longer wishes to turn his neighbour into a frog: he will no longer be the whimsical human attempting to force his ephemeral desires upon the universe, but will be a channel for the forces of life to flow as they should. If he has reached this level of being, however, it is difficult to see why he should retain the need to invoke

[3] Seyyed Hossein Nasr, *An Introduction to Islamic Cosmological Doctrines*, pp. 81-2, rev. ed., Thames & Hudson, London, 1978

planetary spirits. The Scriptures make clear that man is superior to the angels, for it is they who have been required to worship him; attempts to invoke the planetary spirits imply a degrading belief in the reverse, while the desire to manipulate the forces of life declares an ego inflated on the grand scale, which would automatically preclude one from achieving the spiritual merit necessary to do so.

Invocatory magic must be utterly condemned on all levels, as it is by the monotheistic religions. Insofar as it is effective, most mechanical astrological magic falls into the category of 'technology that is not understood'; this does not, however, imply that it is safe to use. The scientists' mastering of technology that was not understood takes them increasingly often into places where they have no right to be, cloning and deforming at the shrine of their own cleverness. Astrology was revealed that we might know God, not that we might attempt to stand in His place; the most efficacious of talismans for our own good, and the only one able to discriminate what this is, is prayer.

17

A Guide to Practice

Whatever form of astrology it is that we practice – or rather, whatever form we practice within the tradition – the basic method is much the same. It consists in the application of a few simple principles over and over again. No matter how complex the situation, if applied often enough and carefully enough, these few principles will unravel it. The only difficult part lies in avoiding the temptation – a temptation based solely on presumption – to try to jump ahead and guess at the answer, a technique usually known as 'intuition'.

It is indeed one of the truths of astrology that it is simple. If it starts getting complicated, it is a sure sign that you have gone wrong somewhere. This does not mean that it is necessarily easy: weight-lifting is simple, but nonetheless requires great effort. In the game of cricket there is a phrase 'line and length', which might well be the motto of any aspiring astrologer. If the bowler is finding it impossible to get the batsman out, he will be reminded: "Line and length; line and length." That is: forget all the fancy stuff; just keep bowling the ball in the right direction for the right distance, and sooner or later you will inevitably get him out. So with astrology: the consistent application of the basic rules, resisting the temptation to try to be clever, will reveal all before you.

The astrological chart is like a rock-pool. The planets are the creatures within it going about their lives. All that is asked of the astrologer is that he observe what is happening. Sticking his head into the pool achieves nothing, as all the creatures scurry into hiding. In the same way, intruding his preconceptions into the chart achieves nothing, as truth vanishes before him even quicker than our creatures. The rules which we have discussed are the few simple facts necessary to understand the nature of the creatures which we observe. Given that knowledge, we have merely to sit and watch what they are up to, and all will become clear. Thus the techniques of the astrological tradition enable the practitioner to see beyond his own reflection, dissolving the illusions of preconception and partiality until the clear form of truth becomes visible in all its sharp and rigorous detail.

Before looking closely at the way in which the astrologer sets about his task, we must acquaint ourselves with some more of the tools that he has at his disposal.

We have seen how the planets' *essential* strength varies from place to place in the zodiac, as they enter the dignities of sign, exaltation, triplicity, term and face, or the debilities of peregrination, fall and detriment. The judgement of essential dignity depends on how the planet is placed in the zodiac: that is, how it is placed relative to the non-manifest sphere of the zodiacal signs (not the constellations bearing the same names). We must also consider the planets' *accidental* dignities and debilities, which are determined by how the planets stand relative to the various manifest spheres of the Earth, the other planets and the stars. These accidental dignities and debilities are highly significant. Consider a tiger: it has immense strength in itself (essential dignity), but if it has fallen into a tiger-pit (accidental debility) it still has the same strength, yet is virtually helpless. These accidental qualities are not part of the inherent nature of the thing in question, but affect it, whether for good or ill, at that time and that place.

There are many of these accidental factors; indeed, it would be true to say that everything in the chart has some accidental effect on everything else in it, but the great majority of these effects will be trivial. The table on page 166 shows the relative strengths of these factors, on a scale from 1-5 as weakest to strongest. It must be stressed that the strength of effect of all these points varies considerably, depending primarily on the degree of exactness of the factor in question (that is, for example, a planet exactly on the cusp of the tenth house is strengthened a lot more than one which is twenty degrees inside that house). This table, which is adapted from William Lilly,[1] who took it from the Arab authors, is intended only as a rule of thumb guide for the student and is meant to be used with a good dash of common-sense.

We start by considering the planet's house position, which is where it is relative to the Earth (i.e. where we would find it in the sky: "Up there" or "Over there"). Its position by sign has shown us its essential strength. The planets are all relatively fixed in their signs: Saturn's average stay in each one is over two years; even the Moon, by far the swiftest of the planets, takes two and a half days to move through each sign. Every planet, however, moves through all twelve houses every day. When in one of the angular houses (1st, 10th, 7th or 4th), planets can work easily: I may not be a good driver (weak essential dignity), but if I am on the tenth cusp, I am the one behind the wheel. In cadent houses, by contrast (3rd, 9th, 6th and 12th), the planets have the greatest difficulty in working – most especially in the sixth and twelfth houses. The remaining, succedent, houses fall between these extremes.

On top of this difference between angular, cadent and succedent houses, we have the system of *joys*. As we have seen, each planet joys in one of the houses, where it gains strength, and is weakened when in the house opposite the house of its joy. The joys are: Saturn, 12th house; Jupiter, 11th; Mars, 6th; Sun, 9th; Venus, 5th; Mercury, 1st; Moon, 3rd. As can be seen from this list, the joys can strengthen a planet even in a weak house – Saturn, for example, joys in the twelfth, the weakest of the cadent houses. This is not a contradiction, as these,

---

[1] Lilly, op. cit. p. 115

ESSENTIAL DIGNITIES	RATING	ESSENTIAL DEBILITIES	RATING
Own sign	5	Detriment	-5
Exaltation	4	Fall	-4
Own triplicity	3	Peregrine	-5
Own term	2		
Own face	1		
Mutual Reception[a]		Mutual Reception	
Sign : sign	5	Detriment : detriment	-5
Exaltation : exaltation	4	Fall : fall	-4
Triplicity : triplicity	3		
Term : term	2		
Face : face	1		
Mixed reception[b]	pro rata		

ACCIDENTAL DIGNITIES		ACCIDENTAL DEBILITIES	
In 10th or 1st house	5	In 12th house	-5
In 7th, 4th or 11th house	4	In 8th or 6th house	-4
In 2nd or 5th house	3		
In 9th house	2		
In 3rd house	1		
In the house of its joy	2	In opposite house to its joy	-1
Direct in motion (not ☉ or ☽ [c])	4	Retrograde	-5
Swift in motion	2	Slow in motion	-2
Increasing north latitude	2	Increasing south latitude	-2
Halb or Hayz	2/3		
Partill[d] ♂ ♃ or ♀	5	Partill ♂ ♄ or ♂	-5
Partill ♂ ☊	4	Partill ♂ ☋	-4
Partill △ ♃ or ♀	4	Partill ☍ ♄ or ♂	-4
Partill ✶ ♃ or ♀	3	Partill □ ♄ or ♂	-3
Beseiged by ♃ and ♀	5	Beseiged by ♄ and ♂	-5
Free from combustion or sunbeams [e]	5	Combust	-5
Cazimi	5	Under the sunbeams	-4
☽ Occidental (increasing in light)	2	☽ oriental (decreasing in light)	-2
♄ ♃ ♂ oriental	2	♄ ♃ ♂ occidental	-2
♀ ☿ occidental	2	♀ ☿ oriental	-2
♂ Regulus (29 Leo)	6	♂ Caput Algol (26 Taurus)	-5
♂ Spica (23 Libra)	5		

a The benefits from mutual reception vary widely with the strength of the planets concerned
b Such as sign: exaltation; triplicity: face etc.
c Because they are always direct.
d A *partill* aspect is formed between two planets in degrees of the same number in their respective signs.
e This does not, of course, apply to the Sun.

like all dignities and debilities, are matters of quality as well as of quantity; that is, they differ in kind as well as in strength. In practice, Saturn in the twelfth will often still have great difficulty acting, but, being in its joy, it does have some strength, almost as if it were a beleaguered garrison driven back to the last citadel from where its enemies will have extreme difficulty in dislodging it.

The speed and direction of the planet must be considered. The faster it is moving, relative to its average speed, the stronger it is; the slower, the weaker. All the planets except the Sun and Moon appear to turn round and travel backwards through the sky from time to time, an optical effect arising from the relative motion of the Earth and the planet in question – just as when your train pulls out of the station, the station appears to be travelling backwards. A planet travelling *retrograde* is weaker than when in *direct* (i.e. normal) *motion*. When about to change direction, planets gradually lose speed until they become stationary: these stationary points are times of great weakness. A planet in its *first station* (when it is turning round to go backwards) is traditionally likened to a man taking to his sick-bed: he feels dreadful and is going to get worse. A planet in its *second station* (turning back to forward motion) is likened to a man rising from his sick-bed for the first time: he still feels wobbly and vulnerable, probably worse than he did when still lying in bed, but from now on he knows that things will get better.

A planet is gaining strength if it is increasing in *north latitude* and weakening if increasing in *south latitude*. Almost always in astrology, we are concerned with measure of longitude: that is, movement across the sky. Giving a planet's position as so many degrees of Aries or Taurus is to define its position by longitude. Latitude is the up or down movement. North latitude, in the northern hemisphere where astrology was born and has resided through most of its history, lifts the planet higher in the sky and so makes it more clearly visible.

The Arab authors in particular put great significance on *hayz* and *halb*. A planet is in its halb if it is in its 'correct' position relative to the horizon: that is, if it is a diurnal planet (Saturn, Jupiter or the Sun) it should be above the horizon by day and below it by night; *vice versa* if it is a nocturnal planet (Mars, Venus or the Moon). Hayz is similar but more demanding: a masculine, diurnal planet (Saturn, Jupiter or the Sun) should be in a masculine sign and also in its halb; a feminine, nocturnal planet (Venus or the Moon) should be in a feminine sign and in its halb. Mars is masculine and nocturnal, so is in its hayz if it is in a masculine sign and above the Earth by night or below it by day. Mercury is diurnal when it rises before the Sun, nocturnal when it sets behind the Sun. The masculine signs are: Aries, Gemini, Leo, Libra, Sagittarius and Aquarius; the others are feminine.[2] A planet in its hayz or, to a lesser extent its halb, has a certain power of command and ability to shrug off dangers.

The other accidental dignities relate to a planet's position relative to other

[2] The definition of hayz and halb is commonly misquoted. See Abu'l-Rayhan Muhammad Ibn Ahmad Al-Biruni, *The Book of Instruction in the Elements of the Art of Astrology*, p. 308; trans. R. Ramsey Wright, Luzac, London, 1934; reprinted Ascella, Nottingham, n.d.

planets and individual stars. Close contact, especially by conjunction, sextile or trine, with the two benefics, Jupiter and Venus, is helpful. Close contact with Mars or Saturn, on the other hand, is a hindrance, especially by conjunction, square or opposition. If we are considering a man about to have a fight, a fortunate contact from Jupiter might show that his big brother is there to back him up; if there is a difficult contact from Saturn, however, he might be ill or overwhelmed by fear. The Moon's North Node (the point where it crosses the ecliptic heading north) acts much like Jupiter; its South Node (where it crosses the ecliptic heading south), much like Saturn: planets falling on these points are strengthened or weakened accordingly. The Nodes affect planets only by conjunction.

A planet can be *besieged* either harmfully or beneficially. It is besieged beneficially when it is between the two benefics, Venus and Jupiter. The closer together the three planets are, the stronger the effect; whichever way the planet turns, something good is bound to happen to it. Getting caught between Saturn and Mars is just the reverse – this is the astrological version of 'a rock and a hard place'. One of the benefics casting its aspect to a planet besieged by the two malefics, however, can alleviate the situation: as if the planet is besieged in his castle, but there is plenty of food and water. If a planet is not bodily placed between the two besieging planets, but casts its aspect between them, it is *besieged by the rays*. This is similar to besiegement proper, but rather more mild.

The Sun confers both great strength and great debility. Being too close to the Sun is most unfortunate: within eight and a half degrees of the Sun, if within the same sign of the zodiac, a planet is said to be *combust*. There is no greater affliction than this: it is as if all its power is burnt up and destroyed. Within seventeen and a half degrees, it is *under the sunbeams*. This too is unfortunate, but much less so than combustion. A planet within seventeen and a half minutes of arc of the Sun, however, is immensely strong: it is said to be *cazimi*, or *in the heart of the Sun*. This is likened to a man raised up to sit beside the king: it has great power to act.

The Moon's strength varies according to its position relative to the Sun. At New Moon, when it has no light at all, it has no power. As it moves away from the Sun, it gradually *increases in light*, and thence in strength. At full, however, when it has its maximum amount of light, it is just as weak as at new. It is totally filled with the Sun's light and has no strength of its own. After full, the Moon at first picks up strength again, but gradually loses it as it decreases in light.

When the Moon is increasing in light, it is also *occidental;* when decreasing, it is *oriental*. These terms describe any planet's position relative to the Sun. Any planet that would be in the sky at dawn is said to be oriental, as it rises before the Sun. Any planet under the Earth at dawn is occidental. Mars, Jupiter and Saturn are strengthened by being oriental and weakened by being occidental; with Venus, Mercury and the Moon it is the other way round. To find out which is which in any particular chart, just mentally revolve all the planets until the Sun is on the Ascendant (its position at dawn). Any planet above the Earth is then oriental, or below it occidental.

Some of the *fixed stars* can greatly influence judgement. As staring into the night sky shows, there are any number of stars. Those of particular astrological significance are the brightest and those closest to the ecliptic. They are brought into play only by conjunction, whether by a planet, house cusp or Arabian Part. The stars become more important the higher in our astrological hierarchy we climb. Most of the time, most stars will play little part in horaries. They become influential in natal charts at the major events of the life or when examining the spiritual nature. In mundane astrology, they come into their own.

The three stars whose powers most often extend downwards into even horary charts are *Regulus*, the 'Heart of the Lion', the brightest star in Leo (currently at 29.51 Leo[3]); *Spica*, the 'Virgin's Spike', the brightest star in the constellation of Virgo (now at 23.51 Libra); and *Caput Algol*, 'Medusa's Head', an unremarkable-looking star in Perseus (26.11 Taurus). Regulus is strongly fortunate for action in the world, although such action may eventually come to a sticky end. Spica is not so goal-oriented, but it too is strongly fortunate, with a powerful protective influence. Algol is thoroughly malefic, traditionally associated with losing one's head, either literally or metaphorically. Astronomically, it is a variable star; it is never very bright, but dims almost to invisibility. This is the key to its malign nature, for it is like a permanent eclipse.

Regulus and Spica are two of the *Royal Stars*, which, as the name suggests, lead to the throne. The others are *Aldebaran*, the 'Eye of the Bull', in the constellation of Taurus (9.48 Gemini); *Pollux*, one of the 'Heavenly Twins' (23.15 Cancer; also known as *Hercules*); *Lucida Lancis*, or the *South Scale*, in Libra (15.06 Scorpio); and *Antares*, the 'Heart of the Scorpion' (9.47 Sagittarius). In effect, they are much like the trumps in a game of cards: the first son of the king may have X or Y in his birth-chart, but if the second son has a prominent Royal Star, he wins. King Charles I gives an example: with Regulus on his Ascendant, he was born to reign; the death of his elder brother brought him unexpectedly to the throne – yet Regulus had its customary unfortunate end. This does not, of course, mean, gentle reader, that the Royal Star on your Ascendant will make you President or Prime Minister: had Charles been the second son of a tailor, he would have inherited the shop.

Weighing up each planet's dignities and debilities, essential and accidental, will tell us how strong or weak it is, and enable us to learn much about what it is that is making it strong or weak. The prime significance of the sign in which each planet falls is to enable us to determine its essential dignity. Often, we will not concern ourselves with the particular nature of the sign at all; the modern

---

[3] Despite being 'fixed' the stars do move slightly, at a rate of approximately one degree every 72 years, or 50 per year – a negligible amount over the life of a man, but of great importance over the life of a nation. Positions given are for the year 2000. Note that Spica, although being in the constellation of Virgo, falls into the part of the zodiac known as Libra, an example of the distinction between constellations and zodiacal signs – an example repeated by most of the other stars mentioned here.

over-emphasis on the zodiacal signs has much to do with selling newspapers and little to do with astrology. The signs do not have the lovable rounded personalities which popular magazines are wont to attribute to them. They do, however, all fall into various groups, which share certain characteristics. These can be important in judgement.

There is a basic division into *male and female:* Aries and every alternate sign (Gemini, Leo, Libra, Sagittarius and Aquarius) are male; Taurus and every alternate sign (Cancer, Virgo, Scorpio, Capricorn and Pisces) are female. If we wish to determine the gender of an unborn child, or to know whether the thief was a man or a woman, for instance, we simply add up the indications of the relevant planets: lots of masculine planets in masculine signs, we have a boy; feminine planets in feminine signs, a girl.

The division into the *elemental triplicities* of fire (hot and dry), air (hot and moist), earth (cold and dry), and water (cold and moist) gives simple judgement on many issues. If on checking the weather I find a hot dry planet in a hot dry sign, I draw the obvious conclusion. If looking for a lost object, its significator in an earth sign will tell me it is on or under the ground; in an air sign, it is high up, or somewhere associated with intellectual pursuits; a fire sign shows somewhere hot; a water sign somewhere wet, or associated with emotions or comfort. So if the significator of the object were in the fifth house, the object might be in a place of recreation. If the significator were also in an air sign, it might be in a cinema or library; in fire, a restaurant; in water, a pub or swimming-pool; in earth, a park or garden.

The division into *cardinal* (Aries, Cancer, Libra, Capricorn), *fixed* (Taurus, Leo, Scorpio, Aquarius) and *mutable* (Gemini, Virgo, Sagittarius, Pisces) is an important indicator of timing. A fixed illness will drag on for ages; a cardinal one will be short and sharp; a mutable one will come and go. If electing a chart for something that is to last – building a house, perhaps – we would have fixed signs in the important places; for something that was to be over quickly, like an operation, we would choose cardinal signs. The mutable signs are also *double-bodied,* showing duality. The ruler of the tenth house of career in a double-bodied sign would be one indicator of someone who free-lances (more than one boss) or has more than one job.

Similarly, these signs show the amount of resolution someone possesses. If an enemy were to take me to court and I cast a horary about this, I would be worried if I found both his house cusp and his significator in fixed signs, for I would know that he was determined to pursue the case till the end and would not be swayed from his course. Much more reassuring to find both cusp and significator in cardinal signs, proclaiming him "unstable, and of no resolution... a wavering, unconstant man".[4] The mutable signs, as usual, would show a medium between the two. Of course, if the significator were at the very end of a fixed sign, it would have to be judged accordingly. This is typical of horary

[4] Lilly, op. cit. p. 89

charts where someone is about to lose a job they have held for many years: they have reached the end of a stable (fixed) situation.

Some of the signs (the water signs: Cancer, Scorpio and Pisces) are *fertile;* some (Gemini, Leo, Virgo) are *barren.* The others are in-between. This has obvious connotations, but not only with child-birth: if I want my investments to grow, I should be pleased to find their significator in a fertile sign. It is notable that the barren signs are those of human image, while the in-between signs are mostly animals, as humans tend to produce fewer offspring than animals, who themselves produce far fewer than scorpions, crabs or fish.

The signs with animal images (Aries, Taurus, Leo, Sagittarius and Capricorn) are *bestial;* those of human form (Gemini, Virgo, Aquarius – and also Libra, as the scales are a man-made object) are *humane.* This is important for telling which branch of creation will suffer from, for instance, the effects of an eclipse or a comet. More immediately, if I am choosing the moment to ask my large and unpleasant neighbour to mend his ways, a humane sign rising will increase the likelihood of my escaping without a punch on the nose. Of the bestial signs, Leo and the latter part of Sagittarius are also *feral,* so introducing the idea of unruliness into appropriate charts. Leo, Scorpio and Capricorn are *dark and anxious,* while "there is a suspicion of trouble in Virgo and Libra".[5] We might note how the modern picture of Libra as the first of the 'impeccably behaved' signs seems to have quite forgotten this, as was clearly demonstrated in our example reading of Hitler's birth-chart.

There are many more such divisions, but the last of those which have common practical importance concerns the degree of voice the signs possess. The water signs are all *mute;* Gemini, Virgo and Libra *loud-voiced,* of which Gemini is *capable of speech.* This distinction is relevant in any matter of communication. When should I make that phone-call? Not when mute signs dominate the chart. Am I born to be a singer? With my significators of vocation in voiced signs, quite possibly.

These various meanings underline the significance of the exact image pertaining to each of the signs, reminding us that this image is not a random doodle around a collection of stars, but is a mnemonic of powerful symbolic value showing, for those who have eyes to see, the nature of that sign, which is the essential nature of one twelfth of creation, the essential nature of one of the three modes of creation working in one of the four elements. These images are carefully and precisely formed: fanciful 'artistic' interpretations of them add nothing, but are merely a symptom of the growing inability to understand imagery. These pictures do indeed tell more than a thousand words, as they embody – all at once, not consequentially – a mass of meanings which is to any articulated statement what a sphere is to a straight line. The attempt to spin out these meanings into words does, indeed, exactly mirror the spinning out of the potential indicated by the signs that is seen in the movements of the planets;

[5] Al-Biruni, op. cit. p. 214

but by the very nature of the task this rendering articulate, whether in microcosm or macrocosm, must always fall far short of realising even a fraction of this potential. The images of the signs, then, demand contemplation, not articulation; but contemplation only of what is in these images, so perfectly fitted to that which they represent, not of the sentimental baggage that we carry with us: contemplation of what is there, not of ourselves.

It is a rare chart on which at least one of the *Arabian Parts* cannot shed some light. The Arabian Parts, so called because they were much used by the Arab astrologers, are particular points in the chart each of which tells us about one particular subject. We arrive at these points by means of a simple calculation. For instance, if a horary chart is set for the question, "Is my marriage over?" we would cast the Arabian Part of Marriage and study its condition.

Parts exist for any number of subjects: Al-Biruni, writing in the Eleventh Century, says: "It is impossible to enumerate the lots (i.e. Parts) which have been invented... they increase in number every day."[6] They range from those dealing with obviously important matters, such as the Parts of Victory, Death, or Marriage, to those that are at first puzzling, such as the Parts of Apricots and of Cucumbers. But if you were the farmer wondering when it would be best to take his apricot crop to market, or the Royal Astrologer casting the Aries Ingress chart to examine the nation's fortunes over the coming year, when the size of the cucumber harvest might be of some significance, the importance of even these recondite Parts would become clear.

The position of each Part is determined by a formula which adds the distance between two places in the chart – usually the positions of two of the planets – to a third place, which is usually the Ascendant. The best-known of the Parts, for instance, the Part of Fortune, takes the distance from the Sun to the Moon and then adds this distance to the Ascendant (so Asc + ☽ – ☉). Once the Part has been calculated, we look to see what is happening to it (it is a principle that Parts do not do; they are done to). If our Part of Cucumbers falls conjunct Jupiter, we are suitably delighted; if conjunct Saturn, we are grateful that we chose to diversify this year. Just as with a planet, we will examine its strength – accidental only – and receptions. Most importantly, we will also look to its *dispositor*, the planet that rules the sign in which it falls. The dispositor of the Part represents that thing in the chart: so if the Part of Marriage falls in Aries, its dispositor is Mars, so Mars signifies the marriage. If Mars is strong, in a fixed sign, and with both the spouses' planets showing by reception a strong interest in it, all well and good. If Mars is badly placed and the spouses' planets have no interest in it, there is cause for concern. Similarly with the dispositor of the Part of Cucumbers: if that planet is making a good connection between me and the other people's money, I know it is time to sell.

The greatest value of the Arabian Parts, however, is found when we seek to

---

[6] Al-Biruni, op. cit. p. 282. Al-Biruni gives a list of the most useful Parts with their formulae. Modern lists of Arabian Parts incorporating Uranus, Neptune and Pluto lack all foundation and are to be disregarded.

peer beneath the superficial reality of the material in order to examine the spiritual reality within. The key Parts are geared to exactly this end, their very existence being evidence of an awe-inspiring knowledge of, and clarity about, spiritual states – a knowledge utterly different from anything contained in the so-called 'esoteric' astrology of the moderns.

The Part of Fortune, based on the Moon, shows the soul; its reverse formula,[7] the Part of Spirit, shows the Spirit (that is, Asc+☉-☽. This is also called the Part of the Sun, or the Part of the Future, the latter presumably because one's final end depends, precisely, on the Spirit). The Part of Faith (Asc+☊-☽) shows the correct or incorrect orientation of the mind. The Ascendant + Part of Spirit – Part of Fortune gives the Part of Love, Friendship and Affection. Its reverse formula, Ascendant + Part of Fortune – Part of Spirit, gives the Part of Despair, Fraud and Penury. Ascendant + Part of Fortune – Mars shows courage or greatness of soul (Part of Valour, Courage). Ascendant + Jupiter – Part of Spirit shows victory and aid from Above (Part of Victory and Aid). Ascendant + Saturn – Part of Fortune shows imprisonment and escape, the wisdom that is born of experience (Part of Captivity and Escape). These are the traditional seven pillars of the spiritual assessment by Arabian Parts, though many other Parts provide important additional information.[8]

Adding the Arabian Parts to the planets completes the cast of players in our drama. We now have all our participants assembled, and have evaluated their strengths by assessing their dignities and their inclinations by assessing the receptions between them. All that remains is to see how these planets and Parts relate to each other by aspect. Aspects are what draw the planets together, allowing them to interact. On many occasions, often but by no means exclusively in horary charts, we shall be looking for specific actions: these will be shown in the chart by aspects reaching exactitude or *perfection*. In many charts, however, we shall be more concerned with describing situations; in these cases, aspects show influence of one thing on another, whether these aspects are exact or not. The closer the aspect, the stronger the influence. An example clarifies the difference in treatment: if I ask a horary question "Did my dog steal the sausages?" and find the planet that signifies my dog just separating from aspect with the planet that shows the sausages, I would find her guilty, as she and the sausages have been in contact in the recent past (a separating aspect showing past action). If, however, I were thinking "What is this dog like? Should I buy her?" this close aspect would help describe her nature, according to the planet concerned.

An important addition to our repertoire of aspects is the *antiscion,* which we saw in action in Hitler's birth-chart. The antiscion of a planet or Arabian Part is

---

[7] Many astrologers, including Bonatus, reversed these two formulae in night-time charts, such that each became the other; but both the reasoning behind this reversal and its practical application are unconvincing.

[8] Of these, perhaps the most important is the Part of Death, which is given as Asc+8th cusp-Moon and Asc+Saturn-Moon, either (or both) of which can be used.

found by reflecting its position in an imaginary mirror stretched between the two solstice points, 0 degrees of Cancer and 0 degrees of Capricorn. For example: a planet that is placed 25 degrees on one side of the mirror (at 25 Cancer or Capricorn) will have its reflection at 25 degrees on the other side of the mirror (so 5 Gemini or Sagittarius). As any contact with an antiscion must be close – nothing much more than a degree away will concern us – it takes, given a little practice, just moments to glance around a chart to see if the antiscia of any relevant points are doing anything of note. What we are looking for is conjunction or opposition to another important point; other aspects to antiscia are worth noting, but are of only secondary significance. An antiscion is, literally, a shadow; so, as might be suspected, contact with the antiscion of a planet typically carries a sense of the covert, revealing to us hidden motives and hidden actions: if boy meeting girl is shown by an ordinary aspect they might marry; if by an aspect involving an antiscion, they would be more likely to have a secret affair.

have now assembled a tool-box which will prove sufficient for any astrological eventuality. Further elaboration of technique is not necessary; all that is necessary is the application of a large amount of common-sense in all our work – or, in the traditional phrase, combining 'discretion with art'. Celestial science as it may be, keeping one's feet firmly on the ground at all times is essential for correct practice.

Whatever form of chart we are judging, practice can be described in a few basic principles. The planets show the nature of the force in question. The signs qualify that force, as an adjective qualifies a noun. The houses locate that force, showing where it is operating. The aspects connect that force with an object, as verbs connect nouns.

The essential nature of the planets is:

> Saturn, the principle of contraction
> Jupiter, the principle of expansion
> Mars, the principle of energy
> The Sun, the principle of power
> Venus, the principle of love
> Mercury, the principle of articulation
> The Moon, the principle of generation.

In practice, we will almost always identify the planets more by the houses with which they are connected than their essential nature, but this nature is always there and always of some significance. That is, when looking at, say, Mars in a chart, we will be more concerned with the fact that it happens to rule the sixth house and so signifies a tradesman (for instance) than with its being the principle of energy. But there will be a qualitative difference between the tradesman as signified by Mars and the tradesman as signified by Venus or Saturn. This difference may or may not be relevant in practical terms to our particular enquiry. The location of the particular force is shown by the house or houses which that planet rules and the house in which it happens to fall. Mars rules the sixth house, so it shows the tradesman; Mars is in the tenth house (mother) from the sixth, so the tradesman has gone to visit his mother. From there it casts an opposition (unfortunate) to the planet that rules the fourth house (my home). So my home is suffering because the tradesman has gone to visit his mum.

The signs act as adjectives, qualifying the nature of the planets. This is primarily by giving or denying them strength, but also by certain characteristics of their own. Mars is in Scorpio, and so is very strong (essential dignity): the tradesman controls the situation. Scorpio is a mute sign, so he has not told me that he has taken the day off to go visiting. The assessment of strength is elaborated by considering the accidental dignities.

Apart from giving or denying strength when the planet falls in its own dignities or debilities, the signs also indicate the interests of the planet by the other dignities in which it falls. Mars is in Scorpio, its own sign and triplicity, so the tradesman's over-riding concern is with himself. If it is at 20 degrees of Scorpio, it is also in the terms and face of Venus, so he is also concerned with whatever Venus signifies in this chart. He is also in the detriment of Venus, so he does not like Venus. We see Venus separating (past action) from a square (difficult) to Mars; Venus rules the seventh house (partners) from the sixth (tradesman): so we see that he has had a row with his wife and gone to see Mum to grumble about her.

Concerned, we might then cast the Arabian Part of Marriage for the tradesman, adding the degree of his first cusp (the sixth cusp of the chart) to the degree of his seventh cusp and subtracting the degree of Venus. This falls in Scorpio. Its dispositor, Mars, we have already found in Scorpio. Both Part and dispositor in a fixed sign is a strong indication that the marriage will last. The Part is in the sign and triplicity of Mars, so the marriage is dominated by the husband. It is in the detriment of Venus, so we see it is detrimental to his wife.

Sometimes, however, we use a manifestation of the essential principle of the planet by taking it in one of its *natural rulerships*. We might turn to Mars, not because it rules a particular house in the chart, but because we are enquiring about a soldier, or the army, or surgery, or iron, or any of its myriad rulerships.

By considering house rulership and natural rulership we will, in any enquiry in any branch of astrology, usually turn up three or four planets that are 'in play' and three or four with which we are not, at the moment, concerned. The situation is much as it is in a theatre: we have a group of characters in heated conversation by the footlights, while the others occupy themselves upstage until it is their turn to speak. As we proceed with our investigation of the chart, we will often find some of these other characters being drawn into the action.

Whatever the subject, we shall almost always be concerned with the ruler of first house. In a horary, this represents the querent; in a nativity it shows the native himself; in a mundane chart it is the nation and the prevailing state of affairs. The other houses concerned will vary according to the nature of our enquiry. If, for example, the querent in a horary asks "Is my brother trying to cheat me?" we would look to the third, the house of brothers, with its ruler and Mars, which is the natural ruler of brothers. So also in a natal chart if we wish to find out about the state of the native's brothers and how he relates to them. In a mundane chart, we might be concerned about the pernicious influence of the press upon the nation, so we would investigate by again turning to the third house and its ruler, this time in company with Mercury, the natural ruler of journalists.

Having identified the relevant planets, we judge them according to the three guiding principles:

Dignity shows power to act
Reception shows inclination to act
Aspect shows occasion to act.

No matter what branch of astrology we are practising, whether it concern the most trivial horary question or the most momentous of mundane events, the study of these three factors will bring us, if God wills, to the correct conclusion. Whether our chart be horary, natal, electional or mundane, the approach is essentially the same, the only difference being a certain shift in focus depending on what it is that we are investigating within the chart. We judge any chart by studying these three principles. If we find that this brings us to a dead-end, the answer is simple: we must study them some more. They will invariably yield results. The following examples of a horary and a nativity show how this is done at different levels of astrological enquiry.

The Horary

The question was a complex one: "Mr X, an agent, claims he can get my business's product onto the national TV shopping channel. Can he do this, will it be worth doing it, and can I trust him not to cut me out of the deal by going direct to the manufacturers of the product?"[9]

The querent, as ever, is shown by the planet ruling the first house: Saturn. *How is Saturn?* Essentially, it is weak: it has no dignity of its own, and so is peregrine. This weakness reflects the querent's inability to achieve anything in this situation by his own efforts. He does have a certain amount of accidental dignity, however: being within five degrees of the fourth cusp puts him on the angle; Saturn is direct in motion; it is moving swiftly and is oriental of the Sun (turn the planets to put the Sun on the Ascendant, and you will see Saturn above the horizon). This accidental strength suggests that he might be in the right place to achieve something. So far, so good.

We now need to locate Mr X. He is an agent: that is, someone with whom our querent can work; but he is not a boss (tenth house), nor is he our querent's employee (sixth). He is someone on more or less the same level, with whom the

---

[9] June 15th 1999, 10.21 pm BST, London.

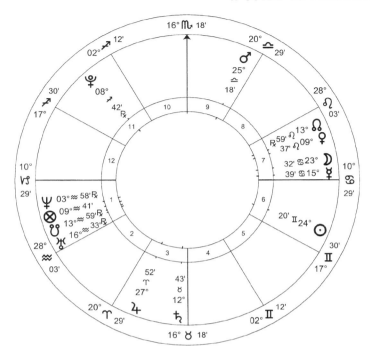

Chart 17: Example of Method

querent may enter a mutually beneficial relationship: so he is shown by the seventh house and its ruler, the Moon. The Moon is usually co-significator of the querent, but if it rules one of the other houses involved, that house has first claim to its services.

How is the Moon? Very strong indeed. It has lots of essential dignity, as it is in its own sign and face. It has accidental dignity, being in an angular house, swift in motion and increasing in light. This accidental dignity is limited by its applying square to Mars. With so much strength, the agent has a lot of power to act: this suggests that he can do what he claims he can do by putting the product on TV. The Moon's immediate aspects confirm this: it is separating from conjunction with Mercury and applying to square Mars. Mercury is the natural ruler of all forms of communication, including television. It is in the Moon's sign and house, showing that (in the context of this question) television is under the control of the agent. Mars rules the querent's tenth house, and so signifies his business. The Moon's movement, then, connects television to the business.

We have seen that the agent can live up to his promises. *What is he interested in?* We tell this from the receptions. The Moon is in its own sign, showing that his prime concern is with himself – much what we would expect. The Moon is in its own house, so he is unlikely to put himself out much on our querent's behalf. The Moon is in the exaltation of Jupiter: that is, the agent exalts whatever Jupiter represents in this chart. Jupiter rules the eleventh house, which is the second from the tenth: the business's money. The agent is keen on the business's money – again, this is no surprise. That the reception in question is an exaltation, however, suggests that he may be over-valuing this money. He thinks he can get more out of the deal than he actually will.

But can he be trusted? That his planet, the Moon, is so strong is a clear indicator that he can: all the planets behave themselves better the stronger they are. Even the malefics, Mars and Saturn, show their best sides when essentially strong, as the benefics, Jupiter and Venus, can display a corrupted virtue when they are weak. The Moon is strong, and there are no malefics in the seventh house, so we have no reason to suspect him of untoward behaviour. He is out for himself; but he would be an unusual agent if he were not.

So what is the bottom line? We have seen that the agent can put the product on TV. But will this be worthwhile? In any question of profit we must look to the money that we hope to make. This will be shown by the second house (money) from one of the other houses, depending on whose money it is that we want. Here, we want the money of the viewing public, a collection of undetermined 'others'; so we locate this public in the seventh house ('other people' in general) and so the eighth shows its money. Yes, it also shows the agent's money (second from the seventh, the house of the agent); but we are not concerned with that. A house can mean any number of things: what matters to us is what it means *in this context.*

The Sun rules the eighth house, and is applying immediately to make a trine aspect to Mars. Mars is the querent's business; the Sun is the other people's money: they are coming together. All things being equal, this is just what we want to see – but all things here are not at all equal. The money comes easily enough (trine aspect shows things happening smoothly): once the product is on TV, all our querent has to do is sit back and wait for the phone to ring. But the Sun is dreadfully weak. It has essential dignity only by face and is seriously debilitated accidentally by being in the sixth house. If the Sun were strong, it would show lots of money coming to the business; here, there will be little. The dignity by face shows that there will be some, but not enough to justify the operation. This is confirmed by Mars (the business) and Jupiter (the business's money) applying to opposition. If Mars and Jupiter represented two people coming together by opposition, we would expect them to argue or divorce: we might foresee a similar falling out between the business and its bank balance.

Our judgement is clear: the agent can do exactly what he says he can do; but he cannot drag customers to the querent's door. The financial return will be limited – too much so to justify the outlay and effort.

The Nativity
Let us take the same chart to demonstrate natal method. An exhaustive natal reading, if there can be such a thing, would take as long as the life itself, just

as even a thousand-page biography will leave many stones unturned. When the chart is read, however, the astrologer will usually be pointed towards particular areas of interest: "Tell me about myself," is a less productive enquiry than "Am I really suited to accountancy and why do all my girl-friends desert me?" We may liken the investigation to a trip to the doctor's: his first question is usually "Where does it hurt?" This narrows his investigation to a manageable scope.

As we saw in our consideration of Hitler's chart, we begin by drawing in the broad outlines. This basic assessment of, as it were, the material from which the person is cut, may not provide the titillating details that he might wish to hear, but will give us the bulk of our information about him. It is like the bottom level of a pyramid, of which the details are the peak; the details make sense only when seen in the context of the basic outline. We begin, then, by assessing the native's temperament.

For this, we must consider:

    1 the first house and its ruler
    2 the Sun and Moon
    3 the *Lord of the Geniture*, which is the strongest planet in the chart.[10]

At this stage, we are concerned only with the extent to which these places are hot, cold, moist and dry.

1. The Ascendant is in Capricorn, a cold, dry sign. It is ruled by Saturn, a cold, dry planet falling in a cold, dry sign (Taurus). The Ascendant is aspected by Saturn itself, which increases its coldness and dryness, and by Mercury. Mercury is occidental, increasing its dryness; but this is balanced by being in a moist sign (Cancer). It is a little cold, increased by being in a cold sign, so this aspect cools the Ascendant further. As the aspect to Mercury is five degrees from perfection, the effect will be slight.

Saturn is moistened by being oriental. It too is aspected by Mercury, cooling it further, and also by Venus. Venus is cold and moist, these qualities both moderated by falling in a hot, dry sign (Leo). It gains a little moisture by being occidental. So these aspects, neither of which are close, make Saturn colder still and slightly less dry. If there were any of the seven traditional planets in the first house, we would bring them into our judgement, but there is not. So far, the temperament is strongly cold and dry.

2. The Sun is by nature hot and dry, but as this is a 'given' in anybody's chart, we need to look at other factors to determine the Sun's influence. These factors are the sign in which the Sun falls and the season. Here, it is in Gemini, a hot, moist sign. Both heat and moisture are increased as Gemini is one of the Spring

---

[10] Strongest, that is, by essential *and* accidental dignity, in contrast to the *almuten* of the chart, which is the planet with most essential dignities (*almuten*, from the Arabic *al-mateen*, meaning 'the inherently strong', and thus 'the tough'). Obviously enough, these are, however, often the same planet. Neither of these is to be confused with the *hyleg*, which indicates the 'vital force' of the person, which, as we might expect, need not be strong at all.

signs (Aries, Taurus and Gemini), all of which have this effect on the Sun apart from that of their individual natures.

The Sun is aspected quite closely by Mars, and with more separation by Jupiter. Mars is hot and dry by nature, its dryness emphasised and heat moderated by being occidental. It is in Libra, a hot, moist sign. Overall, Mars increases the Sun's heat and makes it slightly drier. Jupiter oriental is hot and moist, in a hot, dry sign. Again, it increases the Sun's heat and roughly balances out the drying power of Mars. So the Sun has added a good deal of heat to the mixture and made it moister.

The Moon is cold and moist by nature, but again we need to find distinctive qualities for its effect in the individual chart. Here, it is in Cancer, a cold, moist sign. It is between New and First Quarter, increasing its heat and moisture. It too is aspected by Mars, making it hotter and slightly drier. The aspect to Jupiter is of minor significance, but can be taken into account as it is an applying aspect and Jupiter has strong dignity in the Moon's sign: hotter and a little moister. The Moon, then, adds heat and moisture to the temperament. Between them, the lights have considerably moderated the cold, dry nature shown by the Ascendant and its ruler.

3. Finally, the Lord of the Geniture. There is only one feasible candidate in this chart: it has to be the Moon, the only planet with any major dignity. So we can count in again the Moon's effect as above.

Putting this all together, cold and dry wins by a short head, giving a predominantly melancholic (in the technical sense of the word) nature. If the heat and moisture had been coming from the same sources as the cold and dryness, they could have balanced each other out. Here, one set of testimonies gives us one nature, another another; so we see two contrasting strands in the nature: melancholic-sanguine. With Saturn, the bringer of much of the coldness and dryness, right at the bottom of the chart, and the lights, purveyors of heat and moisture, clustered around the seventh cusp, we can judge that the sanguine side of the nature comes out in company, while left to his own devices the native sinks into a natural melancholy.

The sanguine nature is, in modern terms, 'airy': pleasant, affable, existing predominantly on a mental level (which is not necessarily the same as being intelligent). The melancholic nature is 'earthy': stolid, cautious, prudent, fearful, 'down to earth'. This is the background against which all else that we find must be read.

The *manner* is the outward polish put over the temperament, the veil through which the temperament speaks. To determine the manner, we look first to any planet in the Ascending sign. Here, there is none. Our next possibility is whatever planet is connected with the Moon or Mercury. This gives us no satisfactory outcome either: they are connected with each other, but the dominant partner (because it is the dispositor of both) is the Moon, and neither Sun nor Moon can act as indicator of manner: their role is as the power-source to the chart, rather than to show how that power is used. We turn then to the Lord of the Ascendant, Saturn. Saturn is aspected by its own dispositor (Venus) and close to an angle, so it is quite influential enough to serve our purpose here.

Now we must begin to consider the nature of the planets. Saturn is the principle of contraction. This can manifest in positive or negative fashions. If Saturn is strong, we will find a positive contraction, showing as self-discipline, order, respect and similar virtues. If it is weak, it shows timorousness, dullness of response, inflexibility, churlishness and the like. Saturn here has no essential dignity, but is accidentally strong by being on the fourth cusp and oriental. This combination of essential weakness and accidental prominence puts an unfortunate side of Saturn in an influential place. It could be much weaker, so what we will find here is failings rather than active malice. On the fourth cusp, the cusp of the house of the father, it shows an deep concern for tradition; but the weakness of the planet shows this to be a strait-jacket to the nature, the native hiding in the past, fearing to face the world. In the aspect to Mercury, planet of communication, on the seventh cusp, we see the cultivation of a curmudgeonly manner and (remembering the sanguine side of the temperament) a dry wit. The square to Venus, which dominates Saturn by ruling its sign, suggests a particular fear of women and that this awkward manner will be displayed most clearly in their company.

We now assess the quality of the native's mind. A favourable aspect between the Moon and Mercury is a positive sign. This conjunction being accidentally strong by its angularity and both planets being essentially dignified and swift in motion improves the mental capacity. With the Moon the stronger partner (essential dignity by sign and face, against Mercury's dignity by term and face) we have someone who is bright and ingenious enough, but not a rigorous thinker: remembering the placement of Saturn, we have someone who might top the class in history, but certainly not in arithmetic. The sextile from Saturn gives a capacity – albeit limited by Saturn's weakness – for mental effort. The conjunction being in a mute sign limits the loquacity we might have expected from an angular Mercury, the aspect from Saturn (contraction) increasing the tendency to the laconic. Despite this, Mercury receiving Saturn into the sign of its detriment suggests that the melancholic side of the nature (Saturn) is pained by the exposure given it by the sanguine half (Mercury). Mercury and the Moon are both on prominent fixed stars (Canopus and Pollux respectively): these, on top of the curmudgeonly manner, increase the aggressiveness of the mind, leading it into contentious and unpopular areas. The square from Mars reinforces this testimony. With the conjunction falling so close to the seventh cusp (other people), we see a determination to get the message across, but know that the message will often not be well received.

We have so far assessed the raw materials of the personality. We now turn to the matter of faith, for without the spiritual context the life is meaningless. For this we look first to the ninth house. This house is seriously afflicted by a badly debilitated Mars: energy in this area, but not working well. The ruler of the ninth, Venus, is essentially weak and squares Saturn, the Lord of the Ascendant, which it also disposits. The native, then, has great concern with religious matters, but is unable (fixed Saturn, melancholic temperament) to shift his ego (Ascendant ruler) into conformity with faith, but is set in rebellion against religion (Mars in ninth square Moon; Venus, ninth ruler, square Saturn). This is confirmed by the opposition between debilitated Mars and Jupiter, natural ruler of religion, and by the position of the Part of Fortune, which signifies the soul. This is at 9 degrees of Aquarius, uncomfortably close to the South Node, opposing Venus, ruler of the ninth, and square to Saturn, ruler of the Ascendant. The existence of these aspects again shows the importance of religion in this life, but their nature shows the battling against it. The absence of any substantive mutual reception, which would have enabled one planet to come to the aid of another, suggests that the native will make little attempt to alter his situation, thus confirming the indications of dogged inflexibility given by Saturn.

No matter how mundane might be the actual area of the life that we are investigating, a consideration of the religious nature is essential, as this alone can tell us what amount of constructive effort the native has taken to transmute his lead into gold. In this case, there is no evidence of this happening, so we can judge whatever we find in the chart in basic terms, rather than in any higher light. It is this that provides what the moderns assure us is impossible to find in the chart: the knowledge of the 'level' at which the life is lived. For example, had there been evidence of spiritual effort here, we might have judged the trine aspect from the Sun (Spirit) in the sixth house to a planet in the ninth as showing the dawning of the Spirit through dealing with the vicissitudes of practical life (sixth house); here, it would suggest that the blasphemous tendencies (weak Mars in ninth) are fuelled by a liking for low company (trine aspect from sixth).

These points would be drawn out in rather more detail, but only through the consistent application of the same methods over and over again. This done, the astrologer can now proceed to judgement of the area of the life that is currently of interest. Whichever house this concerns, the manner of judgement is much the same, assessing the condition of the house itself and of its ruling planet according to those same basic principles. We may, as an example, examine the prospects for offspring.

This is a fifth house matter. The cusp of the fifth house is in a barren sign (Gemini), which is one testimony against there being children; but it is the only one. Mercury, ruler of the fifth, is conjunct the Moon, natural ruler of procreation, in a fertile sign (Cancer), close to an angle, with both planets swift in motion and the Moon increasing in light: it would take a good deal to negate so powerful a testimony of fertility as this. The applying aspect from the Moon to Jupiter, even though it is a square, adds even more to the indications of fertility, more than outweighing the square from Mars, a barren planet in a barren sign, because Jupiter disposits the Moon and Mercury by exaltation. The Arabian Part of Children (Ascendant + Jupiter − Saturn in a night-time chart like this one: 25 Sagittarius) is disposited by Jupiter, who also trines it. Jupiter could be a lot stronger, but this is still a persuasive argument of fertility. With such strong testimony, we can expect three or more children. The main significators are in a feminine sign and are the Moon, which is feminine and Mercury, which takes its nature from those planets with which it is in contact – in this case, the Moon, a feminine planet. We can expect the majority of the children to be girls. The Part of Children, however, is in a masculine sign and is disposited by a masculine planet in a masculine sign: we would expect at least one boy.

With the ruler of the fifth house just inside the seventh (wife of the native), the children will cleave more to her than him. The sextile between Mercury and Saturn shows native and children getting along tolerably well, but the reception shows difficulties: Saturn is in the terms of Mercury, but is received into the sign of its detriment. As Mercury exalts Jupiter, which rules most of the second house (money) we see the children's interest in their father being centred around his wallet.

Or we might consider the native's financial prospects by looking at the second house. As with the fifth, there are no planets in that house. A benefic would have improved prospects, a malefic hindered them, according to its nature and the houses that it rules. The ruler of the second, Saturn, is (being within 5 degrees of the cusp) in the fourth, the house of the father. This can indicate gain from the parents; but here this is seriously limited by the weakness of Saturn and the square it receives from Venus, ruler of the fourth. Jupiter must also be considered, as it rules Pisces, which takes up most of the second house, and would always be considered here in its role as natural ruler of wealth. Jupiter is in the third house – benefit from siblings; but this too is seriously limited, in this case by the opposition from Mars, ruler of the third and natural ruler of brothers. So we have a clear picture of the family falling out over money. Venus (ruler of the fourth, and so the native's father) opposes the Part of Fortune, whose worldly significance is with wealth. But the Part is also squared by Saturn, the native himself, so we see that although his wealth is jeopardised by the father, he is far from blameless, sharing responsibility for the situation.

So there is not much money coming from the family. The Part of Fortune being disposited by Saturn, significator of the native, shows him earning his own bread. What he does earn, however, will last: both Fortuna and Saturn, its dispositor, are in fixed signs. The Moon rules the seventh, and so shows the wife. In the sign of Cancer, she exalts Jupiter and casts a square aspect to it: the marriage will be a drain on his resources. As the reception in question is an exaltation, we have the sense of exaggeration. Jupiter is in no dignity of the Moon, so, as it were, the wife likes the money but the money has no interest in her. So we have a wife who is dissatisfied with the state of the husband's finances. This brings us back to the square aspect from Mars to the Moon: Mars rules the tenth house of career and is badly debilitated. So the husband's inadequate career prospects annoy the wife (square to the Moon) and afflict his wealth (opposition to Jupiter).

In this way we can continue, exploring layer on layer of meaning as we approach the chart from every side. As Al-Biruni warns: "In all conditions there is always an admixture of good and bad, often difficult to interpret, and requiring all the resources of the art as well as experience and industry."[11] But astrology is in essence simple. What distinguishes a good astrologer from a poor one has little to do with elaboration of technique and much to do with integrity of approach, as evinced by a willingness to accept what the chart offers rather than seeking to impose himself and his preconceptions upon it. The study of astrology is less about putting in more techniques than of gradually learning how to leave one's ego out of the reading. For this reason, the soundest piece of astrological advice ever offered is that of the great master of the craft, William Lilly:

> *"My Friend, whoever thou art, that with so much ease shalt receive the benefit of my hard Studies, and dost intend to proceed in this heavenly knowledge of the Stars, wherein the great and admirable works of the invisible and all-glorious God are so manifestly apparent. In the first place, consider and admire thy Creator, and be thankful to Him, be thou humble, and let no natural knowledge, how profound and transcendent soever it be, elate thy mind to neglect that divine Providence, by whose all-seeing order and appointment, all things heavenly and earthly have their constant motion; but the more thy knowledge is enlarged, the more do thou magnify the power and wisdom of Almighty God, and strive to preserve thyself in His favour, being confident, the more holy thou art, and more near to God, the purer Judgement thou shalt give."[12]*

---

[11]   Al-Biruni, op.cit. p. 316
[12]   Lilly, op. cit., introductory matter: *To the Student in Astrology*

18

Appendix:
Some Popular Fallacies

"I was born on a cusp."

No you weren't. The idea of a fuzzy area of shared stellar responsibility around the boundaries of the zodiacal signs is a creation of newspaper astrology. Sun-signs are used in the press for one reason only: the great majority of people can know into which sign they fall simply by knowing their own date of birth – something which is not possible for any of the other astrological variables.

Everyone born on, say, the 5th, 15th or 26th of the month can be quite certain of which sign the Sun was traversing at their birth. But the exact time at which the Sun moves from sign to sign changes slightly from year to year. If you were born around the 21st of the month, you cannot be sure of your Sun-sign without checking the exact time at which it changed signs in the year of your birth. In one year, for instance, a person born at 3am on May 21st might have the Sun in the first degree of Gemini; in another year, someone born at that same time could have the Sun still in the last degree of Taurus. It is not that there is any fuzziness about where it falls; it is that by knowing only the day of birth, without the time or the year, we do not have sufficient information to determine where that might be. The Sun is quite definitely in one sign or the other: you just don't know which.

"Saturn's coming over my Ascendant/Sun/Moon, so I'm going to have a really rough time."

No you're not. You're going to have a really rough time because you didn't do your homework/pay your rent/clean your teeth. You can't blame all this on poor Saturn, who has been plodding around the cosmos minding his own business. His passage over some sensitive point in your natal chart may well mark the moment when these various unwelcome pigeons come home to roost, but these problems are of your making, not his. Astrology is not a way of abdicating responsibility for your life.

"We tested 500 astrologers..."

Competent astrologers are few and far between; but somehow the scientists who run the supposed tests on astrology seem to have no trouble in finding them. "We tested 50/500/5000 astrologers," they proclaim "and found that only two of them knew what day of the week it was." Exactly where they find these competent astrologers, unless they breed them like mice in their laboratories, is a mystery. There may – possibly – be 500 competent astrologers in the world; but it is most certain that scientists lack either the inclination or the necessary criteria to determine who they are. Even more certain is that most astrologers of any competence will have better things with which to occupy themselves than running through mazes for the edification of men in white coats.

Astrology, as a true science, is not open to testing by the criteria of modern 'science': the tools with which such testing might validly be done simply do not exist. Modern science deals with quantity; true science deals with quality. No amount of quantity can comprehend distinctions of quality: we might as well judge the value of the Bible by the number of pages it contains. For this reason we lament not only the mockery that is the scientific testing of astrologers, but the more pernicious growth of 'scientific astrology', in which even astrologers who claim to work within the tradition justify their conclusions by producing statistics. As René Guénon explains, "Statistics really consist only in the counting up of a greater or lesser number of facts which are all supposed to be exactly alike, for if they were not so their addition would be meaningless."[1] In astrology more than anywhere the meaninglessness of statistical study is plainly apparent: if the basis of astrology is that whatever happens in any given moment has the particular qualities of that particular moment, where do we the find the identical facts to which we may add our results in order to produce our statistics?

"My knowledge of astrology is intuitive."

No doubt. But would you ride a bus driven by someone whose knowledge of driving was intuitive?

"An aspect must be judged according to whether the person is an evolved or an unevolved soul."

This idea of the evolved or unevolved soul was dragged into astrology by the Theosophists, who dominated astrological writing for the first two-thirds of the Twentieth Century. The centrality of the concept of evolution to their thinking demonstrates the anti-spirituality of Theosophy. This concerns us not only if we happen to be consciously directing our attention towards the Divine, but always; for as the cosmos is founded on the spirit, what is not in accordance with the spiritual must be a lie. As all the revealed faiths make plain, it is not in the nature of the cosmos to evolve.

It is an endearing foible common to writers on any number of subjects to imagine that mankind's ultimate goal is to be just like them. So the Theosophist astrologers, being in the main middle-class Englishmen, assumed quite naturally that the mark of an evolved soul is to behave like a middle-class

---

[1] René Guénon: *The Reign of Quantity & the Signs of the Times,* p.89, third edn. Sophia Perennis, Ghent NY, 1995

Englishman. Their descriptions make it quite clear that learning which fork to use and the appropriate word for a water-closet are the signs of a most advanced spiritual evolution. Whether the Divine plan is really that all mankind should become as late-Nineteenth Century English bourgeois must be open to question: the sacred books seem to have kept surprisingly quiet on the direction in which the after-dinner port should be passed.

It is, however, reassuring to note that all astrologers who have written on this subject are themselves evolved souls, and are capable of distinguishing which of their fellows share this elevation.

"The outer planets – Uranus, Neptune and Pluto – are the higher octaves of the inner ones, to which mankind has been vouchsafed access through its increasing spirituality."

Is mankind really more spiritual now than it was 2000 years ago?

"Ophiuchus, Arachne, or whatever this year's version might be, is the thirteenth sign of the zodiac, knowledge of which has been suppressed by ignorant astrologers/the Catholic Church/the male sex/the Wicked Witch of the West. This revolutionises the whole of astrology."

No it doesn't. The zodiac is divided into twelve equal sections, which through the indescribable majesty of creation are mirrored in the constellations that bear the same names. It is not possible to discover a thirteenth twelfth.

Twelve is the number of celestial manifestation on Earth: the outward, expansive and returning facets of the Divine action – which we know as the three modes of cardinal, fixed and mutable – manifesting through the quaternary of earth, air, fire and water give (3x4) twelve. No amount of sleight of mind can make 3x4 produce thirteen.

"The sidereal zodiac is an accurate reflection of the heavens, so astrologers should use that."

No it isn't. Both zodiacs contain the same twelve signs, each spanning exactly thirty degrees, in the same order; they differ only in where they locate the 'start' of the zodiacal circle. The sidereal zodiac, favoured by the Indian schools of astrology, takes as its start the point of the Sun's apparent entry into the constellation of Aries. The tropical zodiac, which is that with which we are familiar in the West, takes as its starting point the Spring Equinox. The precession of the equinoxes – a phenomenon occasioned by the fall of man – results in these two points being in different places.

The one is as good a place to start as the other. But while the coincidence of astrological and astronomical 'first point of Aries' might seem a tempting reason for adopting the sidereal zodiac, the connection between this zodiac and astronomical reality stops right there. The astronomical constellations are not neat divisions of the zodiac into twelve equal, thirty-degree sections, as are both of the astrological zodiacs; the only difference between the sidereal and tropical zodiacs is where these twelve neat equal sections are held to start. In skilled hands, both systems work excellently well.

"Astrology is a religion."

Only if you believe in idol-worship, confusing the material with the divine; worshipping God's creatures, not God.

"Astrology denies my free-will."

The discussion on whether or not astrology allows free-will is, in modern times, customarily conducted with a complete ignorance of what 'free will' actually means. As we might expect, such ignorance does not lead to a high level of debate.

The assumption is made that free-will is something that we already have (an assumption made most freely and most heatedly by those who most apparently lack all trace of it). What is commonly meant by free will is more akin to 'free whim'. And have it we most definitely do not. "I have free will – I'm going to achieve marvels... oh, she's pretty, I wonder if she's busy just now... goodness me, I'm hungry; what's for dinner?... I know, Pop-o-crunch, that'll fill me up till lunch while curing my bad breath..." and so goes our supposed free will.

While astrology does not by any magic instantly provide us with free will, by showing clearly and dispassionately the reality of our situation, it is a powerful tool with which we may work to acquire it. Most importantly, without the awareness of the relation of Man and God such as is implicit in and is made explicit through traditional astrology, the idea of free will can only ever be a fantasy. Far from denying free will, traditional astrology is one of the few pathways towards it that are still open in the modern world.

Further Reading

William Lilly, *Christian Astrology*, (1645). For the practical student there is no substitute for this book, which, adapted with varying degrees of fidelity, formed the basis of most astrological text-books written in English from the mid-Seventeenth Century to the dawn of the Twentieth Century. Lilly had read virtually everything that had been published on astrology and filtered his reading through a vast practical experience. He is also an engaging writer, with an obvious passion for his subject. The facsimile edition of 1985 is now out of print. *Christian Astrology Books I and II*, Ascella, Nottingham 1999 covers the general introduction and horary section; the section on nativities is forthcoming.

Abu 'Ali Al-Khayyat, *The Judgments of Nativities,* (9th Century) trans. James H. Holden, American Federation of Astrologers, Tempe, 1988. The clearest, soundest and most most concise of the readily available texts on natal astrology.

Titus Burckhardt, *Mystical Astrology According to Ibn 'Arabi,* Beshara, Abingdon, 1977. As indispensable as Lilly for practice is this for theory. Brief, but broad in its scope, it explains the cosmological basis for astrology. A clearer translation is promised for the near future.

It must be noted that more books does not necessarily equal more knowledge. Repeated study of these three texts will bring more reward than the expansion of one's library: effort, not money, is the only legal tender for the student of astrology. In particular, the pursuit of ever more recondite tricks of technique will profit far less than an increase in understanding of the traditional view of life, without which astrology can never seem real, no matter how accurate the results which it offers. There is not a new technique, nor an old technique hidden in some dusty tome, that will suddenly make astrology easy: the key is work; the only other key is more work.

For an understanding of the tradition the Scriptures are, of course, the primary source. Secondary literature such as Frithjof Schuon's *Understanding Islam* (Allen & Unwin, London, 1963) gives a valuable introduction; we might wish for a similar *Understanding Christianity.* Plotinus, being relatively concise, is perhaps the best starting-point among the philosophers; then back to Plato and Aristotle and forward to Ficino, whose *Commentary on Plato's Symposium*

(Spring, Woodstock, 1985) is of immense value. René Guénon's *The Reign of Quantity and the Signs of the Times* (Luzac, London, 1953) provides a comprehensive discussion of the difference between traditional and modern views of the world, and the fatal short-comings of the prevalent intoxication with the latter.

This said, there are other astrological texts of value, though the shelves of the traditional practitioner will never bear either the weight or the peacock hues of those of his modern counterpart. Most of the following have the virtue of being comparatively easy to obtain.

Abu'l-Rayhan Muhammad Ibn Ahmad Al-Biruni, *The Book of Instruction in the Elements of the Art of Astrology,* (1029); trans. R. Ramsey Wright, Luzac, London, 1934. Reprinted Ascella, Nottingham, n.d. More of a compendium of astrological knowledge than a text-book, this is full of valuable information.

Al-Kindi, *On the Stellar Rays,* trans. Robert Zoller, Golden Hind, Berkeley Springs, 1993. Although this work contains 'the Theory of the Magic Arts', the seeker after magic will be disappointed (no recipes!); the seeker after wisdom will find much here to reward him. A valuable discussion of areas of the background philosophy.

Henry Coley, *Key to the Whole Art of Astrology,* (1676); reprinted Ascella, Nottingham, n.d. Much of Coley's book reproduces what is better expressed in the work of his mentor, William Lilly; but in addition to this, there is an interesting section on electional astrology and – most valuable of all – the aphorisms (*Centiloquum*) of both Ptolemy and Hermes Trismegistus. These are key texts in astrology's history, and are correspondingly hard to find today.

Nicholas Culpeper, *Astrological Judgment of Diseases,* (1655), Ascella, Nottingham, n.d. Contains much of value on astrology in general, although dealing specifically with only medical matters. As with *Christian Astrology*, apart from edification there is much delight to be had from meeting the author amid his work.

Claudius Ptolemy, *Tetrabiblos,* trans. F.E. Robbins, Heinemann, London, 1940. Although far from comprehensive, this is by far the most influential book in the history of astrology. That its influence outweighs its value does not diminish the importance of much that it contains. That so few modern astrologers have even opened this book is a matter for astonishment.

Vivian E. Robson, *The Fixed Stars and Constellations in Astrology,* (1923), Ascella, Nottingham, n.d. Although supplanted in the book-stores by more colourful works, this remains the standard text on fixed stars. Accept no substitute.

Richard Saunders, *Astrological Judgement & Practice of Physick,* (1677), JustUs, Issaquah, 1997. A (very) comprehensive text-book of medical astrology by a man much admired by William Lilly. More for the aspiring medical practitioner than the general astrological reader. Some knowledge of Latin is helpful.

The first reliable and comprehensive history of astrology has still to be written. Patrick Curry's *A Confusion of Prophets: Victorian and Edwardian Astrology* (Collins & Brown, London, 1992) provides an entertaining account of various luminaries in English astrology of the period, fleshing out the early history of astrology's distortion into its modern form. The same author's *Prophecy and Power: Astrology in Early Modern England* (Polity, Cambridge, 1989) suffers from an overly political thesis, but is nonetheless interesting on English astrology's apparent Golden Age in the Seventeenth Century and its rapid decline at the dawn of the 'Enlightenment'.

Thomas S. Kuhn, *The Copernican Revolution* (Harvard University Press, 1957) is a clear and detailed account of the Ptolemaic model of the Solar System, together with a discussion, which corrects many common misconceptions, on the rise in popularity of the Copernican model. It is remarkable that few, if any, astrological book-shops stock what should be a standard text.